PLOTINUS

ENNEAD II.9

I0894210

THE *ENNEADS* OF PLOTINUS

With Philosophical Commentaries

Series Editors: John M. Dillon, Trinity College, Dublin and Andrew Smith, University College, Dublin

Also Available in the Series:

I.6: *On Beauty* by Andrew Smith
II.5: *On What Is Potentially and What Actually* by Cinzia Arruzza
IV.3–4.29: *Problems Concerning the Soul* by John M. Dillon & H. J. Blumenthal
IV.4.30–45 & IV.5: *Problems Concerning the Soul* by Gary Gurtler
IV.7: *On the Immortality of the Soul* by Barrie Fleet
IV.8: *On the Descent of the Soul Into Bodies* by Barrie Fleet
V.1: *On the Three Primary Levels of Reality* by Eric D. Perl
V.5: *That the Intelligibles are not External to Intellect, and on the Good* by Lloyd P. Gerson
VI.4 & VI.5: *On the Presence of Being, One and the Same, Everywhere as a Whole* by Eyjólfur Emilsson & Steven Strange

Forthcoming Titles in the Series include:

I.1: *What Is the Living Being, and What Is Man?* by Gerard O'Daly
I.2: *On Virtues* by Suzanne Stern-Gillet
I.3: *On Dialectic* by Pauliina Remes
I.4: *On Well-Being* by Kieran McGroarty
I.5: *On Whether Well Being Increases With Time* by Danielle A. Layne
I.8: *On the Nature and Source of Evil* by Anne Sheppard
II.4: *On Matter* by Anthony A. Long
III.4: *On Our Allotted Guardian Spirit* by Wiebke-Marie Stock
III.5: *On Love* by Sara Magrin
III.7: *On Eternity and Time* by László Bene
III.8: *On Nature and Contemplation* by George Karamanolis
V.3: *On the Knowing Hypostases* by Marie-Élise Zovko
V.8: *On Intelligible Beauty* by Andrew Smith
V.9: *On Intellect, Ideas, and Being* by Matthias Vorwerk
VI.1–2: *On the Genera of Being (I+II)* by Damien Caluori & Regina Füchslin
VI.3: *On the Genera of Being (III)* by Riccardo Chiaradonna
VI.7: *The Forms and the Good* by Nicholas Banner
VI.8: *On Free Will and the Will of the One* by Kevin Corrigan & John D. Turner
VI.9: *On the Good or the One* by Stephen R. L. Clark

PLOTINUS
ENNEAD II.9

Against the Gnostics

Translation with an Introduction
and Commentary

SEBASTIAN GERTZ

PARMENIDES
PUBLISHING

Las Vegas | Zurich | Athens

PARMENIDES PUBLISHING
Las Vegas | Zurich | Athens

© 2017 Parmenides Publishing. All rights reserved.

This edition published in 2017 by Parmenides Publishing
in the United States of America

ISBN soft cover: 978–1–930972–37–7
ISBN e-Book: 978–1–930972–64–3

Library of Congress Cataloging-in-Publication Data

Names: Plotinus, author. | Gertz, Sebastian Ramon Philipp.
Title: Ennead II.9 : against the gnostics / Plotinus ; translation with an introduction and commentary Sebastian Gertz.
Other titles: Ennead. II, 9. English
Description: Las Vegas : Parmenides Publishing, 2017. | Series: The Enneads of Plotinus with philosophical commentaries | Includes bibliographical references and indexes.
Identifiers: LCCN 2016024902 (print) | LCCN 2016029954 (ebook) | ISBN 9781930972377 (pbk. : alk. paper) | ISBN 9781930972643 (ebook)
Subjects: LCSH: Plotinus. Ennead. II, 9.
Classification: LCC B693.E52 E5 2017 (print) | LCC B693.E52 (ebook) | DDC 186/.4--dc23
LC record available at https://lccn.loc.gov/2016024902

Typeset in Warnock and Futura by Parmenides Publishing
Printed by Edwards Brothers Malloy, Chicago, IL
www.edwardsbrothersmalloy.com

www.parmenides.com

Contents

Introduction to the Series With a Brief Outline of the Life and Thought of Plotinus (205–270 CE)

PLOTINUS WAS BORN IN 205 CE in Egypt of Greek-speaking parents. He attended the philosophical schools in Alexandria where he would have studied Plato (427–347 BCE), Aristotle (384–322 BCE), the Stoics and Epicureans as well as other Greek philosophical traditions. He began his serious philosophical education, however, relatively late in life, at the age of twenty-seven and was deeply impressed by the Platonist Ammonius Saccas about whom we, unfortunately, know very little, but with whom Plotinus studied for some eleven years. Even our knowledge of Plotinus' life is limited to what we can glean from Porphyry's introduction to his edition of his philosophical treatises, an account colored by Porphyry's own concerns. After completing his studies in Alexandria Plotinus attempted, by joining a military expedition of the Roman emperor Gordian III, to make contact with the

Brahmins in order to learn something of Indian thought. Unfortunately Gordian was defeated and killed (244). Plotinus somehow managed to extract himself and we next hear of him in Rome where he was able to set up a school of philosophy in the house of a high-ranking Roman lady by the name of Gemina. It is, perhaps, surprising that he had no formal contacts with the Platonic Academy in Athens, which was headed at the time by Longinus, but Longinus was familiar with his work, partly at least through Porphyry who had studied in Athens. The fact that it was Rome where Plotinus set up his school may be due to the originality of his philosophical activity and to his patrons. He clearly had some influential contacts, not least with the philhellenic emperor Gallienus (253–268), who may also have encouraged his later failed attempt to set up a civic community based on Platonic principles in a ruined city in Campania.

Plotinus' school was, like most ancient schools of philosophy, relatively small in scale, but did attract distinguished students from abroad and from the Roman upper classes. It included not only philosophers but also politicians and members of the medical profession who wished to lead the philosophical life. His most famous student was Porphyry (233–305) who, as a relative latecomer to the school, persuaded him to put into writing the results of his seminars. It is almost certain that we possess most, if not all, of his written output, which represents his mature thought, since he didn't commence writing until the age of forty-eight. The school seemingly had inner and outer circles, and Plotinus himself was clearly an inspiring and sympathetic teacher who took a deep interest in the philosophical and spiritual progress of his students. Porphyry tells us that when he was suffering from severe depression Plotinus straight away visited him in his lodgings to help him. His concern for others is also illustrated by the fact that he was entrusted with the personal education of many orphans and the care of their property and careers. The reconciliation of this worldly involvement with the encouragement to lead a life of contemplation is encapsulated in Porphyry's comment that "he was present to himself and others at the same time."

The *Enneads* of Plotinus is the edition of his treatises arranged by his pupil Porphyry who tried to put shape to the collection he had inherited by organizing it into six sets of nine treatises (hence the name *"Enneads")* that led the reader through the levels of Plotinus' universe, from the physical world to Soul, Intellect and, finally, to the highest principle, the One. Although Plotinus undoubtedly had a clearly structured metaphysical system by the time he began committing himself to expressing his thought in written form, the treatises themselves are not systematic expositions, but rather explorations of particular themes and issues raised in interpreting Plato and other philosophical texts read in the School. In fact, to achieve his neat arrangement Porphyry was sometimes driven even to dividing certain treatises (e.g., III.2–3; IV.3–5, and VI.4–5).

Although Plotinus' writings are not transcripts of his seminars, but are directed to the reader, they do, nevertheless, convey the sort of lively debate that he encouraged in his school. Frequently he takes for granted that a particular set of ideas is already familiar as having been treated in an earlier seminar that may or may not be found in the written text. For this reason it is useful for the reader to have some idea of the main philosophical principles of his system as they can be extracted from the *Enneads* as a whole.

Plotinus regarded himself as a faithful interpreter of Plato whose thought lies at the core of his entire project. But Plato's thought, whilst definitive, does according to Plotinus require careful exposition and clarification, often in the light of other thinkers such as Aristotle and the Stoics. It is because of this creative application of different traditions of ancient thought to the interpretation of Plato that Plotinus' version of Platonism became, partly through the medium of later Platonists such as Porphyry, Iamblichus (245–325), and Proclus (412–485), an influential source and way of reading both Plato and Aristotle in the Middle Ages, the Renaissance, and up to the early 19th century, when scholars first began to differentiate Plato and "Neoplatonism." His thought, too, provided early Christian theologians of the Latin and particularly of the Byzantine tradition, with a rich variety of metaphysical concepts with which to explore and express difficult doctrinal ideas. His fashioning of Plato's ideas into a consistent metaphysical structure, though no longer accepted as a uniquely valid way of approaching Plato, was influential in promoting the notion of metaphysical systems in early modern philosophy. More recently increasing interest has centered on his exploration of the self, levels of consciousness, and his expansion of discourse beyond the levels of normal ontology to the examination of what lies both above and beneath being. His thought continues to challenge us when confronted with the issue of man's nature and role in the universe and of the extent and limitations of human knowledge.

Whilst much of Plotinus' metaphysical structure is recognizably an interpretation of Plato it is an interpretation that is not always immediately obvious just because it is filtered through several centuries of developing Platonic thought, itself already overlaid with important concepts drawn from other schools. It is, nevertheless, useful as a starting point to see how Plotinus attempts to bring coherence to what he believed to be a comprehensive worldview expressed in the Platonic dialogues. The Platonic Forms are central. They become for him an intelligible universe that is the source and model of the physical universe. But aware of Aristotle's criticism of the Platonic Forms as lifeless causes he takes on board Aristotle's concept of god as a self-thinker to enable him to identify this intelligible universe as a divine Intellect that thinks itself as the Forms or Intelligibles. The doctrine of the Forms as the thoughts of god had already entered Platonism, but not as the rigorously argued identity that Plotinus proposed. Moreover the Intelligibles, since they are identical with Intellect, are themselves actively intellectual; they are intellects. Thus Plato's world of Forms has become a complex and dynamic intelligible universe in which unity and plurality, stability, and activity are reconciled.

Now although the divine Intellect is one it also embraces plurality, both because its thoughts, the Intelligibles, are many and because it may itself be analyzed into thinker and thought. Its unity demands a further principle, which is the cause of its unity. This principle, which is the cause of all unity and being but does not possess unity or being in itself, he calls the One, an interpretation of the Idea of the Good in Plato's *Republic* that is "beyond being" and that may be seen as the simple (hence "one") source of all reality. We thus have the first two of what subsequently became known as the three Hypostases, the One, Intellect, and Soul, the last of which acts as an intermediary between the intelligible and physical universes. This last Hypostasis takes on all the functions of transmitting form and life that may be found in Plato, although Plato himself does not always make such a clear distinction between soul and intellect. Thus the One is the ultimate source of all, including this universe, which is then prefigured in Intellect and transmitted through Soul to become manifest as our physical universe. Matter, which receives imperfectly this expression, is conceived not as an independently existing counter-principle, a dangerously dualist notion, but is in a sense itself a product of the One, a kind of non-being that, while being nothing specific in itself, nevertheless is not simply not there.

But this procession from an ultimate principle is balanced by a return movement at each level of reality that fully constitutes itself only when it turns back in contemplation of its producer. And so the whole of reality is a dynamic movement of procession and return, except for matter, which has no life of its own to make this return; it is inert. This movement of return, which may be traced back to the force of "love" in Plato or Aristotle's final cause, is characterized by Plotinus as a cognitive activity, a form of contemplation, weaker at each successive level, from Intellect through discursive reasoning to the merest image of rational order as expressed in the objects of the physical universe.

The human individual mirrors this structure to which we are all related at each level. For each of us has a body and soul, an intellect, and even something within us that relates to the One. While it is the nature of soul to give life to body, the higher aspect of our soul also has aspirations toward intellect, the true self, and even beyond. This urge to return corresponds to the cosmic movement of return. But the tension between soul's natural duty to body and its origins in the intelligible can be, for the individual, a source of fracture and alienation in which the soul becomes over-involved and overwhelmed by the body and so estranged from its true self. Plotinus encourages us to make the return or ascent, but at the same time attempts to resolve the conflict of duties by reconciling the two-fold nature of soul as life-giving and contemplative.

This is the general framework within which important traditional philosophical issues are encountered, discussed and resolved, but always in a spirit of inquiry and ongoing debate. Issues are frequently encountered in several different contexts, each angle providing a different insight. The nature of the soul and its relationship to the body is examined at length (IV) using the Aristotelian distinctions of levels of soul (vegetative, growth, sensitive, rational) whilst maintaining the immortal nature of the transcendent soul in Platonic terms. The active nature of the soul in sense-perception is maintained to preserve the principle that incorporeals cannot be affected by corporeal reality. A vigorous discussion (VI.4 and 5) on the general nature of the relationship of incorporeals to body explores in every detail and in great depth the way in which incorporeals act on body. A universe that is the product of design is reconciled with the freedom of the individual. And, not least, the time-bound nature of the physical universe and human reason is grounded in the life of Intellect, which subsists in eternity. Sometimes, however, Plotinus seems to break outside the framework of traditional metaphysics: the nature of matter and the One, each as non-being, though in a different sense, strains the terminology and structure of traditional ontology; and the attempt to reconcile the role of the individual soul within the traditional Platonic distinction of transcendent and immanent reality leads to a novel exploration of the nature of the self, the "I."

It is this restless urge for exploration and inquiry that lends to the treatises of Plotinus their philosophical vitality. Whilst presenting us with a rich and complexly coherent system, he constantly engages us in philosophical inquiry. In this way each treatise presents us with new ideas and fresh challenges. And, for Plotinus, every philosophical engagement is not just a mental exercise but also contributes to the rediscovery of the self and our reintegration with the source of all being, the Platonic aim of "becoming like god."

While Plotinus, like Plato, always wishes to engage his audience to reflect for themselves, his treatises are not easy reading, partly no doubt because his own audience was already familiar with many of his basic ideas and, more importantly, had been exposed in his seminars to critical readings of philosophical texts that have not survived to our day. Another problem is that the treatises do not lay out his thought in a systematic way but take up specific issues, although always the whole system may be discerned in the background. Sometimes, too, the exact flow of thought is difficult to follow because of an often condensed mode of expression.

Because we are convinced that Plotinus has something to say to us today, we have launched this series of translations and commentaries as a means of opening up the text to readers with an interest in grappling with the philosophical issues revealed by an encounter with Plotinus' own words and arguments. Each volume will contain a new translation, careful summaries of the arguments and structure of the treatise, and a philosophical commentary that will aim to throw light on the philosophical meaning and import of the text.

John M. Dillon
Andrew Smith

Abbreviations

DK	H. Diels, *Die Fragmente der Vorsokratiker*, 6th ed, revised by W. Kranz. Berlin: 1952.
HS2	P. Henry and H.–R. Schwyzer, *Plotini Opera* I–III (editio minor, with revised text). Oxford: 1964–1982.
LS	A. A. Long & D. N. Sedley, *The Hellenistic Philosophers*, 2 vols. Cambridge: 1987.
MacKenna	S. MacKenna, *Plotinus. The Enneads.* English Translation revised by B. S. Page. London: 1962.
NHC	J. M. Robinson, *The Coptic Gnostic Library*. 5 vols. Leiden: 2000.
SVF	H. F. A. von Arnim, *Stoicorum Veterum Fragmenta*. 4 vols. Leipzig: 1903–1924.

Acknowledgments

I WISH TO THANK THE SERIES EDITORS, John Dillon and Andrew Smith, for their offer to work on *Ennead* II.9 and for their helpful comments on the manuscript. My thanks are also due to Gale Carr at Parmenides Publishing, for her patience and advice. Finally, I am grateful to John Turner, who kindly answered my questions on *Zostrianus* in correspondence.

Introduction to the Treatise

IN *AGAINST THE GNOSTICS*, PLOTINUS undertakes no less than a defense of the Platonic heritage against (as he sees it) an arrogant and mischievous clique of usurpers. The stakes are high: as the rhetoric of the treatise develops, we are presented with a clash between reasoned argument and irrational self-assertion, between the time-honored tradition of Greek philosophical inquiry and the superfluous innovations of inspired visionaries. Plotinus himself never names his opponents, and instead refers to them in vague terms, usually in the third person plural ("they"), sometimes in the singular ("if someone should say . . . "). Only in a single instance (at 15, 22–23) does he identify them by their claim to possessing revealed "knowledge" (*gnōsis*, from which the Greek *gnōstikoi*, "those in possession of knowledge," derives, which in turn is the origin of the English word "Gnostics"). Gnosticism can be considered a religious movement in its own right, with distinctive positions on the place of human beings in the universe and the nature of salvation, although its utility as a category has been questioned.[1] For the purposes of this volume, the word "Gnostics," unless otherwise qualified, is simply a convenient way of referring to Plotinus' opponents, and nothing more.

Rhetoric seldom matches reality, and only careful study of *Ennead* II.9 and the Gnostic texts themselves will allow us to judge how well the polarities that Plotinus constructs map onto the actual differences between Gnostics and Platonists. The little that we know about the unnamed opponents mostly comes from Chapter 16 of Porphyry's *Life of Plotinus*, our most important source in this regard, and worth quoting here:

> There were in his time Christians of many kinds, and especially certain heretics who based their teachings on the ancient philosophy. They were followers of Adelphius and Aculinus who possessed a lot of writings by Alexander the Libyan, Philocomus, Demostratus and Lydus, and also brandished apocalyptic works by Zoroaster, Zostrianus, Nicotheus, Allogenes, Messus and others of that kind. Deceiving many and themselves deceived, they claimed that Plato had not

1 See, for example, Williams (1996); King (2003).

reached the depths of intelligible being. (*Life of Plotinus* 16.1–9; tr. Edwards)

What Porphyry tells us is that the Gnostics were Christians, that they were regarded as "heretics" by other Christians, and that they took the inspiration for their teachings from the "ancient philosophy" (that is, from Greek philosophy), while at the same time accusing Plato, the "ancient philosopher" par excellence, of not fully grasping intelligible being.[2] Nothing in *Against the Gnostics* suggests that Plotinus' opponents gave any particular role to Christ in their writings, which may at first sight cast doubt on Porphyry's report. Overt Christian references are equally absent from two of the apocalyptic works that Porphyry mentions, namely those by Zostrianus and Allogenes, which are both preserved for us as part of the collection of texts found in the Egyptian desert near Nag Hammadi in 1945. The two texts belong to a group of Gnostic writings that make significant use of Platonic vocabulary and concepts, and which give some prominence to the figure of Seth, also called "the one of another race" (the literal meaning of "Allogenes").[3] But it

2 For detailed discussions of Chapter 16 of Porphyry's *Life of Plotinus*, see Schmidt (1900, 13–17.19–26); García Bazán (1974); Igal (1981) and Tardieu (1992). See also Burns (2014, 161–163).

3 For a thorough study of these Platonizing Sethian treatises, see Turner (2001).

has recently been argued that they were "written by and for an audience familiar with and receptive to Judaeo-Christian ideas and themes,"[4] such that the absence of overt Christian references and themes may not license the inference to a non-Christian origin or readership of these texts.[5] In sum, we have no reason to question this part of Porphyry's report.

Due to lack of evidence, it is more difficult to assess his claim that the Christian heretics brandishing apocalypses were "followers of Adelphius and Aquilinus." The two are little more than names to us, although Aquilinus is mentioned by Eunapius as a disciple of Plotinus in Rome (see *Lives of the Sophists* 4.2.2 Giangrande).[6] If Eunapius is in fact talking about the same Aquilinus as Porphyry, it is possible that there were close ties, but also an undercurrent of rivalry, between Aquilinus the Gnostic teacher and Plotinus. More speculative is the suggestion put forward by Tardieu, that Adelphius and Aquilinus may have

---

4 Burns (2014, 147).

5 See Abramowski (1983, 2), with reference to *Zostrianus.*

6 The veracity of Eunapius' report has been questioned on good grounds; see Schmidt (1900, 15–17); Puech (1960, 164.177). See also Edwards (1989, 231), who suggests that Aquilinus, far from being a student of Plotinus, may have belonged to the same generation as Origen, Plotinus' somewhat older fellow-student under Ammonius Saccas in Alexandria.

continued the teaching of the Gnostic Valentinus, who was active in Rome between ca. 135–160 CE.[7]

Before turning to the Gnostic views that are refuted in II.9, some comments on the purpose of the treatise are in order. *Against the Gnostics* is not, in the first instance, directed at the Gnostics themselves: as Plotinus makes clear, he has no confidence that rational argument will persuade them, presumably because he thinks that their views are not ultimately arrived at by reasoned reflection.[8] Instead, the treatise is aimed at those of his students who have sympathies with Gnostic views but who are also amenable to rational persuasion. By refuting the views of the Gnostics, Plotinus thus demonstrates the superiority of his own philosophy over that of the rival systems known to some of his students. It is difficult to judge just how influential these Gnostics were in Plotinus' circle, but Plotinus at one point in II.9 advises his students to read the Gnostic apocalypses for themselves, suggesting that the latter were readily available (see 14, 36–37).

As far as the views of the Gnostics themselves are concerned, we can do no better than turn to the outline of their ideas that makes up the first part of II.9, from Chapters 1–6. It is frequently difficult to distinguish between instances where Plotinus reports what he takes

7 See Tardieu (1992, 519–520); the possibility is already discussed by Schmidt (1900, 49–50).

8 See II.9.9, 60–64.

to be his opponents' views, and instances where he considers for dialectical purposes what they might say in response to his objections. In addition, it is likely that he is not interested in presenting the particulars of any one sect, but concentrates on the essential features of the type of theory that various Gnostic sects are committed to.[9] Any attempt to construct a Gnostic "system" from the disparate materials scattered across the first six chapters of II.9, and the treatise as a whole, thus faces insurmountable problems, and the following remarks should be read with this proviso in mind.

The opening chapter of the treatise begins abruptly with the recapitulation of an earlier discussion ("It has become clear to us then . . .") on the identity of the One and the Good in V.5, the treatise immediately prior to II.9 in chronological order.[10] But the real focus of the

9 See Puech (1960, 181).

10 According to an influential proposal put forward by Harder (1936), II.9 completes a "great treatise" that Plotinus' editor Porphyry had somewhat arbitrarily separated into the treatises that are now *Enneads* III.8, V.8, V.5 and II.9. This proposal continues to be widely discussed; two noteworthy critical discussions of Harder's thesis are those by Wolters (1981), and Appendix 1 in *Plotin Traités 30–37*. Porphyry, Plotinus' editor, makes plain that the treatise he titled *Against the Gnostics* was composed as a single work (*Life of Plotinus*, 16.9–11), a piece of evidence that seems to decide the case against the "great treatise," as Narbonne (2011, 2–3) points out. Whether or not II.9 originally belonged to a larger work, it is worth noting the important connection between III.8 and II.9 in particular. Treatise

debate is on the nature of Intellect. Plotinus suggests that the Gnostic opponents would divide Intellect into a potential, contemplated part, and an active, contemplating one (see 1, 23–57). If a comment later in II.9 represents the views of the same opponents, they would also have distinguished a third part of Intellect that uses rational deliberation and has a demiurgic function (see 6, 19–24). In addition to this tripartite division of the Intellect, they may also have posited an intermediary rational principle (*logos*) between Intellect and Soul, which may or may not be identical with the third (demiurgic) part of the Intellect (see 1, 30–33.57–63). They further suppose that Soul, the principle that succeeds Intellect (and the intermediary *logos*), creates the universe as the result of a "fall" (*sphalma*) or a "decline" (*neusis*), terms which Plotinus takes as equivalent. This "fall" is apparently conceived of as a temporal event, which implies that the universe is created in time. Once the soul repents of its "fall," it goes on to destroy the world, not however without saving the souls of the elect, who are gathered in a heavenly abode called the "new earth," from which they ascend to the intelligible world after the end of the world (see 4, 1–22;

III.8 sets out how nature, the lowest aspect of the world soul, creates the visible universe through its activity of contemplating Intellect, and this conception of creative action provides the theoretical backdrop for many of Plotinus' attacks on the Gnostics' conception of the demiurge in II.9. See O'Meara (1980) for a lucid discussion of this topic.

5, 23–26). This "new earth" is itself the creation of the Soul, and acts as the paradigm of the visible universe. Plotinus seems unsure whether his opponents viewed its creation as prior or posterior to the visible universe, and dismisses both options as absurd. They agree with Plato in some respects, for example when they hold the soul to be immortal and maintain that it must separate itself from its association with the body (see 6, 36–43). But in Plotinus' view, they either misinterpret Plato's teaching, as, for example, when they read Plato's *Timaeus* as suggesting a tripartite division of the Intellect, or disguise some of their debts to Plato under new terminology (see 6, 5–10).

The core of the disagreement between Plotinus and the Gnostics is best summed up by the alternative title *Against those who say that the creator of the cosmos and the cosmos are evil*. The central chapters of the treatise, from 7–18 (with the exception of Chapter 14, which is something of a digression), are all in various ways concerned with refuting the view that the cosmos, and anything that has a body quite generally, is to be despised and regarded as evil. Plotinus himself concedes that the Gnostics may have found support for their views in Plato's own texts, especially the *Phaedo*, but he insists that the universe must be regarded as an image of the intelligible reality that it reflects. As an image, the universe is different from, and less perfect than, its intelligible model, but that does not overturn its claim to being the most beautiful image of the intelligible world that there is. Throughout these chapters, Plato's own account, in the *Timaeus*, of the creation of the universe by a divine craftsman who creates out of his own goodness, provides a key point of reference for Plotinus' own discussion.

The structure of this second part of II.9 is somewhat difficult to discern in detail, but I suggest that it falls into three broad sections. To begin with, Chapters 7–9 survey various reasons why the Gnostics might blame the universe. It may be because the world soul's concern with a material body could in some sense be troublesome and a departure from its natural state. But, as Plotinus argues in Chapter 7, one cannot conceive of the world soul's governance of the universe by analogy with the rule of individual souls over their bodies. Nor can sufficient grounds for blaming the universe be found in the reason for the soul's creation, which, for the Gnostics, is its decline away from intelligible reality. Chapter 8 thus argues that to think of the world's creation in terms of a decline and a deliberate undertaking on the part of the world soul is to fundamentally misconceive what it means for intelligible entities to create. Plotinus' theory of double activity, according to which an entity has its own internal activity that is part of its own essence while also producing an image of that activity in external effects, is here employed to give an alternative account of creation.[11] On this picture, creation does not require the fallible and imperfect reasoning that accompanies the production of craftsmen; rather, the production of the world is the necessary consequence of the world soul's contemplation of the intelligible world, and the beauty and orderliness of the cosmos a direct reflection of the great power of its producer. If the Gnostics should wish to object that the world displays some manifest imperfections, such as inequalities in wealth and the injustices many people suffer, Plotinus, in Chapter 9, urges them to consider that the wise man's happiness does not depend on good fortune, and is consequently not harmed by the eventualities whose occurrence the Gnostics decry. But even so, any injustices in this life will be made up by punishments and rewards in the afterlife. For Plotinus, the Gnostics' censure of the universe goes hand in hand with their claims to being the sole possessors of a divine substance, and it is this aspect of their teaching that the rest of Chapter 9 discusses.

The second section of the second half of II.9 spans Chapters 10–14. It begins with a transitional section in Chapter 10, where Plotinus refuses, perhaps not with the utmost sincerity, to offer a point-by-point refutation of his Gnostic friends because of the "respect" that he feels for them. He instead offers to examine one point

11 For two important formulations of the theory of double activity in the *Enneads*, see V.1.6, 30–39 and V.4.2, 27–33.

in particular, how the Gnostics compromise the purity of the intelligibles, by attributing to them responsibility for the (in their view) evil creation. For this reason, Plotinus proceeds to examine their account of creation in considerable detail (from the end of Chapter 10 to the end of Chapter 12), probably drawing on a text that has close parallels with our version of the Nag Hammadi text *Zostrianus*. Chapter 13 brings this discussion to a conclusion, and offers a diagnosis of the Gnostics' error: they blame the cosmos because they do not understand that there is a gradual and necessary succession of entities, from the One to Intellect, from Intellect to Soul, and from Soul to the universe. Tagged on to this diagnosis are observations on the nature of the stars and evil. Chapter 14 then returns to the larger topic, how the Gnostics render the intelligibles impure, and discusses their views on magic, which, he argues, imply that the intelligibles can be affected by human actions and words. The source of their error lies in a mistaken ambition to appear holy, which Plotinus goes on to link with their claims of being able to cure diseases by expelling demons.

In the third and final section, from Chapters 15–18, Plotinus explores the practical consequences of the Gnostics' contempt for the world and their corresponding belief that they possess a privileged spiritual nature. In the domain of ethics, he argues in Chapter 15, their belief in a special providence that rewards the elect few can give no meaningful place for the pursuit of virtue. Against this view, Plotinus thinks that providence is universal and rewards individuals in accordance with their character, which is the result of natural dispositions that are trained through habituation and cultivated by the development of the intellectual faculties. The notion of a special providence that extends only to the Gnostics but not to the world at large continues to come under attack in Chapter 16, which culminates with an account of how an understanding of intelligible realities leads to an appreciation of their perceptible imitations. In some cases, such as that of lovers, appreciation of sensible beauty can trigger our recollection of intelligible reality, but the Gnostics, we are to infer, are barred from gaining knowledge of reality in this way because of their contempt for worldly beauty. If this contempt is the result of a mistaken understanding of Plato, Plotinus continues in Chapter 17, the opponents should consider that just as the world soul has the marvelous power of bringing the whole universe into motion, so it is able to make it beautiful to the greatest possible extent. Beauty, then, should move the soul, and if the Gnostics claim to be unmoved by it, their position is irrational, and may be an overcorrection of some prior tendency toward excess. Chapter 18 concludes the treatise by arguing that contempt for the world and everything that is bodily does not result in a greater ability to contemplate the intelligibles. Our condition of embodiment is a necessity that should be accepted and that does not prevent us from contemplation if we prepare ourselves appropriately through virtue. Thus the Gnostics' contempt for the body blinds them to the real possibility of happiness while being embodied.

So much about the structure of II.9. I conclude with a few remarks on the character of Plotinus' engagement with the Gnostics, and its significance in his wider philosophy. The overall tone of the treatise is, I think, one of puzzlement. Plotinus struggles to understand both what it is that the Gnostics believe, and, when failing to find any rational justification, why they believe it at all. Many of his criticisms assume the validity of his own philosophy, which is unsurprising given that the treatise is addressed in the first instance to his own students. He occasionally glosses over possible differences between Gnostic accounts, for example when equating the idea of a "fall" of the soul with its "decline" in Chapter 4, and at times he simply refuses to engage with his opponents on their own terms (see, for instance, 12, 41, where the notion of a pre-existing darkness is dismissed by asking, "Where did it come from?"). But his overall method is a sound one: he assumes that the Gnostics' claims have a meaning, that this meaning can be expressed in propositions, and that these propositions ought to be consistent. In this way, he treats them as he would any other school of philosophy, such as the Stoics and the Peripatetics. It may be objected that the Gnostics, like Plato in his *Timaeus*, did not intend their creation narratives to be read as literal truths, but rather as myths that describe reality through symbols. Yet even if the Gnostic narratives are ultimately to be read as symbolic, they must be symbolic *of* something, and Plotinus is surely right to demand an explanation of what it is that is being symbolized. He himself attempts such an explanation when he discusses the possibility that the "sojourns, repentances and copies" that Gnostic texts such as *Zostrianus* and the anonymous untitled text in the Bruce Codex mention are meant to describe the soul's progress toward the intelligibles, rather than actual locations (6, 2–5).

Finally, what significance should we attribute to II.9 within Plotinus' philosophy in the *Enneads*? We can begin by noting that Plotinus' debate with the Gnostics did not begin with II.9 and did not end there. Polemical asides that seem directed at views endorsed by the Gnostics can be found both before and after *Against the Gnostics*, which suggests a more continuous engagement with their views rather than a single skirmish.[12] It is reasonable to think that some of his ideas, for example those regarding the

12 To take but one example, Plotinus formulates his views on the productive activity of intelligible causes in opposition to views that, if not exclusively Gnostic, would certainly have been shared by his Gnostic opponents. See, for instance, IV [28] 4.10 and 12, and VI [38] 7.1. See more generally the passages listed in Puech (1960, 183).

generation of matter, had been formulated more carefully as a result of the Gnostic confrontation.[13] But the larger question to what extent this engagement shaped Plotinus' own views and affected the development of his philosophy would exceed the confines of this introduction. Suffice it to say here that it is an area of lively research, in which much work remains to be done.[14]

13 On this point, see Puech (1960, 182–185); Narbonne (2011, 5–6).

14 Narbonne (2011) is a fine example of how the study of Plotinus' engagement with the Gnostics can open up new perspectives on the development of his thought.

Note on the Text

LINE NUMBERS IN THE TRANSLATION are approximate and do not always match the original Greek text. Since the commentary follows the sequence of the English translation, there may sometimes be a slight discrepancy in the ordering.

The Greek text adopted is that of the Oxford edition (taking into account the Addenda ad Textum in vol. 3, 304–325). Deviations from the text are noted in the commentary. Each *Ennead* is referred to by Roman numerals, followed by the number of the treatise, the chapter of the treatise, and, finally, separated by a comma, the line number or numbers, e.g, V.1.3, 24–27.

It is customary to add the chronological number given by Porphyry in his *Life of Plotinus* (*Vita Plotini*), so that, for example, V.1 is designated V.1 [10]. In this series the chronological number is given only where it is of significance for Plotinus' philosophical stance. The following chart indicates the chronological order.

Chronological Order of the *Enneads*

Enn.		*Enn.*		*Enn.*		*Enn.*		*Enn.*		*Enn.*	
I.1	**53**	II.1	**40**	III.1	**3**	IV.1	**21**	V.1	**10**	VI.1	**42**
I.2	**19**	II.2	**14**	III.2	**47**	IV.2	**4**	V.2	**11**	VI.2	**43**
I.3	**20**	II.3	**52**	III.3	**48**	IV.3	**27**	V.3	**49**	VI.3	**44**
I.4	**46**	II.4	**12**	III.4	**15**	IV.4	**28**	V.4	**7**	VI.4	**22**
I.5	**36**	II.5	**25**	III.5	**50**	IV.5	**29**	V.5	**32**	VI.5	**23**
I.6	**1**	II.6	**17**	III.6	**26**	IV.6	**41**	V.6	**24**	VI.6	**34**
I.7	**54**	II.7	**37**	III.7	**45**	IV.7	**2**	V.7	**18**	VI.7	**38**
I.8	**51**	II.8	**35**	III.8	**30**	IV.8	**6**	V.8	**31**	VI.8	**39**
I.9	**16**	II.9	**33**	III.9	**13**	IV.9	**8**	V.9	**5**	VI.9	**9**

	Enn.		*Enn.*		*Enn.*		*Enn.*		*Enn.*		*Enn.*
1	I.6	**10**	V.1	**19**	I.2	**28**	IV.4	**37**	II.7	**46**	I.4
2	IV.7	**11**	V.2	**20**	I.3	**29**	IV.5	**38**	VI.7	**47**	III.2
3	III.1	**12**	II.4	**21**	IV.1	**30**	III.8	**39**	VI.8	**48**	III.3
4	IV.2	**13**	III.9	**22**	VI.4	**31**	V.8	**40**	II.1	**49**	V.3
5	V.9	**14**	II.2	**23**	VI.5	**32**	V.5	**41**	IV.6	**50**	III.5
6	IV.8	**15**	III.4	**24**	V.6	**33**	II.9	**42**	VI.1	**51**	I.8
7	V.4	**16**	I.9	**25**	II.5	**34**	VI.6	**43**	VI.2	**52**	II.3
8	IV.9	**17**	II.6	**26**	III.6	**35**	II.8	**44**	VI.3	**53**	I.1
9	VI.9	**18**	V.7	**27**	IV.3	**36**	I.5	**45**	III.7	**54**	I.7

Changes to the Greek Text

1, 19–20 Punctuate, with Heigl and Kirchhoff: *Loipon de . . . tōn triōn toutōn. Tines an . . . par'autas;*

1, 25–26 Punctuate: *phuseis poieisthai pleious · all' oude en tois meta tauta.*

1, 36 Reading *de* in place of *gar*, with Harder.

1, 45–46 Following two suggestions by Heigl, I am reading *eimen* in place of *eien*, and *aitian echoi* in place of *aitian echoien.*

3, 11–12 Punctuate, with Heigl: *Anagkē toinun . . . kai aei. Genēta . . . .*

4, 7 Reading *gar* in place of *de*, with Harder.

5, 1 Inserting *alogon* after *Alla*, as proposed by Creuzer.

9, 35 Reading *endeiknumenon* with M and C, in place of *endeiknumenous.*

9, 45 Accepting Kirchhoff's insertion <*kai tous theous*> before *kai anthropous.*

9, 59 Reading *hotan* for *eita,* as proposed by Harder-Beutler-Theiler (1960, 430), and reading a period after *alloi* at 9, 60 rather than a question mark.

9, 60–64 Ignoring the changes proposed in the *Addenda* to HS$_2$ and reading *ti an, ei chiliopēchus einai nomizoi, tous* <*d'*> *allous pentapēches einai akouoi; monon de phantazoito hōs ta chilia arithmos megas.*

9, 81 Ignoring the reading *polloi* that is proposed in the *Addenda* to HS$_2$, and maintaining *polla.*

10, 25 Excising *hoion mē neusai.*

10, 25–26 Reading *to skotos* in place of *tōi skotōi,* with Heigl and Kirchhoff.

11, 9 Reading *autē* in place of *autēi,* with R and J.

11, 14 Reading a question mark after *poiēsantas,* not a period.

11, 24 Reading *gar* in place of *de.*

12, 9–10	Accepting Heigl's punctuation: *ekeina—ē kai tēn mētera autou—. . . .*
12, 11	Reading <*ek*> in place of the second *kai*, with Kirchhoff.
12, 25	Reading *ekeino* in place of *ekeinos.*
13, 21	Accepting Bréhier's insertion of *dei* before *nomizein.*
14, 9	Reading *hois* in place of *hoi*, with A and Q.
14, 25	Reading a question mark after *tēkesthai*, not a comma.
14, 45	Inserting *ouk* after *hēmin*, with Mueller.
15, 7	Reading Volkmann's *pōs* in place of *hōs.*
15, 34	Reading *kai pōs* with Volkmann, in place of *pōs kai.*
16, 4	Emending *pas kakos* to *pagkakos* instead of excising it, as suggested by Heigl.
16, 14	Ignoring the deletion of *hoti* proposed in the *Addenda* to HS_2.
17, 7	Reading *kai to noēton* in place of *kata to noēton*, with Kirchhoff *et al.*

17, 8–9	Reading *to genomenon tōi amerei tōi tou paradeigmatos* in place of *tou genomenou tōi amerei to tou paradeigmatos*, as suggested by Harder-Beutler-Theiler (1960).
17, 28	Inserting <*kai*> after *an poioien tou.*
17, 31	Reading *kakōs diatethentes*, in place of *kai pōs diatithentes*, as suggested by Kirchhoff.
17, 45–46	Reading *allōs . . .* <*tou*>*tous kallous* in place of *allous . . . tous kallous* with Bury (1945, 53).
18, 13	Reading <*pros*>*poieitai* in place of *poieitai*, as suggested by Dodds.
18, 38	Accepting Creuzer's conjecture <*tois*> *aei.*
18, 46–48	Transposing lines 46–48 to come after 18, 40.

Synopsis

Chapters 1–6: Main series of critiques of Gnostic views

Chapter 1—*The three hypostases, and the indivisibility of the Intellect*

1–11 The nature of the Good is simple and primary, and the same as the One. It does not depend on anything else for its existence or exist in anything else.

11–16 The natural order of principles is: the Good, Intellect, and Soul. No more and no fewer principles should be sought.

16–19 It has been shown elsewhere that no two of the three principles can be equated; hence at least three principles are necessary.

19–23 It is not reasonable to introduce principles beyond these three, for a number of reasons: (1) There is nothing beyond the Good.

23–26 (2) Dividing immaterial principles that are always in actuality into potential and actual parts would be ridiculous; *a fortiori*, such a division cannot be made at the level of the One.

26–33 (3) Intellect cannot be divided into parts that are in motion and at rest.

33–40 (4) Intellect cannot be divided into a part that thinks and a part that thinks that it thinks.

40–57 (5) No sensible account can be given of an intellect divided into thinking and thinking that it thinks, even at a conceptual level.

57–63 (6) There is no rational principle (*logos*) between Intellect and Soul.

Chapter 2—*Individual souls compared with the world soul*

1–4 Therefore there are exactly three principles, and Intellect cannot be divided.

4–10 Individual souls have three parts; if the lowest part, concerned with the body, becomes dominant, it will affect the intermediate part that brings the highest part's activity of contemplation to our awareness.

10–18 The world soul, on the other hand, always remains concentrated on its contemplation of the intelligible world, and maintains the universe as a result of this contemplation.

Chapter 3—*The world of generation is eternal*

1–11 The world soul always gives life to the universe, just as it is in the nature of the One to engender Intellect, and in the nature of Intellect to produce Soul.

11–15 There is no absolute coming into being or perishing.

15–21 Not even matter is perishable, nor is it ever cut off from divine influence.

Chapter 4—*This universe did not come to be in time and will not be destroyed*

1–17 The world soul did not create the universe in time nor in order to further some goal.

17–22 The universe is not going to be destroyed at a particular point in time.

22–32 The opponents are wrong to censure the world for its imperfections, because it is as good an image of the intelligible world as there can be.

Chapter 5—*Arrogance of the Gnostics, and two mistaken views*

1–8 The opponents wrongly claim for themselves an intelligence greater than that of the heavenly bodies.

8–16 In the same way, they are wrong to reserve immortality for themselves, without extending it to the heavens.

16–23 The notion of a soul made of elements faces problems:

(a) How can life result from a composite of elements?

(b) How can the soul be created from the elements if it is one and the same thing as their combination?

(c) How could such a material soul possess mental faculties such as apprehension and will?

23–37 The concept of a "new earth" as the afterlife destination for elect souls is riddled with inconsistencies:

(a) If the "new earth" is also the paradigm of the perceptible world, why would the opponents wish to ascend to the paradigm of a world they despise?

(b) Did the soul create the paradigm of the cosmos before or after the perceptible world, in order to keep the elect safe? Either way it is useless.

Chapter 6—*Their unacknowledged dependence on Plato and contempt for the Greeks*

1–10 What are the "repentances," "copies" and "sojourns"?

10–24 Some of the opponents' doctrines derive from Plato, and of those, some are based on a mistaken reading of his texts, for example the *Timaeus*. Other doctrines of theirs, not taken from Plato, are simply wrong.

24–34 Intellect is a unity, and should not be divided into plurality.

35–43 Divine men have already laid down sound doctrines regarding the soul.

43–52 In discussions, the Gnostics should seek to establish the truth of their claims like philosophers, rather than insulting the Greeks.

52–62 Although they have taken many doctrines from Plato, they have also added mistaken views.

Chapters 7–9: The universe should not be censured

Chapter 7—*The world soul is not affected by the body*

1–4 It has been said before the Gnostics that embodiment is not best for the soul.

4–27 We cannot think of the world soul as similar to our own souls. There are differences: unlike us, the world soul is unaffected by its body.

27–32 Nor is the constitution of the world's body the same as that of the bodies of individual beings.

33–39 Conflicts between the universal order and partial beings do not show that the universe is imperfect.

Chapter 8—*The universe is a beautiful image of the intelligibles*

1–5 The soul creates of necessity; no further reason is needed.

5–18 The universe displays the greatness of the intelligible world.

18–29 The universe exists necessarily and is unique.

29–39 What reason could there be for denying that the stars are divine?

39–46 If the world soul has forced the souls of the elect to descend, it is better and more powerful. If the souls have come down willingly, they have only themselves to blame.

Chapter 9—*The nature of providence*

1–11 The wise man is not concerned with the goods of fortune.

11–17 Vicious people exist, but the wise man has nothing to fear from them.

17–26 A just order bestows rewards and punishments in the universe.

26–64 Many beings are able to contemplate, not just the elect. The opponents should not exalt themselves at the expense of others.

65–69 How could god's providence extend to a part of the universe (the opponents) but not the whole?

70–83 If the opponents respond that they do not need providence because of some innate spiritual power, they are deluded.

Chapters 10–14: How the Gnostics render the intelligibles impure

Chapter 10—*Two ways of engaging with the Gnostics, and Sophia's fall*

1–14 There is another way of refuting the Gnostics, by close scrutiny of their doctrines, which is not pursued here.

14–33 Instead, one must consider their most absurd doctrine, that regarding Sophia's fall, and the creation of the universe.

Chapter 11—*The Gnostics' illumination of the darkness*

1–14 What does it mean to say that the soul "illuminated the darkness"?

14–17 How could matter produce psychic images?

17–23 What is the "image in matter"?

23–25 Why is the Demiurge at all necessary?

26–29 Why is one thing created before another?

Chapter 12—*The creation of the world by an "image"*

1–12 How could the Demiurge or his mother create the world on account of their memory of the intelligibles?

12–25 The opponents wrongly reduce creation to the manner of production characteristic of the crafts.

25–30 How could an image bring about the order that obtains in the heavens?

30–44 The responsibility for the creation of the world must be referred back to intelligible causes. The same applies to matter.

Chapter 13—*Their ignorance of the succession of entities, the stars and the nature of evil*

1–6 Censuring the cosmos displays one's ignorance of the order of succession among beings.

6–25 There is nothing frightening about the heavenly bodies, and they do not impose a tyranny.

25–33 Evil is not simply a diminution in goodness; otherwise evil would exist in the intelligible world.

Chapter 14—*Magic and demons*

1–11 The intelligibles cannot be influenced by magic.

11–36 Diseases are not caused by demons.

36–45 The philosophy of Plotinus' school, as based on reason and the pursuit of the holy, is opposed to that of the Gnostics, as can be seen from their books.

Chapters 15–18: The effects of the Gnostics' arguments

Chapter 15—*The Gnostics' disregard for virtue*

1–27 There are two schools about the end of actions, one (including Plotinus' own) that pursues virtue, another (including Epicurus and the Gnostics) that pursues bodily pleasure.

27–40 The Gnostics' contempt for virtue and the fine is further evidenced by their lack of writings about virtue.

Chapter 16—*Contempt for the world, and the special providence of the Gnostics*

1–5 Despising the world is not the same as becoming good.

5–12 The opponents' so-called reverence for the intelligibles has no connection with anything else in the universe.

12–32 Their notion of a special providence for the elect is confused, since providence deals with wholes and not parts.

32–39 One cannot seriously compare oneself to the universe.

39–43 Experts in music and geometry delight in perceptible representations of intelligible order.

43–56 Perceptible beautiful things can lead us toward the intelligibles.

Chapter 17—*Beauty leads to the intelligibles*

1–21 If the Gnostic despise the cosmos because of its bodily nature, they should abstract its corporeal features in order to appreciate the intelligible reality beneath it, particularly the great power of the world soul, which is able to make the cosmos beautiful.

22–31 There is nothing noble in being unmoved by beauty; rather it reveals an ignorance of intelligible causes. The opponents' contempt for worldly beauty is the result of past excesses.

32–56 Beauty is not the same in part and whole. Individual things face obstacles that may hamper the full development of their beauty. The same is not true for the universe, which contains everything within itself.

Chapter 18—*The body is no obstacle for contemplation*

1–14 Embodiment is a necessity one has to put up with. The Gnostics are either ignorant of this fact, or secretly drawn to the body, despite their ostensible contempt for it.

14–35 We should not seek kinship with base people, but with the world soul, to which we can liken ourselves when through virtue we become impassive to the blows of fortune.

35–40.46–48 The Gnostics fail to see that the soul of the stars and the world comes from outside this perceptible universe, because it is not located in space, just as they misconceive the ascent of individual souls after death in spatial terms.

40–46 Embodiment is no obstacle to the good life, and we should not deny the stars the ability to contemplate.

Translation of Plotinus
Ennead *II.9 [33]*

Against the Gnostics, *or* Against those who say that the creator of the cosmos and the cosmos are evil[15]

1. It has become clear to us, then, that the nature of the Good is simple and primary (because everything that is not primary is not simple); that it has nothing within itself, but is some sort of unity; and that it is the same as the nature of what is called the One, since this nature [*sc.* the One] itself is not something or other, | and then one, nor is the Good something or other, and then good. We must think of the same nature when we talk about the One and when we talk about the Good, and call it one, even though we are not attributing anything to it,

15 Porphyry, in his *Life of Plotinus*, records two different titles for this treatise (at 5.33 and 24.56–57). The first, *Against the Gnostics*, identifies the opponents, who are never named in the treatise itself, while the alternative title *Against those who say that the creator of the cosmos and the cosmos are evil* identifies the main subject matter.

but revealing it to ourselves as far as possible.[16] So in this way we say that the One-Good is primary, since it is most simple, and self-sufficient, since it is not composed of many things, or else it would be dependent | on its component parts. And we say that it does not exist in something else, because everything that exists in something else also takes its own existence from that thing.

If, then, the primary nature neither takes its existence from something else nor exists in something else nor is any kind of composite, there must not be anything beyond it. Therefore, we should not proceed to other principles, but put the Good above all, and first after it Intellect and thinking, and then—since this is the natural order—| Soul after Intellect, without positing any more or any fewer principles than these in the intelligible world.

For if they posit fewer they will have to say either that Soul and Intellect are the same, or that Intellect and the primary nature are the same. But it has been shown in many ways that they are different from each other.

Now it remains to consider if there are more principles | than these three. Then what natures would belong to them? No one would succeed in finding any principle

16 The opening of *Against the Gnostics* recapitulates some of the conclusions of V.5 [32], in particular Chapters 12–13 of that treatise, which comes immediately prior in chronological order. See especially V.5.13, 33–36.

simpler and higher than the one principle of everything we have thus described.

They are surely not going to say that there is one principle of everything in potentiality, and another in actuality, since in the case of beings in actuality and without matter it would be ridiculous to multiply natures | by dividing them into potentiality and actuality. But we should not even attempt such a division in what comes after these.

Nor should we conceive of a kind of intellect in some sort of rest, and another as if it were in motion.[17] For what would be Intellect's rest and motion and procession? What would be the idleness of the one intellect and what the function of the other? No, Intellect is as it is, always the same and | remaining in stable activity. Motion toward it and around it is already the function of Soul, i.e. a reason-principle coming from Intellect into the Soul makes the Soul intellective, but does not produce some other nature intermediate between Intellect and Soul.[18]

Nor indeed should we multiply Intellect on the ground that one intellect is thinking, and the other thinking that it thinks.[19] Even if in our world thinking is one thing, | and thinking that one thinks another, it is still a single mental application that is well aware of its own activity. But it would be ridiculous to assume this division in the

17 See Numenius, fr. 15 des Places.

18 Cf. Eusebius, *Preparation of the Gospel* 11.19.

19 See Numenius, fr. 22 des Places.

case of the true Intellect; rather, the intellect that thinks that it thinks will absolutely be the same as the one that was thinking. Otherwise there would be one intellect that only thinks, and another that thinks that it thinks which is different and not | the one that has been thinking.

But if they should say that this distinction exists only in thought, they should first renounce their multiple realities; then, they should consider whether these distinctions allow for the possibility of an intellect that only thinks, without being conscious in itself that it is thinking. If this happened amongst ourselves who are always | attentive to our impulses and thoughts, even if we are not particularly wise, it would invite the charge of foolishness. Now when the true Intellect thinks itself in its thoughts and the object of its thinking is not outside it, but Intellect is itself its object of thought, it possesses itself and sees itself in the act of thinking by necessity. When it sees itself | it is not unthinking: it sees while thinking. So in the primary act of thinking Intellect would also possess its thinking that it thinks, since it is one. And in the intelligible world there is no duality in thought. Further, if Intellect were always thinking what it is, what possibility would there be of separating in thought its thinking from its thinking that it thinks? Indeed, if one were to introduce a third distinction | besides the second one that distinguishes "thinking that it thinks," i.e. "thinking that it thinks that it thinks," the absurdity would become even more manifest. And why not proceed like this to infinity?

Further, anyone supposing that the reason-principle comes to be from Intellect, and that from this reason-principle another reason-principle comes to be in the Soul (so that the first is intermediate between | Soul and Intellect) will deprive the Soul of thinking: it will not receive the reason-principle from Intellect, but from another principle, the intermediate. The Soul will have the image of the reason-principle, but it will not have the reason-principle itself, and it will not know Intellect at all nor think at all.[20]

2. Therefore one must not posit more principles than these three [*sc.* the One, Intellect, and Soul] nor make superfluous distinctions among intelligible beings that do not apply to them. Rather, one must posit one Intellect that remains the same, unswerving in every way and imitating the Father as far as it can.

One part of our soul is always | directed to the intelligible beings, another part to the things in this world, and another to what is intermediate between those. Since the soul is one nature with many powers, sometimes the whole soul is brought together in the best part of it and of being, and sometimes when the worst part of it has

20 See above, lines 30–33.

become dragged down, it drags the intermediate part along with it; for the whole soul is not allowed | to be dragged down. This affliction befalls the soul because it did not remain in the best place, where the soul that is not a part remains—and of which we are no more a part either—and allows the whole body to receive as much as it can from the soul. There the soul remains free of care, because it does not govern with rational calculation, nor does it restore anything to order, but | with its marvelous power it brings about order through the contemplation of that which comes before it. The more the soul is engaged in contemplation the more it grows beautiful and powerful. It gives what it has received from the intelligible world to its successor, and it illuminates just as it is itself always illuminated.

3. So because the soul is always illuminated and possesses the light perpetually, it is able to give it to its successors. They are always held together and nourished by this light and, as far as they can, have the benefit of living because of it. It is just as when a fire is placed in the open somewhere and those who | can are warmed by it. The fire is limited indeed: yet in the case of powers that are not measured or separated from real beings, how could they exist while nothing participates in them? No, it is necessary for each thing to give a part of itself to another. The Good would not be a good, and Intellect not an intellect, and Soul

not what it is, | unless there is also some secondary life along with the primary living, for as long as the primary exists. Therefore it is necessary that all things succeed one another, and for eternity.

Now the others have come to be by taking their existence from other things. Therefore things said to "have come to be" did not come to be, but were coming to be and will come to be. They will not perish, except those that have something into which they can dissolve. But what has | nothing it can dissolve into will not perish at all.

If someone should say that it could dissolve into matter, why cannot matter itself also perish? And if someone should say that matter also perishes, we will reply: "By what necessity did matter come to be?" If they are going to say that matter came about as a necessary consequence, the same necessity obtains now also. And if it is going to be left alone, the | divine realities will not be everywhere, but limited to a particular place and "walled out,"[21] as it were. But if this is not possible, matter will be illuminated.

4. But if they are going to say that the soul created the world when it "had shed its wings,"[22] as it were, we reply that the soul of the world does not suffer this; and if they are going to say that the soul created the world when it fell down, let them tell us the cause of this fall. When did

21 Aristophanes, *Birds* 1576.

22 Plato, *Phaedrus* 246c2.

it fall? If it did so from eternity, then | by this argument of theirs it remains in a fallen state. But if the soul began to fall, why did it not fall before then? We say that its decline is not creative; rather its non-decline is. <For> if the soul declined clearly it did so by forgetting the intelligible realities. But if it had forgotten them, how could it create? Where could its creative power come from if not from the realities that it sees in the intelligible world? If the soul creates by remembering these, it did not | decline at all. Even if it possesses only a faint memory of them, it will all the more incline toward the intelligible world, so as not to see dimly. For why did the soul not want to return there, given that it possesses some sort of memory of the intelligible world? What advantage would it expect from the creation of the world? It would be ridiculous to think it was in order to be honored,[23] and characteristic of people who extrapolate from sculptors | in our world. Otherwise, if the soul was making the cosmos with the aid of rational calculation, and making and the power of making were not in its nature, how could it have made this cosmos?

And when is the soul going to destroy the cosmos? If the soul has repented of having made the cosmos, what is it waiting for? If it has not yet repented, it would not do so in the future, because it has already become accustomed to the cosmos and grown fonder of it over time. But if | it

23 See Clement of Alexandria, *Stromata* 4.13.89.

is waiting for the individual souls, they should no longer come back to the world of generation, given that in their former births they have already experienced the evils therein. So they would already have given up coming here.

Nor must we grant that this world has been badly made on account of the many troubles within it, since this is the opinion of those who give too much honor to it, | in as much as they think that this world is the same as the intelligible world, rather than its image. Yet what other image could be more beautiful than this?[24] What other fire is a better image of the intelligible fire than the one in our world? Indeed, what other earth besides this one could come after the intelligible earth? What sphere more precise and venerable, more harmonious | in its movement could come after the self-containment of the intelligible world? What other sun could there be after the intelligible but before the visible sun?

5. But it is <unreasonable> that these people who have a body, as men do, and desires and pains and impulses, think so highly of their own power. They claim that they can reach the intelligible world, but that the sun's power is no more | impassible, orderly and unchanging than ours, and that it does not have greater intelligence than we do

24 See Plato, *Timaeus* 29a5.b3; 30a7.

who have just been born and are hindered from getting to the truth by so many delusions.

Nor is it reasonable to say that their soul and that of the meanest of men is immortal and divine, but that the | heaven and the stars up there do not share in immortality even though they are much more beautiful and pure. Seeing the order and grace and harmony up there, they greatly censure the disorder in this world, as if the immortal soul had chosen the worse place | on purpose, and wished to yield the better one to the mortal soul.

But their surreptitious introduction of that other soul, which is composed of the elements, is also unreasonable: for how could a composite made up of the elements possess any form of life? The blending of the elements produces the hot or | the cold, or a mixture of both; or the dry or the wet, or a mixture of both. How then can the soul be the same as the union of the four elements if it has later come to be from them? When they attribute apprehension and will and countless other things to this soul, what should one say in response?

Because they do not honor this creation or this earth, they say that, supposedly, they will depart from this world to a "new earth"[25] | that has been created for them, and that this is the rational model of the world. Why do they have to get there, though, to the paradigm of the cosmos

25 See Anonymous, *Untitled Text* 249.21 Schmidt-MacDermot (Bruce Codex), and 11, 12 below.

that they despise? Where does this paradigm come from? According to them this paradigm came into being when its maker had already declined toward the things in this world. If | the maker himself really was so eager to make another cosmos after the intelligible one that he possesses—and why should he have been?—and if [he made the paradigm] before our world, for what end [would he have done so]?

—So that the souls may be kept safe.

Then how is it that they did not stay safe? The paradigm has come to be in vain. If he made the paradigm after the cosmos, taking away its form | while depriving it of its matter, the experience would have sufficed to keep the souls that had undergone it safe. But if they think that they have received the form of the world in their souls, what novelty is there in their account?

6. What are we to understand by the other basic elements that they introduce, the "sojourns" and "copies" and "repentances"?[26] If they say that affections of the soul are [repentances] when it is in a state of repenting, and copies when it receives as it were images of reality, but does not | in any way see the real beings themselves, they follow the custom of people who invent new terminology for the

26 See *Zostrianus* (NHC VIII,1) 5.17–29; 8.13–16; 12.10–22; Anonymous, *Untitled Text* 263.11–264.6 Schmidt–MacDermot (Bruce Codex).

promotion of their particular sect. They fabricate these things as if they did not have contact with the ancient Hellenic [tradition], even though the Greeks understood such matters clearly and spoke without pretense about ascents from the cave and the gradual progress toward a truer and | truer contemplation.[27]

In general, some of their doctrines have been taken from Plato, while they have invented others with a view to establishing their own philosophy, and we have found these to be far from the truth. For the judgments and rivers in Hades and the reincarnations also come from Plato.[28] And creating a plurality in the intelligible world, i.e. Being, | Intellect, and the Demiurge who is different from Intellect and Soul,[29] this is taken from what is said in the *Timaeus*, since he said: "The maker of this universe intended that it should possess all the forms that Intellect perceives in the real Living Being."[30] But these people did not understand and took there to be one intellect at rest | that contains all reality within itself, and another intellect next to it that contemplates [the first], and another one that reflects. With them, it is often the creative soul that takes the place of the intellect that reflects. And they

27 See Plato, *Republic* 514a–520d.

28 See Plato, *Gorgias* 523a–527a; *Phaedo* 81d–82a; 107a–115a; and *Republic* 614a–621d.

29 Cf. Numenius, fr. 22 Des Places.

30 Plato, *Timaeus* 39e7–9.

think that according to Plato this is the Demiurge, since they are far from knowing who the actual Demiurge is.

In general, they are wrong about the manner of | creation and many other doctrines of Plato. They drag his opinions into the mire, pretending that they have fully grasped the intelligible nature, while he and the other blessed men have not. When specifying a plurality of intelligible beings they think that they have discovered accuracy in their beliefs, while | they are in fact reducing the intelligible nature to likeness with the perceptible and lesser nature, on account of that same plurality. One must seek to have the least number in the intelligible world and to get rid of plurality by referring everything to what comes after the first, which is all things: the first Intellect and being and all other beautiful things that come after the first nature. |

The form of Soul is in the third place. But these people should look for the differences among souls in their affections or in their nature, and not disparage divine men. Rather, they should graciously receive the opinions of these men, since they are more ancient, and accept what they have stated well: the immortality of the soul; the intelligible world; the first god; that the soul must | flee its association with the body; its separation from the body; that it must flee from the world of generation to being. For they do well when they repeat these doctrines laid down so clearly by Plato.

We bear no ill will toward those who say they want to disagree, but in meetings with their audience they should not recommend | their own doctrines by disparaging and insulting the Greeks. Rather, they should show the correctness of all doctrines that they consider peculiar to themselves and different from those of the Greeks on their own merits. They should set down their own doctrines courteously and in a philosophical manner, and those that contradict them with fairness. They should look toward the truth, and not chase | after glory gained from censuring men judged to be good by other great men since ancient times, while claiming that they themselves are better than these men.

For what was said by the ancients about the intelligible world is much better and more educated. Those who are not deluded by the deception that | prevails among men will easily understand that [the Gnostics] later took these doctrines from the ancients, although with some unbefitting additions. This is the case, for example, when they want to contradict the ancients: they introduce absolute generations and destructions; they berate this universe and | blame the soul for its kinship with the body and censure that it dwells in this universe; and they equate the Demiurge with the soul and transfer to this universal soul the same affections that also affect the particular souls.

7. We have said before that this cosmos did not have a beginning and is not going to end, but exists always, as long as the intelligibles exist.[31] Further, it has been said before these Gnostics that the communion of our soul with the body is not better for the soul.[32] But to conceive of the soul of the universe | from a similarity with our own soul is as though someone were to take the class of potters or coppersmiths and censure a whole well-governed city. One should rather grasp the differences in how the universal soul governs bodies: its manner of doing so is not the same as that of individual souls, and the universal soul is not tied to bodies as individual souls are. Besides the other differences, which we have discussed countless times | elsewhere, we must consider this point in particular, that the body which has become a bond has tied us down already when we were born.[33] The nature of the body, being already bound in the universal soul, binds whatever it embraces. But the soul of the universe could not be bound by the bodies that it binds itself, since it is in command.

This is why | the universal soul is unaffected by bodies, while we are not their masters. The part of the universal soul that is turned to the transcendent divine remains pure and unhindered, while that which gives

31 At 3, 11–12 above.

32 See Plato, *Laws* 828d4–5.

33 Cf. Plato, *Phaedo* 67d1–2.

life to the body receives nothing from it in turn. Because in general, what exists in something else is necessarily affected by that other thing but does not transmit | its own affection, given that the other thing has its own life. It is as if the shoot of a tree were grafted onto another: when the tree is affected, the shoot is affected with it, but when the shoot dries out, it leaves the tree with its own life. In fact, when the fire in you is quenched, the universal fire is not quenched; and if the universal fire were to perish, the soul in the intelligible world would not suffer anything, | but only the constitution of its body.[34] And if it were possible that some cosmos be composed out of the remaining elements, this would not concern the soul in the intelligible world. For the constitution of the universe and of each living being is not the same: in the universe the soul runs, so to speak, along the surface, ordering each being to remain in its place, but here living beings are tied | by a secondary bond for the preservation of their order, as though they were in flight. But in the universe there is nowhere to escape to. Therefore the soul does not need to hold all beings together from the inside nor push them inside through outward pressure, but from the beginning they remain where the nature of soul wanted.

34 See Plato, *Philebus* 29b–c.

If some of its parts move naturally, those parts for which the movement is unnatural suffer. The former are carried along excellently, as parts | of the whole, but the latter perish because they are not able to conform to the order of the whole. It is as if, when a large group of dancers is moving in order, a turtle that has been caught up in the middle of the procession was trampled upon because it was unable to flee the company of dancers. If, however, the turtle were to co-ordinate its movement with the group of dancers, it would not suffer anything from them.

8. To ask "why did the soul create this cosmos?" is the same as to ask "why does the soul exist?" and "why did the Demiurge create?" Firstly, this question is characteristic of people who conceive of perpetuity as having a beginning. Secondly, they think it was by turning from one thing to the next and changing that the soul | has come to be the cause of creation. They must be taught, if they should bear themselves reasonably, what the nature of these beings is, so that they may cease to abuse them lightly, rather than treating them with the great reverence that is appropriate. One could not rightly censure the ordering of the universe, because it demonstrates in the first place | the greatness of the intelligible nature. If in fact the universe came to live in such a way that it did not have an inarticulate life—like the smallest living things in the universe, which always come to be day and night

on account of the abundance of life in it—but a life that is continuous, distinct, great and everywhere, and that demonstrates an | enormous wisdom, how could one not say that it is a clear and beautiful image of the intelligible gods?[35] But if the universe is not [the intelligible reality] because it is an imitation of it, this itself is according to its nature, since it would no longer be an imitation otherwise. Yet it is false to say that it is an imitation without likeness, for nothing has been left out of it that a beautiful natural image was able to possess. | Indeed the imitation exists by necessity, not by rational calculation or artifice, since the intelligible world cannot be the last among realities. For the activity of the intelligible world must be double, one within itself, one toward another. Therefore there must be something after it, since only | the most powerless thing of all bestows nothing of itself to what is further below. A marvelous power runs through the intelligible world; this is why it also produces. If there is in fact another cosmos better than this one, what is it? But if it necessarily exists and there is no other cosmos, it preserves the imitation of the intelligible world.

Indeed the whole earth is full of all sorts of living | immortal beings; everything is full of them up to the sky. But why are the stars, both those in the spheres above and those in the highest sphere, not gods, given that they move

35 See Plato, *Timaeus* 37c6–7.

with regularity and circle around in order? Why would they not possess virtue, and what obstacle prevents them from acquiring it? What makes men bad here certainly | does not exist there, nor does the evil of the body, which both experiences and gives trouble. Why should the stars not have understanding in eternal leisure, and why should they not grasp with their minds god and the other intelligible gods? Will our wisdom be greater than that of the stars? Who could maintain this and not have lost his mind? For if the souls | have been forced to come down to this world by the world soul, how could they be better, seeing that they have been forced? In souls, the ruling part is better. If the souls have come down willingly, why do you blame this cosmos into which you have come willingly, and which also allows one to depart, if one does not like it? But if this universe is in fact such that we can also | possess wisdom in it, and live in accordance with intelligible realities while we are here, how does this not bear witness to its dependence on the intelligibles?

9. If someone censures wealth and poverty, that is to say, the fact that there is an unfair distribution in all such matters, he is in the first place ignorant that the wise man does not seek a fair distribution in these things; and further, that he does not think the rich have the advantage, nor that those in power have the better | over private citizens. Rather, the wise man allows that others

have such concerns, and understands that life here takes two forms[36]: one life belongs to the sages, the other to the bulk of mankind. The life of the sages tends toward the highest and what is above, while the more human life takes two forms again: one is that of the man who shares | in some good by being mindful of virtue, the other that of the common crowd, which is like a manual laborer who provides the necessities of life for those who are better.

If someone commits a murder or gives way to pleasure by reason of his weakness, what is surprising about the fact that errors are not in the intellect, but in souls that are like "beardless children"?[37] If the world is a gymnasium with winners and losers, | how is it not well made in this respect? If you are wronged, what does the immortal part have to fear? But if you are murdered, you got what you wanted. If you are complaining about the world now, nothing compels you to remain a citizen in it. Moreover, it is agreed that there are judgments and punishments in this world. So how can one rightly censure a city that is rewarding each citizen according to merit? In such a city, | virtue is honored, and vice receives appropriate dishonor; not only statues of the gods are there, but also the gods themselves[38] who observe from on high, and who will "easily be acquitted"[39] from

36 See Plato, *Gorgias* 500d.

37 Heraclitus, DK B117.

38 See Plato, *Epinomis* 983e5–984a1.

39 Cf. Theognis, *Elegies* 1034.

the charges levied against them by men, as the poet says. They bring everything into order from the beginning to the end and give to each individual the destiny in the changes of life that is due to them | in consequence of prior actions. Anyone ignorant of this is very reckless and boorish in his judgments concerning divine matters.

No, one must try to become as excellent as possible, and not think that one alone can become so—for in this way one is no longer excellent. Rather, one should consider that there are also other excellent men, and good daemons, | and much more so gods, both those that exist here while looking up to the intelligible world and most of all the ruler of this universe,[40] a most blessed soul. Then one must also praise the intelligible gods, and right above these the great king in the intelligible world | whose greatness <is displayed> most of all in the multitude of gods. The task of those who know the power of god is not to try to reduce him to a unity, but to show that the divine is as multiple as the god has himself shown when, while remaining what he is, he creates many other gods that depend on him, exist because of him and take their origin from him. This cosmos | exists because of him and looks to the intelligible world, and the whole cosmos and each of the gods proclaim the intelligibles to men and announce through oracles what is dear to them.

40 See Plato, *Phaedrus* 246e4.

But if these gods [*sc.* the stars] are not what this god [*sc.* the One] is, this is itself in accordance with nature.

If you want to despise the gods and boast that you are no worse than them, I reply first that in so far as someone is excellent, he is | well disposed toward all <gods> and men. Next I reply that a noble person should ascend to the right extent and not with boorishness, going only as far as our nature is able to. One should recognize that there is space for other people by god's side, and that one must not set oneself up as alone coming after god as though taking flight in dreams, while robbing | oneself of the chance to become a god as far as the human soul is capable: that is, to the extent that Intellect guides it. To think that one is above Intellect is already to be removed from It. But stupid people are convinced by these ideas as soon as they hear: "Not only will you be better than all men, but also than the gods"—| for the presumption among men is great. And a man who was humble, moderate and a private citizen before would be convinced, if he should hear: "You are a child of god, but the others, whom you admire, are not his children, nor are the beings which they honor in the tradition of their fathers, but you are greater even than heaven without making any effort," <when> others also join | the chorus. It is as if, in a group of people who do not know how to count, one man without the knowledge of counting had heard that he is a thousand cubits tall.[41] What would happen if he thought he was a thousand cubits tall, but had heard that the others are five cubits tall? He would only imagine that a thousand cubits is a great number.

Next, if god exercises his providence toward you, why is he not concerned | with the whole cosmos in which you also exist? If it is because he does not have time to look at the cosmos, no more is he allowed to look at what is below. Yet why, when he is looking at you people, does he not look beyond, that is, look at the world in which you exist? But if he does not look beyond, so that he does not oversee the cosmos, then he does not look at you either. |

—But they have no need for god.

Yet the cosmos needs god and knows his order, and the people within the cosmos know to what extent they are in it and to what extent in the intelligible realm. Those men loved by god will meekly accept what befalls them in this world, if something inevitable should happen to them because of the changes that pervade everything, since one must not look at individual | preferences but at the universe. A man who honors individuals according to their merit, and is always striving toward the same goal as everything else that is capable of doing so (there are many beings that strive toward the intelligible world, and

41 See Plato, *Republic* 426d8–e1.

those that succeed are blessed, but the others attain the fate that is befitting to them, as far as they can)—such a man does not give the capacity to reach the intelligible world to himself alone. | For one does not have the capacity that one claims to have by virtue of proclaiming it. But even though they know that there are <many things> that they do not have, they say that they have them. They think that they have what they do not have, and that they alone have what they alone do not in fact have.

10. Therefore, if one were to examine many other points, or even all of them, one could abundantly prove what is the case with each of their arguments. [But we will not do this,] since we feel a certain respect[42] toward some of our friends who have fallen in with this doctrine before they became our friends and | remain attached to it I do not know how. They, however, do not shrink from saying what they say, either because they want to make their doctrines seem plausibly true, or because they also believe them to be true. But in what we have said we were talking to our students, not to them (since nothing more would have them persuaded), so that | these people who provide no proofs for their doctrines (for how could they?), but speak arrogantly instead, may not trouble them. There is another way in which one can defend

42 See Plato, *Republic* 595b9.

oneself in writing against those who arrogantly venture to tear to pieces the fine and true doctrines of ancient and divine men.[43] So | let us forego the close scrutiny of their doctrines, since those who have accurately understood what we have said so far will also be able to know what is the case concerning all their other doctrines.

Leaving this aside then, let us talk about the following doctrine, which really surpasses them all in absurdity, if one must call it absurdity. They say that the soul and a so-called "Sophia" have declined, whether | the soul initiated the decline, or whether Sophia is the cause for soul's coming to decline, or whether they hold both to be the same. They maintain further that the other souls descended together and that these are "members of Sophia" which take on bodies such as those of humans.[44] But the soul for whose sake the other souls descended, they say, did not | in turn descend, that is, decline, but it alone illuminated <the darkness>, and then an image from that soul came to be in matter.[45] Next they fabricate an "image of the image"[46] somewhere here below, by way of matter or materiality, or whatever name they wish to use—they call it one thing, and then another, and they refer to it with many other names which they use | to the point of

43 See Porphyry, *Life of Plotinus* 16.9–18.

44 Cf. *Zostrianus* (NHC VIII,1) 27.9–12.

45 See *Zostrianus* (NHC VIII,1) 9.16–27.

46 *Zostrianus* (NHC VIII,1) 10.4–5.

obscurity—and bring their so-called Demiurge into being, representing him as separated from his mother. They drag down the cosmos created by the Demiurge to the status of the lowest images, just so that he who wrote this can make all kinds of reproaches.

11. We reply first, then: If the soul did not descend, but illuminated the darkness, how can it properly be said to have declined? For if something had gushed forth from it such as light, it is not appropriate to say that it had declined by this time; unless perhaps the darkness lay somewhere in the lower world, and | the soul moved toward it spatially and illuminated it once near. But if the soul illuminated the darkness while remaining by itself without purposely contributing anything to this task, why did it alone illuminate, but not those realities more powerful than it? And if the soul was capable of illuminating this cosmos by grasping, and in accordance with, its rational design, why did it | not illuminate and create the cosmos at the same time, rather than waiting for the production of images?

Next, did the rational design of this cosmos, which is called the "alien earth"[47] by these people and has been created by higher beings, as they themselves say, not also lead its makers to decline?

47 See 5, 24 above.

Next, how could matter, once it has been illuminated, | produce psychic images, but not a corporeal nature? An image of the soul would have no need of darkness or matter, but when it comes to be, if it comes to be, it would follow its maker and be joined to him.

Next, is this image a substance, or, as they say, a "conception"? If it is indeed a substance, in what way is it different from its producer? But if it were another form | of soul, perhaps it would be plant-like and generative, supposing that the higher soul is rational. If this is so, how could [the image have created the universe] in order to be honored,[48] and how could it have made it because of arrogance and recklessness? In general, this notion eliminates the possibility that the image created through imagination and even more so through rational planning. Then what further need was there to introduce a maker made from matter and an image? <For> if the image | is a "conception," one must first indicate where it takes its name from, and second, how it can be [an image], unless one is going to give the power of creating to the "conception." But, besides this fiction, how can they account for the creation? They say: "This thing comes first, and this other after that," but they speak quite arbitrarily. Why does fire come first?

48 See 4, 13–14 above.

12. And how can the image set to work just as it comes into being?

—On account of the memory of what it saw.

But it did not exist at all so as to be able to see, neither the Demiurge, nor the mother that they give to him. Next, is it not amazing that these Gnostics should come here into | this world not as images of souls, but as true souls? Scarcely one or two of them are only just able to transport themselves outside this world and, once they have come to recollect, can recall to mind only with difficulty what they knew some other time. And is it not amazing that this image (or even its mother), a material image, should think of the intelligibles—even if only dimly, as they say—just as it comes into being; | that it should not only think of them and derive a conception of the cosmos <from> the intelligible world, but also know the elements from which the cosmos comes to be?

So for what reason did the image make fire first? Was it thinking that fire ought to be first? Why not something else? But if the image could make fire when thinking of it, | why did it not make the cosmos straightaway when thinking of it, seeing that it must first have the whole in mind? Evidently it must have encompassed the elements too in its thinking. Creation takes place in an altogether more natural way, rather than like craft production, because the crafts are posterior to nature and the cosmos. Even now the particular things that come to be from natural principles are not first | fire, then each [remaining] individual element, and then a mixture of them. Rather, there is an outline and a sketch of the whole living being that imprints itself onto the menstrual fluid. Why then, in the case of the creation, was matter not also sketched with an impression of the cosmos, in which earth and fire and the other elements are contained? But perhaps they would so create the world in order to | make use of a more genuine soul, while <this image> would not have known how to create in this way.

Further, to have a prior conception of the greatness of the heavens, or rather their actual size, the obliquity of the Zodiac, the movement of the stars within the heaven, and the earth, such that one can identify the reasons for their order—this is not characteristic of an image, but belongs absolutely to the power | derived from the best principles. Even they agree with this against their will, because when their illumination into the darkness has been thoroughly examined, it will be made to recognize the true causes of the cosmos. Why in fact did the soul have to illuminate, unless it needed to do so absolutely? Either it was necessary by nature or against it. But if it was necessary by nature, it was so always. If against nature, what is against nature will also | exist in the intelligibles; evils will exist prior to this cosmos, and the cosmos will not be their cause. Rather, the intelligibles will be the cause of evil in this world, and evil will not come to soul from this world, but to there from the soul.

The argument will thus amount to referring the creation of the world back to the primary causes. And if this is so, matter, from which [the world] would come forth, [must also be referred back to the primary causes]. For they say that the soul that | declined saw and illuminated a darkness that already existed. Where did the darkness come from? If they are going to say that the soul made it when it declined, there was obviously nowhere for it to decline to, nor would the darkness have been the cause of the decline, but rather the nature of the soul itself. This is the same point as was reached in the compelling arguments before, i.e. that responsibility lies with the primary causes.

13. Someone censuring the nature of the universe, then, does not know what he is doing, or where his insolence leads him. This is because he does not understand that there is an order of successive entities, firsts, seconds and thirds,[49] and ever so on down to the extreme points, and that one must not rail | against those that are worse than the first, but meekly accept the nature of all things. One should oneself rush toward the first principles and stop talking about this tragedy of terrors that takes place,

49 Cf. Plato, *Letters* 2.312e1–4.

as they think, in the cosmic spheres (the spheres that in fact "make all things gentle"[50] for them). What is really frightening about these spheres, that they would inspire fear in those who are inexperienced | in argument and ignorant of educated and refined knowledge (*gnōsis*)? For if the bodies of the spheres are fiery, one must not thereby be afraid of them, given that they are aligned with the universe and the earth. But one should look toward their souls—the Gnostics themselves, of course, also think that they [themselves] are worthy of honor on this account. Yet the bodies of the spheres too stand out in size and | beauty, and they co-operate and collaborate in what comes about by nature, which will not cease to happen as long as the first principles exist; together they complete the universe and are its major parts. If men are more honorable than the other living beings, so much more are the spheres that exist in the universe—not for the sake of imposing a tyranny, | but so as to provide it with order and arrangement. We <must> consider things that people say are caused by the stars as indications of future events, but think that the events differ owing to chance (for it is not possible that the same things should happen to each individual), the moments of birth, the great distance of places and | the dispositions of souls. Nor again must one demand that all men be good; nor,

50 Pindar, *Olympian* 1.30.

since this is not possible, rashly censure [the nature of the universe], thinking that things here are no different from those in the intelligible world; nor again should one deny that evil is something other than a weakness in reasoning and a lesser good, and always tending toward diminution—| as if someone were to say that nature is evil, because it has no perception, and that the perceiving part is evil, because it has no reason. Otherwise they will be forced to say that there are evils in the intelligible world too, since there the Soul is inferior to Intellect and Intellect to another.

14. But they render the intelligibles impure in another way especially. For when they compose incantations to the intelligibles (and not only to Soul, but to what is above Soul also), what are they doing if not making the intelligibles obey and follow people who utter magic spells, enchantments and evocations? | They claim that this will happen if any one of us is able to say with some proficiency the right things in the right way, such as chants, sounds, breathings, hissings of the voice and other such things which are described in their writings as exercising a magical power over the realities beyond. But even if they do not wish to maintain this, how can the incorporeals be swayed by sounds of the voice? <By the same means> they use to make | their own discourses appear holier they have without noticing it taken away what is holy from the incorporeals.

When they say that they can cleanse themselves of diseases, they would be speaking correctly if they mean by moderation and an orderly regimen, like the philosophers. But when they suppose that diseases are daemons, and declare and promise that they can | expel them through magic words, they might appear to be very holy to the many who marvel at the powers of magicians. However, they would not persuade those with real understanding that diseases do not have their causes in either strain or satiety or lack or sepsis, and | generally in changes that originate outside or inside. The cures for diseases also make this plain: for example, the disease moves downward to the outside as a result of stomach purges, the taking of medicine or blood drainage; and lack of sustenance can also be a cure. Was the daemon starving, and did the cure make him | waste away?

Further, does he leave the body at once, or does he stay inside? But if he still remains, how is it possible to be no longer sick when he is inside? But if the daemon has left, why did he? What happened to him?

—The disease nourished him.

So the disease was something other than the daemon.

Next, if the daemon enters when no cause of disease is present, why | is the body he is in not always sick? If a cause is present, why does a daemon need to bring about the sickness? The cause of fever, for example, is sufficient to produce it. It is ridiculous to think that as soon as the cause is present, right away a daemon will be ready as though aiding the cause. But in fact it has become clear how and why | they make these claims: it was for this reason in particular that we have also recalled their daemons.

I leave you to read their books so as to examine their other doctrines and to observe everywhere that the form of philosophy that we pursue exhibits, apart from all other kinds of goods, also simplicity of character | together with pure thinking. Our philosophy pursues the holy, not what is arrogant, and joins daring with reason, great assurance, caution and the greatest circumspection. But I leave it to you to compare the other doctrines to one of this kind. The form of philosophy of these other people [*sc*. the Gnostics], however, has been established in very opposite terms throughout. We should add nothing | more, since it would <not> be appropriate for us to talk about them in this way.

15. This point in particular must not escape our notice, what effect these arguments have on the souls of the listeners and those persuaded to hold the world and what is within it in contempt. There are two schools on how to attain the goal: one | posits bodily pleasure as the goal, the other chooses the fine and virtue, the desire for which depends on god and can be referred back to him—precisely <how> must be considered elsewhere. Epicurus, having done away with providence, exhorts us to pursue what is left, namely pleasure and enjoyment. | Yet this doctrine

[*sc.* of the Gnostics] is even more insolent in its censure of the master of providence and providence itself. It dishonors all the laws here and virtue, which has been gained since the beginning of time, as well as making a mockery of temperance—all to prevent one from seeing anything fine in this world. | This doctrine also does away with the innate justice of character that is perfected by reason and practice, and generally with those things that could make a man wise. As a result, they are left with only pleasure and their own concerns, i.e. what is not shared by other men and merely a demand of utility, | unless someone in their group is superior to their doctrines because of his own natural disposition. For them, nothing in this world is fine, but something else is, and this they will go on to pursue one day. However, those who already have the knowledge (*gnōsis*) should have gone in pursuit of the fine as a consequence; and when pursuing it they should have first set right things in this world, since they have issued forth from a divine nature. For it belongs to that | divine nature to heed the fine while disdaining bodily pleasure. But those who do not partake in virtue are altogether unable to progress toward the intelligibles.

The fact that they have not composed any treatise on virtue also bears witness against these people. They have completely left out any teachings on these subjects, and they do not | state what virtue is, or how many parts it has, or any of the other many fine doctrines considered by the ancients. They do not state how virtue is acquired and how one preserves it, nor how one takes care of the soul or purifies it. Saying "Look to god" certainly does not accomplish anything useful when one does not also teach people *how* to look. Someone might say: | "What prevents me from looking to god while not refraining from any pleasure or being powerless against anger; remembering the word 'god,' yet being impelled by all kinds of pleasure without making any attempt to remove them?" So really it is virtue that reveals god when it proceeds toward the goal and comes to be in the soul together with wisdom. In the mouth of someone | who is not truly virtuous, god is a mere name.

16. Moreover, despising the world, and the gods and other fine things within it, is not the same as becoming good. Every wicked man would have despised the gods at an earlier time, and even if he was not <completely wicked> before, i.e., if he was not wicked | in all other respects, when he despised the gods he would have become so by that very act.

Further, their supposed reverence for the intelligible gods is practically cut off from anything else. For someone who feels affection for another also welcomes anything that is their kin, for example the children of the father he loves. But every soul is a child of Father Intellect. There are also souls | in the stars, intellective, good, and much more connected to the intelligibles than ours. How then could this cosmos be separated from Intellect? How could the gods within the cosmos be?

But we have already discussed these matters before.[51] For now, [we must say] <that> these people do not know the intelligibles except in speech, because they certainly despise what is akin to them. Otherwise, | how can it be pious to deny that providence extends to the things in this world or anything whatsoever? How are they consistent with themselves? Because on the other hand, they claim that god only looks after them. But does he look after them when they are in the intelligible world, or also when they exist in this world? If he was looking after them when they were in the intelligible world, why did they come down? If he looks after them in this world, how can they still be here? And how is god himself | not also here? How else will he know that they are here? How would he know that, when they are here, they have not forgotten him and become bad? If he knows those that have not become bad, he also knows those that have, so that he can distinguish the one group from the other. So he will be present to all and he will be in this cosmos, | in whatever way; therefore the cosmos will also participate in him. Yet if he is absent from the cosmos, he will also be absent from you people, and you would not be able to say anything about him nor about what succeeds him.

51 At 9, 30–42 above.

But whether some form of providence reaches you from above, or whatever else it is you want, even so the cosmos receives something from the intelligible world and has not been left abandoned nor | is it going to be. For providence deals much more with wholes than with parts, and the world soul participates in it to a greater extent. Its existence and intelligence show this. Who among these unreasonably high-minded people is as ordered and rational as the universe? Even the comparison is ridiculous and very | absurd, and anyone who makes it, except for the sake of argument, will not escape the charge of impiety. Nor is posing this question characteristic of a reasonable person, but rather of some blind man who lacks perception and intellect, and is far from perceiving the intelligible cosmos, since he does not even see this universe. Indeed, could there be a musician | who, once he has perceived the harmony in the intelligible world, will not be moved by hearing the harmony in perceptible sounds? Or could there be an expert in geometry and arithmetic who will not take pleasure in symmetry, proportion and order when he sees them with his eyes? In the case of paintings, people who look at the products of this art with their | eyes do not even see the same things in the same way. Rather, when they recognize a perceptible imitation of something lying in thought, it is as if they are bewildered and coming to a recollection of the truth, which indeed is the same affection that moves lovers. Indeed, when someone sees beauty well represented in a face[52] he is led to the intelligibles. And who will | be so lazy in his mind and impassive to anything else, that on seeing all the beauties in the sensible world, all the symmetry and that great orderliness in it, the form that becomes apparent in the stars even though they are far away, he would not infer in consequence | that such things derive from the intelligibles, and be seized by awe? Then he did not understand these things in our world, nor did he see the intelligibles.

17. However, even if it came into their heads to hate the nature of the body because they have heard Plato often blame the body for the kinds of obstacles[53] it presents to the soul—and he said indeed that every bodily nature is worse than the soul—they ought to have considered what remains, | once they have removed this nature from their thought: an intelligible sphere encompassing the form imposed upon the cosmos; souls in ordered rank, without bodies, who give magnitude to the intelligible <and> lead it into extension, such that <what has come into being> may, by having magnitude, become like its indivisible model as far as it has the capacity. For greatness in the intelligible world | consists in power, but here in mass. And whether they wish to think that this [visible] sphere is in motion and that it revolves around by the power of

52 See Plato, *Phaedrus* 251a2–3.

53 See Plato, *Phaedo* 65a10.

god that is "the beginning, middle and end"[54] of its whole power, or whether they think that it stands still because the power of god is not yet governing anything else, it would be suitable for attaining a correct conception of the | soul that governs this universe. If they have already placed a body inside the soul, they should think about the cosmos in this way: the soul does not undergo any affection, but it gives to the other whatever each particular thing is capable of receiving, because jealousy is not allowed to exist among the gods.[55] They should grant the soul of the cosmos such power that it can make the bodily | nature, which is not beautiful, participate in beauty, to the extent that the soul can make it beautiful.

This very beauty is what stirs souls, which are divine, into motion. Unless perhaps they should say that beauty does not move them, and that they look at ugly and beautiful bodies indifferently. But in this way they would regard with indifference ugly and beautiful ways of life, beauty in sciences,[56] and abstract speculations; | and therefore god. Things here exist because of the primary beings. So if things in this world are not beautiful, neither are these: beautiful things in this world are their successors. But when they claim to despise the beauty in this world, they would do well to despise the beauty of boys and women

---

54 Plato, *Laws* 715e8–716a1.

55 See Plato, *Phaedrus* 247a7 and *Timaeus* 29e1–2.

56 Cf. Plato, *Symposium* 211c4–8.

<too>, so that they do not yield to licentiousness. But one should know that they would not | puff themselves up if they despised something ugly. Rather, they do it because they despise something that they first said is beautiful, <when they were in a bad state>.

Next, we should know that beauty is not the same in part and whole, in each thing and in the entirety; then, that there is such beauty in perceptible and partial things, e.g. the beauty of daemons, that one is astonished | by their maker and confident that they come from the intelligible world; and therefore we should proclaim that the intelligible beauty is "extraordinary,"[57] not clinging to sensible things or berating them, but rather proceeding from them toward the intelligibles. And if sensible beauties are also beautiful inside, we should declare that their inside agrees with the outside; but if their inside is ugly, they are diminished in their best parts. | But perhaps nothing exists that is really beautiful on the outside but ugly inside, because the outside is completely beautiful when the inner beauty prevails. Those who are called beautiful but are ugly on the inside also have a false exterior beauty. If someone is going to say that he has seen really beautiful people who were all the same ugly inside, I think | that he has not [really] seen them, but <wrongly> takes <them> to be beautiful. If he has really seen them, I think it is because the ugliness in them is some accretion to their beautiful

57 See Plato, *Republic* 509a6.

nature. For in this world there are many obstacles to reaching the goal. But what was to hinder the universe that is beautiful from also being beautiful within? Certainly those beings to which nature | has not granted perfection from the beginning may perhaps have been unable to reach their goal, so that it was also possible for them to become bad. But the universe was never imperfect like a child nor did anything extraneous attach itself to it, or add something to its body. Where could this have come from? The universe contained everything. But nor could one imagine | that something attached itself to its soul. If one granted them this possibility, though, it would not be something bad attaching itself.

18. But perhaps they will say that these arguments make us flee the body, so that we can hate it from afar, while ours bind the soul to it. This would be as though two people were living in the same beautiful house, | and one of them objected to its construction and its maker while staying as long in it as the other person. This other person does not object to anything, but says that the maker has made it very skillfully, and waits until the time when he will be delivered and no longer be in need of a house. The first man | might think he is cleverer and more prepared to depart, because he knows to say that the walls are put together from lifeless stones and wood and fall far short of the true dwelling. But he is ignorant that he distinguishes

himself only in being unable to bear necessities, unless in fact he pretends to feel disgust while secretly enamored with the beauty of the stones.

| As long as we have bodies, we must stay in the houses built by our good sister soul who has a great facility for creating without toil. Or do they think it is right to address even the meanest of men as their brothers, while they refuse to call the sun, the heavenly bodies, | and, "with their raving mouth,"[58] even the soul of the world "brothers"? It is right, in fact, not to be joined in kinship with men who are wicked, but with those beings that are good and not bodies, who are rather souls within bodies; souls that are able to inhabit them very much like the world soul inhabits the body of the universe. This consists in not | coming up against or paying heed to the pleasures or sights that assail us from outside,[59] and in not being disturbed if something painful occurs. The world soul certainly is not stricken by any misfortune, since there is nothing from which it could suffer. But we who are in this world may push back the blows of fortune through virtue: some blows are already lessened by our greatness of mind, while others do not even succeed in | striking because of our strength. When we have become nearly immune to blows, we imitate the soul of the universe and of the stars, and when we come very close to achieving

58 Heraclitus DK B92.

59 See Plato, *Timaeus* 43b7–c1.

likeness with it, we rush toward the same goal and are even ourselves able to enjoy contemplation of the same objects, inasmuch as we too have prepared ourselves well in our natures and | pursuits. But for the soul of the universe and the stars this is possible from the beginning.

These people are certainly no better able to contemplate if they should claim that they alone have the capacity; nor will it do so because they say that they can depart from here when they die, while the stars <that> always adorn the heavens cannot. They may say this because they are ignorant what this "outside" can possibly be and how the soul | "takes care of the whole lifeless universe."[60] <It is because they do not see that their soul comes from outside that they also do not think that the nature of the stars looks at what is outside.>[61]

Therefore, it is possible to cease loving the body and to become pure; to despise death; to come to know the better things and to pursue them; not to jealously allege that the beings who are able to pursue them and always do so, are not in fact pursuing them; and not to be under the same | impression as those who think that the stars do not run their course, because perception tells them that these stand still.

---

60 Plato, *Phaedrus* 246b6.

61 Lines 46–48 have been transposed to come after line 40.

Commentary

Chapter 1

In this chapter, Plotinus summarizes his doctrine of first principles, and defends it against any attempts to increase or lessen their number.

1, 1–8 *It has become . . . and then good*: *Ennead* II.9 begins *in medias res*, by summing up some of the main conclusions about the nature of the One that were reached in V.5 [32], the treatise immediately preceding *Against the Gnostics* in chronological order. The claim that the One is "simple and primary" occurs at V.5.10, 10, while the notion that the Good has "nothing within itself" is argued for at some length in Chapter 13 of that treatise. Plotinus is committed to the thesis that anything is ontologically primary if and only if it is also absolutely simple. If a principle had some duality within it, then it could not be what is ultimately primary, because it would not be truly simple. Conversely, a principle that is primary only in some qualified way could not be absolutely simple, because whatever is ontologically superior to it would also have to be simpler. The parenthetical sentence "for everything that is not primary is not simple" expresses this latter claim.

Central to the notion that the Good does not have anything "within itself" is the denial that anything at all can be predicated of it, which is the relevant sense of "being in" here (see Aristotle, *Categories* 1a24–5). Plotinus illustrates this point by saying that "this nature [*sc.* the One] itself is not something or other, and then one, nor is the Good something or other, and then good" (1, 4–5). We are not given an explicit argument to this effect, but with a view to the earlier treatise V.5, one might reason as follows. Suppose, contrary to Plotinus' claim, that one could meaningfully say, "The Good is beautiful," for example. In this case, there would be some property, namely "being beautiful," that the Good shares with other beautiful things. So what makes the Good unique and separate from these other entities? It must be some other feature that the Good has, not included in the predicate "beautiful," and this is the predicate "good." But now the Good is no longer a single unity, but something divided into (a) the property "being beautiful" that it shares with other beautiful things, and (b) whatever else it is that distinguishes it from these, namely its goodness. As a result, the Good would be a composite of "good," which differentiates it from other things, and "not-good," in so far as it has property of "being beautiful," which is different from its "goodness." And so, concludes Plotinus, this composite Good cannot well be the first principle of goodness, since it is not simply good but a composite, such that it must derive its own goodness from participation in some even higher principle. See V.5.13, 20–32, which provides the materials for the above argument.

One might object here that the Good has an essential nature, its goodness, and that it therefore does contain something "within itself," namely goodness. But in Plotinus' view, even this seemingly harmless kind of self-predication must be ruled in the case of the single nature that is the Good. We can see the reason why: take the claim "The Good is good," and then argue in a manner exactly parallel to the one sketched out in the preceding paragraph. If the Good shares its goodness with other good things, some property must distinguish it from them (say, for the sake of argument, its "oneness"). And so again, the Good is a composite, only this time "being good" is what it has in common with other good things, while the property that is other than "being good," its "oneness," differentiates it from them. Hence, even self-predication will make the Good a composite, and thus undermine its claim to being a first principle.

A note on the translation of 1, 4 is in order at this point: Like Harder and Armstrong, I take *hautē* to refer to the nature of the One, and *touto* as referring to the Good. Other translators (Igal, for example) take *touto* to be referring to the One once more. On this reading, Plotinus would be saying that the *One* is not something or other, and then good. Dufour offers a different reading, according to which both *hautē* and *touto* refer to the single nature of the One-Good, such that Plotinus would be denying that the One-Good is first one thing (either good or one) and then another (whichever one of the two properties is left). On this reading, the remark in 1, 4–5 emphasizes the perfect coincidence of the One and the Good.

1, 3 *some sort of unity*: "Some sort of unity" translates the Greek *hen ti*. An alternative translation would be "some one." Harder's translation "ein Eines und Einheitliches" elegantly captures both senses.

1, 5–8 *Since this has . . . as far as possible*: Note here the distinction implied between "attributing" a property to the single nature of the One/Good, and "revealing it to ourselves." We cannot genuinely attribute a predicate to the Good, since even a sentence of the form "The Good is one" implies a kind of internal complexity of subject and predicate that cannot properly reflect the unified nature of the first principle itself (see the note on 1, 1–8 above). However, predication can have some usefulness for us as inquirers into the nature of the Good, by allowing us to single out particular features of the Good, even though the Good, as Good, does not possess these features in the divided manner of our thinking and speech. Cf. V.3.14, 4–8; V.5.6, 11–25; V.5.13, 9–17; VI.9.5, 29–41 on the ineffability of the One and human efforts to refer to it.

1, 10–11 *everything that exists . . . from that thing*: Cf. Plato, *Parmenides* 138a2–4, a passage noted by Dufour (2006, 239n9), where the character Parmenides refutes the thesis that the One can be "in something else," although on very different grounds than Plotinus here.

The converse of the principle that everything which exists in something else also takes its existence from something else is more fully explained at V.5.9, 1–5: "Everything that comes to be by something else is either in that which has made it or in something else, supposing that there were to be something after that which made it. For since that which comes to be by another was also in need of that other for its generation, it needs that other everywhere, for which reason it is in another" (tr. Gerson).

1, 16–18 *For if they . . . are the same*: With this first appearance of "they" in II.9, Plotinus may be referring, in the first instance, to some imagined objectors, rather than to a specific individual or group of individuals. At this point, Plotinus does not yet seem to have his Gnostic opponents in mind (whom he never identifies, consistently referring to them as "they"). Their ontology was, in his view, too permissive rather than too restrictive. One may thus view this section as transitional: the general topic is that of unreasonable departures from the correct account of first principles, and here, the views of other philosophers in antiquity can stand beside Gnostic positions. A great difficulty for interpreters is the fact that Plotinus nowhere signals to his readers when the referent of "they" changes in the course of his discussion. The position of those who make Soul and Intellect the same can perhaps be related to the Stoics, according to whom the soul is chiefly its rational or "governing" (*hēgemonikon*) part (see, for example, Pseudo-Galen, *Philosophical History* 24.41–2). Aristotle, on the other hand, could be described as holding that Intellect is "the primary nature," that is, the first principle of everything (on a plausible interpretation of *Metaphysics* 12.7.1072b–1073a); a similar conflation can also be found among Middle Platonists, e.g. Alcinous, *Handbook of Platonism* 10.3; Numenius, frs. 11, 15, 16.12–17.

1, 18–19 *But it has . . . from each other*: Notable passages where Plotinus distinguishes Soul and Intellect are V.9.4; V.1.10–11. He argues against the identity of Intellect and the One particularly in V.6, a treatise that explains why a principle beyond Intellect is needed that does not itself think. See also III.8.9–10; V.4.2.

1, 19–20 *if there are more [principles] than these three. Then . . .* : I punctuate, with Heigl and Kirchhoff: *Loipon de . . . tōn triōn toutōn. Tines an . . . par'autas*;

Plotinus now goes on to review what possible grounds one might have for wishing to introduce further principles beyond the three he has already singled out, and which he takes to be exhaustive. He proceeds to give five different reasons why neither the One nor the Intellect admits of any further division.

Earlier Platonists were able to find Platonic "proof texts" for a division of the intelligible world into more principles than Plotinus would allow. Particularly relevant here are pseudo-Plato's *Second Letter* (312e) and a passage from the *Timaeus* (39e7–9) that Plotinus will go on to discuss in Chapter 6 of the present treatise (6, 19–24). In the passage from the *Second Letter*, we find the following mysterious description of "Three Kings," which could lend support to the idea that there must be at least three principles in the intelligible world: "Upon the king of all do all things turn; he is the end of all things and the cause of all good. Things of the second order turn upon the second principle, and those of the third order upon the third (tr. Morrow)." *Timaeus* 39e7–9 had likewise been taken to imply a threefold division of principles, according to a strained interpretation of the following lines that describe the actions of the Demiurge: "And so he determined that the living by Porphyry, *Life of Plotinus* 16.6–7—make a threefold division of the intelligible world (what they call the Aeon of Barbelo), into a principle at rest that is contemplated (Kalyptos), a principle in motion that contemplates (Protophanes), and a creative principle that uses rational deliberation (Autogenes). See Turner (2001, 695–697). Such is the debt of the Gnostics to the Platonist Numenius in their construction of the intelligible world that the latter has been given the sobriquet "a half-Gnostic" (*ein halber Gnostiker*); see Harder-Beutler-Theiler (1960, 426). Plotinus returns to the Gnostics' threefold division of the Intellect at 6, 14–24.

1, 21–22 *For no one . . . have thus described*: Plotinus' first argument against attempts to multiply realities is to deny that any principles beyond the One can be discovered. See VI.9.1–2 for a representative argument for the claim that the One is the highest and simplest principle of all things. Cf. V.3.12, 9–14; V.4.1, 5–15.

1, 23–25 *They are surely . . . potentiality and actuality*: Having ruled out the possibility of a principle beyond the One, Plotinus now rejects the view that some kind of duality may be found in the "principle of everything," which for him is the One. The passage can be read as presenting the following *a fortiori* argument: given that a division into actuality and potentiality in intelligible beings is ridiculous in general, so much more will it be ridiculous to apply such a division to the One in particular. In the case of intelligible beings, the Intellect for example, which, for Plotinus, is always actively thinking (or thinking "in actuality"), there would be no sense in making a further division into one aspect of the Intellect that is potentially actively thinking and one that is actually actively thinking, since Intellect is always actively thinking, and never potentially. On the other hand, if Intellect could be so divided, it would have to be preceded by an intellect that is always thinking, since actuality is prior to potentiality (see V.9.5, 1–4 for an argument to this effect).

He does not specify what the relationship between the potential and actual parts of a principle would be on the kind of account he is considering. Is the actual part prior to the potential part, or vice versa? In light of the suggestions that are discussed in the remainder of the chapter (1, 26–57), it seems that the potential part would be prior to the active one, just as the intellect at rest is prior to the intellect in motion (1, 26–33), and the intellect that thinks is prior to the intellect that is actively aware that it thinks (1, 33–57). For Gnostic parallels for the idea of a first principle in potentiality, see, for example, Irenaeus, *Against the Heresies* 1.1.1, reporting the views of the Valentinian Gnostic Ptolemy, who posited a "Pre-Principle" or "Pre-Father" as his first Aeon.

intellective through a reason-principle (*logos*). Crucially, he does not think that this *logos* has any independent existence of its own (cf. III.2.6, 12–17; IV.4.2, 27–29; V.1.3, 12–23; V.1.6, 49); he rather describes it as the product of both Intellect and Soul, although some passages, hastily read, could suggest that the *logos* acts as an independent principle (see, for example, III.2.2, 15–18; III.5.9, 1–8). On the established text, we are, rather oddly, given an argument against such an intermediate principle only at the end of the chapter, at 1, 57–63, rather than following 1, 33, where one should expect it.

1, 34–40 *Nor indeed should. . . . has been thinking*: The Greek *en toutois* literally means "in these matters"; from the context, the words most likely refer to thinking in the human realm, since Plotinus is contrasting human thinking with the thinking of the true Intellect, where it would be "ridiculous" to introduce a distinction between thinking and awareness of thought. An alternative translation of *en toutois* would be "among these people." On this reading, Plotinus would ascribe the claim "Thinking and thinking that one thinks are different things" to his opponents, rather than endorsing it in so far as it applies to our world. See Spanu (2012, 56–57).

"Mental application" here translates the Greek term *prosbolē*; alternative translations would be "intuition" or "awareness." From the context, it is difficult to decide which translation is preferable, and not much may depend on the choice of either alternative (although to speak of an "awareness" that is "well aware of its own activities" is more tautological in English than in Plotinus' Greek). In what sense, though, is thinking "one thing," and thinking that one thinks, "another," given that the two do not in fact come apart but are united in a single "mental application"? Plotinus has not yet turned to discussing the "conceptual" (*epinoiai*) distinctions that his opponents wish to make (in lines 40–57), so presumably the question in the present passage cannot be whether thinking and thinking that one thinks are to be conceptually distinguished. Perhaps we can understand Plotinus to be saying that both thinking "This rose is red," for example, and thinking "I think this rose is red" are intrinsically self-aware, such that any instance of thinking is a single "mental application" that is aware of its activities, whether it is expressly self-reflexive or not. Nevertheless, there is a real distinction between the two thoughts: one is about the red rose, the other about the thought (or my thinking) about the red rose.

Plotinus evidently considers absurd the view that one part of Intellect is thinking, while another part (not identical with the thinking part) is only thinking that it thinks. But at this stage, Plotinus is not providing an independent argument against the division of the Intellect into thinking and self-thinking parts. Rather, he is simply pointing out that this division is incompatible with a view of Intellect that he elsewhere defends (notably in V.3 and V.5), namely that it is a complete unity in the act of thinking. However, see Commentary on 1, 46–52 below for an explicit argument against the position under attack here.

Finally, something must be said about the origin of the distinction within the Intellect that Plotinus discusses. It seems to me that Numenius is once again our best source for the distinction between an intellect that thinks, and a lower intellect that thinks that it thinks. The main evidence is worth quoting here: "Numenius assigns to the First [*sc.* Intellect] a rank corresponding to the Living Being and says that it thinks by using (*en proschrēsei*) the Second; the Second corresponds to Intellect and this principle in turn creates by using the Third, which corresponds to discursive intellect" (fr. 22 des Places, tr. Perry). Now on one interpretation of the fragment, the first intellect generates a second intellect in order to contemplate *itself*; the first intellect only gains self-awareness of its thinking "by using" the second intellect. Cf. Perry (2012, 175–177). Behind this theory is an attempt to explain how Intellect and the objects of its thinking, namely real beings, are related. Numenius thinks that the objects of thoughts in the first intellect must be "at rest" and prior to any activity of contemplation, which is the task of the second intellect. Plotinus himself comes very close to adopting such a solution at III.9.1, 19–20, where he says that the intellect that contemplates the intelligible intellect is "in a way the intellect of that intellect, because it thinks it." On such a view, one may well conclude that the contemplating intellect is an intellect that thinks that it thinks. The influence of Numenius is palpable in III.9.1; see also Commentary on 1, 19–20. See also Dodds (1963, 277–278). For an interesting parallel in the system of the Gnostic Marcus, see Irenaeus, *Against the Heresies* 1.14.1 (=1.8.1.11–17 Harvey): "When first the unoriginated, inconceivable Father, who is without material substance and is neither male nor female, willed to bring forth that which is ineffable to Him, and to endow with form that which is invisible, He opened His mouth, and sent forth the Word similar to Himself, who, standing near, showed Him what He Himself was, inasmuch as He had been manifested in the form of that which was invisible" (tr. Roberts-Rambaut). See also *Zostrianus* (NHC VIII,1) 82.2–83.1. Cf. Elsas (1975, 163–164).

1, 36 *But it would . . . the true Intellect*: This sentence contrasts the true intellect with human thinking; I am thus reading *de* ("but") with Harder, in place of HS_2's *gar* ("for").

1, 40–44 *But if they . . . it is thinking*: The Greek *epinoiai* ("in thought"; *epinoia* in the dative case) in this context comes close in meaning to what in English would be called a "conceptual" distinction, in opposition to a real difference in things. For this use of *epinoia*, cf. Sextus Empiricus, *Against the Professors* 10.255.3–5; Ammonius, *Commentary on Porphyry's* Introduction 40.6–8. See also García Bazán (1977) for a discussion of this term in Plotinus and in Gnostic texts, and Kobusch (2007) for a more general survey of its significance in ancient thought.

The logic of this sentence stands somewhat in need of explanation: it argues that, if Plotinus' opponents defend the distinction between an intellect that thinks and one that is thinking that it thinks as a merely "conceptual" one, they should not at the same time maintain that this distinction marks a real difference between entities, and therefore they should let go of the multiple realities they have introduced in the intelligible world. Next, even if their distinction were merely conceptual, the opponents do not thereby avoid reaching conclusions that are just as absurd as if they were talking about real distinctions in the Intellect.

1, 44–46 *If this happened . . . charge of foolishness*: "Amongst ourselves" presumably refers not only to followers of Plotinus, but to "us" as members of the human species. Plotinus here adduces the psychological fact that we are aware of our "impulses and thoughts" to reject the view that an intelligible principle could somehow contain a part that is unaware of its own activity of thinking.

Following two suggestions by Heigl, I am here reading *eimen* ("we are") in place of *eien* ("they are"), and *aitian echoi* ("it would invite the charge") in place of *aitian echoien* ("they would invite the charge"), to agree with *eph' hēmōn* ("amongst ourselves") at 1, 44.

1, 46–52 *Now when the . . . duality in thought*: The view that the objects of thought are "outside" the Intellect was at one time defended by Porphyry; the task of refuting him fell to Amelius (see Porphyry, *Life of Plotinus* 18.8–14). Plotinus takes up the issue at length in V.5, where he also defends the essential unity of the Intellect with the objects of thought in its thinking. How precisely does the unity of the Intellect with its objects of thought prevent the conceptual distinction that Plotinus' opponents wish to introduce into the Intellect? The analogy with seeing here is helpful. Assume that Intellect thinks itself; then it will be its own object of thought. If thinking is a kind of seeing, Intellect will, by thinking itself, also "see" itself. Now assume further that Intellect is completely transparent to itself, in other words, that it has a complete and true grasp of itself by thinking about itself. Then when it comes to "see" itself, it will also "see" its own activity of thinking about itself. And so, in the case of Intellect, thinking and thinking that it thinks would be intrinsically connected, if we assume the complete transparency of Intellect to itself. Cf. V.6.1, 1–5; V.9.5, 4–16.

Proclus, a later Platonist, may have Plotinus' argument in the present passage in mind when he argues that every intellect is "simultaneously aware of the thing known, of itself as the knower, and of itself as the object of its own intellective act" (*Elements of Theology* 168, tr. Dodds).

1, 52–54 *Further, if Intellect . . . that it thinks*: Why should the fact that Intellect is "always thinking what it is" rule out its conceptual separation into "thinking" and "thinking that it thinks"? I take it that Plotinus here relies on an argument very similar to the one at 1, 46–52 (see my comment above), but that he strengthens it in one respect, with the addition of "always." The point is that, if Intellect always has a complete and true grasp of its own activity, and its activity is thinking about itself, there can never be a time when its self-reflexive thinking could be separate from its thinking.

1, 54–57 *Indeed, if one . . . this to infinity*: From 1, 33–54, Plotinus has already argued that it would be superfluous to separate out a part of Intellect that thinks that it thinks. He concludes his refutation with a final *reductio ad absurdum*: if the opponents admit at least one superfluous distinction in the Intellect, they have no principled grounds for not admitting even further distinctions, such that they will have to accept an infinite regress of higher and higher levels of self-thinking parts.

1, 57–63 *Further, anyone supposing. . . . think at all*: In this argument against an intermediate entity between Intellect and Soul, Plotinus takes it for granted that Soul, if its rationality were due to some intermediary reason-principle derived from Intellect (cf. 1, 31–32), would "not know Intellect nor think at all" (lines 62–63). Both of these claims deserve comment. The first, that the Soul "will not know Intellect" if it is, so to speak, at two removes from it appears to rely on the assumption that a superior entity can only be properly known by those entities directly succeeding it. Knowledge of a principle, on this picture, would be intransitive: if the intermediate reason-principle knows Intellect, and Soul the intermediate reason-principle, then it does not follow that Soul knows Intellect. Plotinus' second claim, that the Soul will not "think at all" if it is at two removes from Intellect, requires the assumption that any kind of thinking that is not appropriately related to Intellect is not thinking at all. Without this assumption, Plotinus would only be entitled to the weaker conclusion that whatever cognitive activity the Soul, on the account he rejects, would possess, it will not be the kind of thinking that is continuous with its procession from the Intellect, but some other, lower and presumably more fallible, form of thinking.

We are now faced with the difficult task of identifying the originator of this *logos* theory. Some such theory was current in both Platonic and Gnostic circles. Particular importance must be given to one member of Plotinus' circle, the Platonist Amelius, who interpreted the prologue of St. John's Gospel so as to make the *logos* an independent principle. In Amelius' view, it is according to the eternal *logos*, the source of "living, life and being," that whatever has come to be has come to be (see Eusebius, *Preparation of the Gospel* 11.19). The little that Eusebius tells us about Amelius' views is perplexing, but it is entirely possible that his *logos* was conceived of as an intermediary between the lowest, demiurgic phase of Intellect (Amelius divides the Intellect into three; see Commentary 1, 19–20 for the background to this division) and the world soul. Cf. Dillon (2009, 33), who suggests that for Amelius, the *logos* was "a projection downward into Soul, and ultimately into the physical world, of the totality of Forms resident in the Intellect." See also Vollenweider (2009). It is worth noting, in this context, that the Valentinians, like Amelius, were eager students of St. John's Prologue in particular, such that an exegesis comparable to Amelius' own could also have flourished in their midst. Cf. Heracleon fr. 1 (= Origen, *Commentary on the Gospel of John* 2.14.102.2–55; 103.5–7 Blanc), which suggests that the *logos* provided the cause for the Demiurge's creation and is the active principle that operates through him. In the *Tripartite Tractate*, on the other hand, the *logos* takes on both a lower, demiurgic aspect and a higher aspect that re-ascends into the intelligible world, making it more similar in its contemplative and creative activities to Plotinus' own world soul than to a principle intermediate between Soul and Intellect. Cf. (NHC I,5) 85.15–90.13.

Chapter 2

After summarizing the results of the previous chapter, Plotinus turns his attention to the nature of individual souls. He briefly alludes to his view that one part of the soul always remains in the intelligible world, before explaining how we may conceive of the activity of the world soul, which is always directed to the intelligible world.

2, 1–4 *Therefore one must. . . . as it can*: This summary of the previous chapter underscores that the main topic of discussion so far has been the nature of Intellect. Two of three characteristics Plotinus ascribes to Intellect in 2, 3–4 are deserving of further comment. There is, first, the peculiar adjective "unswerving" (*aklinēs*), relatively rare in the Plotinian corpus: its other occurrences, at III.7.11, 4 and VI.8.9, 33, also qualify Intellect. "Unswerving" differs from "unmoving" or "unchanging" only slightly; it may here serve to emphasize the constancy of Intellect's activity of thinking, and the impossibility of its decline to a lesser form of existence. In second place, it is worth noting that "the Father," which Intellect is said to imitate, refers to the One. Numenius is reported to have called his first principle "Father" (frs. 12.3–4; 21.1), and his influence can be felt behind the charge (reported by Porphyry, *Life of Plotinus* 17.1–6) that Plotinus plagiarized him.

2, 1 *superfluous distinctions*: As pointed out by Harder, the use of the plural word *epinoiai* ("distinctions") may be subtly mocking, since the singular *Epinoia* (in the sense of "afterthought") is used in a number of Gnostic texts to describe the offspring of the divine principle *Ennoia*. See, for example, *Apocryphon of John* (NHC II,1) 8.11; 9.25; 20.17–28; *Trimorphic Protennoia* (NHC XIII,1) 39.17–32.

2, 4–10 *One part of. . . . be dragged down*: With this transition to the nature of our soul, Plotinus moves on from his refutation of those who seek to multiply intelligible realities beyond necessity to an altogether different subject, the nature and creative activity of individual souls, and their relation to the world soul. Although the soul is briefly described as a single nature with many powers (see 2, 6), the question of its unity is never directly raised. Only the slightest hint of polemic comes through in the chapter (see the comment on 2, 14); for the most part, Plotinus is here content to set out his own views on the soul, which will provide him with a launching point for the more direct engagement with the Gnostics in subsequent chapters, where soul's creation of matter becomes a central topic. Plato's *Republic* and *Phaedrus* contain important accounts of the division of the soul into three parts. In Book 4 of the *Republic*, Socrates argues that, in order to resolve obvious cases of psychological conflict, such as both wanting to eat another slice of cake and not wanting to eat it, we must distinguish different parts of the soul. Instead of saying that I both want to enjoy x and do not want to enjoy x at the same time in the same respect, which would result in contradiction, we can say that my appetitive part, for example, desires the slice of cake, while reason, which looks out for the interests of myself as a whole, instills me with a contravening desire to abstain from more sugary sweets. Between reason and appetite, Socrates argues, exists another set of desires that are concerned with one's social self, and which takes into account other people's evaluations of my actions. This part, the spirited part of the soul, motivates an agent through emotions like anger (the feeling of being wronged by another) and shame (the sense that a particular action or desire of mine would be disapproved of by society at large). In the *Phaedrus*, we find a similar division of the soul into three parts expressed in mythical language. There, Socrates likens the structure of the soul to a charioteer with a team of two winged horses: one of the charioteer's horses "is beautiful and good and from stock of the same sort, while the other is the opposite and has the opposite sort of bloodline" (246b; tr. Nehamas-Woodruff). See also *Timaeus* 41d–42d for a similar division of souls.

Plotinus' division of the soul in the present passage, however, is not primarily concerned with desires and motivations, but rather with the objects toward which each soul part is directed, and the kinds of cognitive activities that are appropriate for these objects. The highest part of the soul is always directed toward the objects of knowledge, "the intelligibles," while the lowest part looks toward thing in this world through sense perception. One of the main functions of the intermediate part of the soul is to make judgments based on the impressions received from sense-perception (see, for example, V.3.2, 7–14; V.3.3, 1–12; V.3.10, 40–44). In this respect, the pertinent Platonic influence is the division of the line in *Republic* Book 6 (509d–511e), where Socrates contrasts the direct understanding (*noēsis*) of Forms with a lower kind of thought (*dianoia*) that proceeds from sensible images to make claims about abstract concepts like the square or the triangle itself, analogous to Plotinus' intermediate part of the soul.

The suggestion in 2, 4–5, that one part of our soul always remains in the intelligible world, has proved to be Plotinus' most controversial legacy to the Platonic tradition. As he explains in IV.8.8, 1–6—apparently contrary to the opinion of certain unnamed "others" who may well be his contemporaries, as Fleet (2012, 183) argues—the undescended part of the soul always contemplates the intelligibles, but our awareness of this contemplation may be affected when the lowest part of the soul "is thrown into turmoil" (tr. Fleet). Why did Plotinus posit an undescended soul-part? Nothing in Plato obviously suggests that one part of the soul is always contemplating even if we are unaware of it, although the famous simile of the sea god Glaucon in Book

10 of the *Republic* may perhaps be taken to suggest that the underlying reality of soul is never separated from the intelligibles. An interpreter of Plato who takes seriously the *Republic*'s suggestion then faces a problem: how can the real nature of soul be divine and pure, and at the same time, as in the myth of the charioteer in the *Phaedrus*, be dragged down to earth by the unruly horse of desire and emotion? And if the whole soul is indeed dragged down and separated from the intelligible world, what is it that enables it to return to its natural state of contemplation? At least part of Plotinus' motivation for introducing this particular doctrine, then, is that it reconciles, on the one hand, different Platonic sources, while also providing an explanation of how the soul's connection to the intelligible world can survive intact through the profound changes that different incarnations will bring about (see *Timaeus* 42a–d for Plato's account of a descending scale of incarnations). It is against this background that we can understand Plotinus' insistence in 2, 9–10 that "the whole soul is not allowed to be dragged down." In less metaphorical terms, he presumably means that even though the whole soul (the collection of soul parts) can become disintegrated, in so far as focus on perception and pleasures disturbs one's ability to reason abstractly, and consequently to become aware of the unified way of thinking that is characteristic of the highest part of the soul, the activity of that part is not itself impaired. Cf. IV.8.8, 6–13.

2, 6 *the soul is one nature with many powers*: Some scholars have viewed the phrase "one nature with many powers" as polemical, for example Igal (1982, 495n21) and more guardedly Dufour (2006, 244–245n33). While some Gnostic sects divide souls in accordance with their powers (the Valentinians, for instance, divide souls into those made of an incorruptible "pneumatic" substance on the one hand, and those made of "psychic" and "material" substances on the other, corresponding to their various capacities to receive spiritual knowledge), Plotinus insists that a single entity, soul, can possess a multiplicity of powers, without its unity being undermined. See Irenaeus, *Against the Heresies* 1.6.1–6.2; *Tripartite Tractate* (NHC I,5) 118.14–122.12. But there is no compelling reason, in my view, to read the phrase in this way. It is, first and foremost, needed as the premise in an argument: given that the soul is capable of doing many things, we can understand why it is able to tend toward being as well as the sensible world.

2, 7–9 *sometimes the whole . . . and of being*: The scope of "being" (*to on*) in this sentence cannot be restricted to "intelligible being" alone. If this were the case, Plotinus would appear to divide the intelligible world into better and worse parts, a result that would be difficult to square with his insistence on the unity and homogeneity of the world of forms. Instead, "being" must be understood in a wider sense, including both the objects of sense perception as well as intelligible being. On this reading, there is no difficulty involved in singling out the best part, intelligible being, of a greater whole comprising things that exist quite generally.

An alternative reading has been suggested by Spanu (2012, 5) who argues that "the whole soul" (*tēn pasan* [sc. *psuchēn*]) should be supplied in thought before "of being" (*tou ontos*), to yield: " . . . the whole soul belongs to being." The present translation, however, supposes that both *autēs* ("of it") and *tou ontos* ("of being") qualify *tōi aristōi* ("the best part"), as is, I think, naturally suggested by the Greek.

2, 10–11 *This affliction befalls the soul*: By "this affliction," Plotinus means the state of souls that have become individual and separate from the world soul ("the soul that is not a part," as it is called at 2, 11). He does not here explain how this individuation is possible, but a passage from IV.8 can shed light on the process and its consequences: "But the individual souls move out of the universal to become partial and to belong to themselves; each of them, as if weary of being with something else, retires into its own place. When it does this over a period of time, fleeing the All and setting itself apart, and does not look at the intelligible—then it becomes a part, is isolated, grows weak, becomes embroiled and looks to the partial [. . .]" (IV.8.4, 10–15; tr. Fleet). See also V.1.1, 3–5, a difficult passage where Plotinus lists "audacity, birth and the first otherness" as the reasons why souls "fall."

2, 12 *and of which we are no more a part either*: What Plotinus denies here is the view that we, as individual souls, are parts of the world soul. At IV.3.1–3, he argues at length that the relation of part to whole cannot properly capture the relation between individual and world soul.

2, 13–18 *There the soul. . . . itself always illuminated*: The remainder of the chapter describes the activity of the world soul, which orders the visible universe. Its power derives from the contemplation of Intellect, and involves neither active deliberation nor periodic interventions to restore the natural order. The world soul is always directed toward Intellect (cf. IV.8.2, 53–54), and "grows more beautiful and powerful" (2, 16) through this contemplation. Ontologically higher causes are endowed with greater causal power; so the world soul, itself the product of Intellect, will in its contemplation of Intellect become more powerful, that is to say, be more fully in possession of the rational principles (*logoi*) that it derives from Intellect. These rational principles (*logoi*) are in turn passed on to nature (cf. II.3.17, 15–17), the "trace" and "lowest expression" (II.3.18, 12) of the world soul, or its "successor," as at 2, 17. By both receiving and passing on rational principles, the world soul thus "illuminates just as it is itself always illuminated" (2, 17–18).

2, 14 *it does not govern with rational calculation, nor does it restore anything to order*: Two strains of thought are joined together in this phrase: there is, first, Aristotle's claim that nature, like art, does not deliberate. An experienced carpenter, for example, will not have to deliberate about the purpose of his art, nor, perhaps, even about the steps he needs to take in order to achieve a particular goal each time. Rather, given a particular product that he wants to make, he will be able to manipulate his materials accordingly. Likewise, nature does not actively deliberate either about the manner in which it produces natural organisms, nor does it deliberate about the purpose for which it brings together different elements in order to create an animal or a plant (see Aristotle, *Physics* 2.8.199b26–33). Like Aristotle, Plotinus thinks that nature so produces living beings. But Plotinus applies this same idea more widely to the principle on which nature itself depends, namely the world soul, which "does not govern with rational calculation" (2, 14). As he explains in IV.8.8, 13–16: "The soul that is whole and belongs to the whole brings order to the whole by the part of it that is on the side of the body; transcending it effortlessly, because it acts on what is below it not through calculation, as we do, but by intellection—for 'art does not deliberate'—organizing what is below it, what belongs to the whole" (tr. Fleet). Other passages in II.9 where the world soul's activity is discussed are 4, 15–17; 7, 27–32; 8, 3–5.20–21; 18, 15–17.

Cf. IV.4.10, 7–29; IV.4.12. See also O'Meara (1980) on the world soul's creative activity.

A second line of thought in the present passage is that the world soul does not "restore anything to order" (2, 14). On one level, this remark supports the general claim that the world soul "remains free of care" (2, 13), in that governance of the universe does not require any active interventions on its part that would somehow distract it from its contemplation (on which see the comment above, on 2, 13–18). But one may also suspect a hint of anti-Gnostic polemic: as Alt (1990, 18) has pointed out, Valentinian accounts of the fall of the divine principle of Sophia presuppose that some subsequent restoration of order is required. See, for instance, Hippolytus, *Refutation of All Heresies* 6.36.1.1–2.1 Marcovich, where the same Greek verb *diorthoun* ("to correct," "to amend") features prominently. On this account, the creation of the universe results from transgressions in the divine realm, principally the illicit desire of Sophia to create an offspring. It is the role of Christ (in his lowest manifestation) to "amend" these transgressions. Plotinus mentions this Gnostic view in another context, only to reduce it to absurdity. In his view, it amounts to thinking of the world soul as a farmer who is "putting right" (*diorthoutai*) the damage caused to his crops by wind and hailstorms, a crudely anthropomorphic account that cannot be seriously entertained. Cf. II.3.16, 33–36. Note that both the idea of rational calculation and restoring things to order are brought together in the Sethian Gnostic text *Allogenes* (NHC XI,3), in the following passage: "Like all [the] aeons, the Barbelo-Aeon is also endowed with the types and forms of the things that truly exist, the image of Kalyptos; and endowed with their intelligent rational principles, it bears the male Intellect Protophanes as an image, and acts within the Individuals either with craft or with skill or with partial instinct; endowed with the divine Autogenes as an image and knowing each one of these (individuals), it acts separately and individually, continually rectifying defects arising from Nature" (51.12–32; tr. Turner).

Chapter 3

The world soul that is always illuminated by Intellect will forever pass on the power that it receives from there, just as all other levels of reality pass on some part of themselves to lower beings.

3, 1–3 *So because the. . . . [because of it]*: This sentence summarizes the results of 2, 13–18, where the creative activity of the world soul is explained. While "the successor" in 2, 17 is best understood as nature as a whole, "the successors" at 3, 2 refer to the totality of natural living beings. "The light" (3, 3) that they receive from the world soul and by which they are "always held together and nourished" (3, 2) stands for the reason-principles which nature implants into matter in order to create living beings. These living beings "have the benefit of living" (3, 3) to varying degrees, because they are not able to receive the whole soul (cf. VI.4.15, 3–6). Underlying this line of thought is an important principle in the *Enneads*: that the degree of participation depends on the suitability of the participating entity. See VI.4.11, 3–14.

3, 4–7 *It is just. . . . participates in them*: The illustration of the fire and the heat that it radiates to those around it helps to imagine how an immaterial power can be present to all. While the heat that the fire gives off decreases with one's distance from it, the same is not true for incorporeal powers, whose greatness is not measurable in quantitative terms, and inexhaustible because derived from intelligible causes. Cf. VI.4–5, which discusses the omnipresence of divine powers in depth.

3, 7–12 *No, it is. . . . and for eternity*: In these lines, Plotinus extends his reflections from the world soul to the Good, Intellect and the hypostasis Soul. It is a curious shift in the argument, to be explained perhaps by the fact that a general understanding of immaterial causes leads to the conclusion that there can be no absolute coming to be or perishing for the universe. How matter links into this line of thought will be considered below at 3, 15–21. What the present passage gives expression to is Plotinus' theory of double activity, which states that, in addition to an internal, primary activity that constitutes each entity, there is also a secondary activity directed outward, which arises as the necessary by-product of the first. To use one of his own illustrations, one can distinguish the heat that makes the fire what it is (that "completes its essence," as Plotinus would have it; cf. V.4.2, 30–31), from the warmth that is generated around it as a result. See V.1.6, 30–39; V.4.2, 27–33.

3, 10 *some secondary life along with the primary living*: MacKenna's succinct "some life after the Primal Life, a second where there is a first" captures the meaning of this sentence admirably. It states that the existence of secondary entities depends on the existence of their causes. Kirchhoff's emendation *meta to prōtōs zōn* ("after the primary living") in place of *meta tou prōtōs zēn* ("along with the primary living") succeeds in capturing this nuance of ontological succession and dependency, but is not necessary to make sense of the Greek.

3, 11–12 *Therefore it is . . . and for eternity*: Plotinus gives a summary of the argument in 3, 7–12: the gradual succession of entities is a timeless fact. This translation follows Heigl's punctuation, reading a period after *aei*, not a comma. With *genēta de* in 3, 12, a new line of argument begins; *de* marks a transition, not a contrast with the *panta* in 3, 11.

3, 12–15 *Now the others. . . . perish at all*: "Coming to be" refers to the dependence of an effect upon its cause, which will continue for all time (it is "coming to be and will come to be"), not to a temporal moment of coming into existence. Nor is anything going to perish, unless there is some material substrate into which it can dissolve (for the sense of "into which," see comment on 3, 14–15). What is the scope of "the others" (*ta hetera*)? Some translators think that it is a way of referring to the sensible world (Harder's *Erdenwelt*, Igal's *las* [sc. *cosas*] *de segundo orden*); an alternative interpretation takes "the others" to include all things other than the One, including the sensible world (Dufour 2006). The difference between these interpretations is largely a matter of emphasis, except in one important respect. If "the others" include intelligible realities as well as the sensible world, Plotinus' argument that the others do not "come to be" in the literal meaning of the words might take on a particular significance. On this reading, he would probably be arguing against Gnostic speculations that introduce a temporal beginning even among intelligible beings. See Dufour (2006, 248n51), to whose comments I here owe a debt, who cites Irenaeus, *Against the Heresies* 1.1.1. In this text, Irenaeus reports the Valentinian claim that a divine entity named Depth ("Bythus") spent countless ages in silence and solitude, before he "decided" (*enenoēthē*) to bring forth the principle of all things. This anti-Gnostic subtext of Plotinus' discussion would be lost if we restricted "the others" to sensible things alone. On this restricted interpretation, the whole collection of sensible things, that is, the universe, does not come to be in a temporal sense, but is rather maintained for eternity by its higher causes.

3, 14 *But what does . . . it can perish*: This sentence is best understood as marking out a subset of "the others" (see comment above, on 3, 12–15). Particular bodies in the world, for example, belong to "the others," in so far as they are made up of component parts that undergo constant transformation, but never come to be temporally, and which depend for their arrangement and cohesion on the formative influence of soul. Unlike the rest of "the others," however, particular bodies, qua composites, have something they can dissolve into, and so they are perishable. To illustrate the idea of one thing "dissolving into" another, we can think of a plant "dissolving into" its component parts, such as its physical elements. Aristotle uses precisely this sense of "dissolving into" when he reports the views of the Pre-Socratics (for him, simply "the first philosophers"): "that of which all things that are consist, and from which they first come to be, and into which they are finally dissolved (the substance remaining, but changing in its modifications), this they say is the element and the principle of things, and therefore they think nothing is either generated or destroyed, since this sort of entity is always conserved, as we say Socrates neither comes to be absolutely when he comes to be beautiful or musical, nor ceases to be when he loses these characteristics, because the substratum, Socrates himself, remains" (*Metaphysics* A.3.983b8–16; tr. Ross, slightly modified). Plotinus' claim would then be that something is perishable only if it can break up into some simpler components. Cf. II.1.4, 25–30.

3, 14–15 *But what has . . . perish at all*: The contrapositive of the principle that something is perishable only if it can dissolve into something else is here asserted. If "what has nothing it can dissolve into" can be understood as referring to the sensible world as a whole, Plotinus is at least implicitly arguing that the Gnostic view of a complete destruction of the universe is impossible, as Kalligas (2014, 377) notes. Since the universe contains everything, there is nothing into which it can dissolve, and so, by the logic of the principle at 3, 14, it is imperishable. Even if it should become disintegrated, perishing will eventually come to a halt at the level of some basic components, for example the four elements. The view of some Gnostics that the universe will end in a final conflagration is well attested; see, for example, Irenaeus, *Against the Heresies* 1.7.1, reporting the opinion of the Valentinian Ptolemy, in whose view the conflagration would take place after the lower Sophia marries Christ and the souls of the elect (the "spiritual seed") re-enter the Pleroma (the Gnostic version of the intelligible world): "When these things have taken place as described, then shall that fire which lies hidden in the world blaze forth and burn; and while destroying all matter, shall also be extinguished along with it, and have no further existence" (tr. Roberts/Rambaud). See also *Gospel of the Egyptians* (NHC III,2), 61.1–15.

3, 15–21 *If someone should. . . . will be illuminated*: A dialectical exchange between Plotinus and an imagined or real objector brings the chapter to a conclusion. The sudden change from third person singular to third person plural (compare "if someone should say" at 3, 15 with "if they are going to say" at 3, 17) may suggest that Plotinus does not have a specific individual in mind; he is rather imagining how a Gnostic would respond to his arguments. The whole exchange in the passage is difficult to reconstruct with complete confidence, as Plotinus, here as elsewhere, presupposes that the views he is discussing will be familiar enough to his readers. But something like the following may be offered as an interpretation. First of all, note that "what has nothing it can dissolve into" (3, 14–15) is probably the intended subject of 3, 15. Plotinus had argued before that what comes to be, in the sense of depending on a cause, is imperishable if there is nothing it can dissolve into. A bronze statue, if melted down, can be dissolved into liquid metal, but the same will not be true for the fundamental material components of the universe, for example the elements. Now comes the objection: why could the elements themselves not dissolve into something even more fundamental, namely matter? But, counters Plotinus, what guarantees that matter itself cannot perish (whether by dissolving into something yet more fundamental, or in some other way, he does not specify)? Presumably, we are meant to infer that the idea of matter perishing is absurd, as he maintains, for instance, at III.6.8, 10–11. But even if the Gnostics wish to uphold that matter can come to perish, they face a dilemma. Either matter exists by necessity, that is to say, as the effect of higher causes, or it does not. If it does, then it must always exist, since the power of these causes is always transmitted to their effects, and so it cannot perish; if it does not exist by necessity, then the power of the divine is limited, which to Plotinus is an intolerable conclusion (on this last point, see the comment on 3, 18–20 below). See also O'Brien (1990, 112) for a discussion of this passage, and his (1993, 78–80) for a French translation with commentary.

3, 18–20 *And if it . . . as it were*: If matter does not exist by necessity, it would be "left alone" in the sense of not participating in the divine causes, having been abandoned by them, so to speak. For Plotinus, the divine realities are everywhere, because their power is not circumscribed by space, as he has explained already at 3, 4–7. Note that it is grammatically possible to understand "soul" as the subject for "left alone" and "illuminated," rather than "matter," a reading that has been adopted by Orbe (1954, 18), and defended by Hadot (1999, 214). But a reading that requires such a sudden and unmarked change of subject is indefensible, in my view; when Plotinus shifts the discussion to soul, as at 4, 1, he makes it quite explicit. The striking expression "walled out" (*apoteteichismena*, a verbal form derived from *apo* ["away from"] and *teichos* ["wall"]) is rare in Greek; one parallel is Aristophanes, *Birds* 1576, where a character is said to have "walled out the gods" (*tous theous apoteichisas*). There is an intriguing possibility that Plotinus may be recasting Gnostic cosmogony in a rather irreverent light: fundamental to a number of Gnostic accounts of the creation of the universe is an emphasis on the gulf between the intelligible and the sensible world, whereas Plotinus insists on continuity between the two. In Valentinus' gnosis, this gulf between the two spheres becomes personified in the divine being Limit (*Horos*), who is said to have "fenced off" (*apostaurōthēnai*) the *Enthymesis* ("Intention" or "Thought") of Sophia from the Pleroma (intelligible world); see Irenaeus, *Against the Heresies* 1.2.4. A similar report by Hippolytus illustrates the rigid separation between the cosmos (also called the Hysterema, after the Greek word for "lack," "need") and the intelligible world: "Now this Aeon is styled Horos, because he separates from the Pleroma the Hysterema that is outside. And (he is called) Metocheus, because he shares also in the Hysterema. And (he is denominated) Staurus, because he is fixed inflexibly and inexorably, so that nothing of the Hysterema can come near the Aeons who are within the Pleroma" (*Refutation of All Heresies* 6.31.6.1–5; tr. MacMahon). See also *Excerpts from Theodotus* 22.4; 42.1, where Staurus ("the Cross") is described as the Limit of the Pleroma, as pointed out by Alt (1990, 20n60), and *Hypostasis of the Archons* (NHC II,4) 94.10, which talks about a "veil" (*katapetasma*) that separates the world above from what is below.

Chapter 4

In this section, Plotinus discusses the opponents' view that the soul created the world as a consequence of its fall.

4, 1–15 *But if they. . . . of this fall*: In the myth of the charioteer in Plato's *Phaedrus* (246c2), Socrates describes how souls that have "shed" their "wings" take on earthly bodies. The creation of the world is not at issue in Plato's text, but later Gnostics made use of the language of "falling" and "declining" in order to describe the creation of the world at the hands of a divine principle called Sophia. See, for example, *Zostrianus* (NHC VIII,1) 9.2–18; 10.20; 27.12 (for "declining"); Irenaeus *Against the Heresies* 1.1.9.15–17 Harvey; and Hippolytus, *Refutation of All Heresies* 6.52.4.3–4 Marcovich (for "falling"). In a later chapter,

Plotinus goes on to consider the relationship between the Gnostics' Sophia and "soul" (in his terminology, the world soul), without reaching any conclusion (see 10, 19–21). In the present passage, however, he presupposes the identity of "soul" with the divine principle Sophia.

The transition from the end of Chapter 3, which had argued that the sensible world could not perish, to the opening of Chapter 4, which now discusses the "fall" (*sphalma*) of the soul, requires some explanation. It is likely that Plotinus' imagined Gnostic objectors are continuing the dialectical exchange that had begun at 3, 15–21. The objectors are now giving another reason why the world should be thought of as perishable: it was created by a soul that "had shed its wings," such that the compromised state of the creator (the soul) will taint the creation itself (the world), rendering it liable to ultimate destruction (see comment on 3, 14–15). In short, the Gnostic view under attack is that the world is perishable because it was badly made, and that it was badly made because it was made by a fallen soul.

Plotinus' report of his opponents' view in 4, 1–2 raises an interesting question: Did the Gnostics themselves use Plato's language, perhaps to give greater credibility to their doctrines, or is Plotinus paraphrasing what they would have said, and substituting Platonic language for whatever terminology would have been used by the Gnostics themselves? On the first view, Plotinus' interlocutors are ready to back up their ideas with Platonic imagery, a fact that would underline the relative closeness of Platonic and Gnostic views. (See also Plotinus' later comment that the Gnostics have taken "some of their doctrines" from Plato, at 6, 10–11 below). Alternatively, and more likely, Plotinus describes in his own words the Gnostic view, using a Platonic expression for the soul's fall with which he is clearly very familiar (see similar references to the *Phaedrus* passage at IV.3.7, 19; IV.8.1, 37; IV.8.4, 22; VI.9.9, 24). The telling use of "as it were" at 4, 1 suggests that Plotinus is not here quoting the precise language of the Gnostic account, but paraphrasing it in a loose manner. Finally, note one peculiarity of Plotinus' account: he speaks about the "fall" (*sphalma*) of the soul at 4, 3–5, whereas in subsequent lines (at 4, 6–7 and 4, 10) he discusses its "decline" (*neusis*). What might seem like a mere verbal difference can be referred back to different Gnostic traditions: as Narbonne (2013) argues, *sphalma* occurs in contexts where Neo-Pythagorean numerology influences Gnostic speculation, while a likely Coptic equivalent of the Greek *neuein katō* can be found in the Sethian Nag Hammadi text *Zostrianus* (NHC VIII,1) 27.12. See also Poirier (2012, 620). But if there ever was some difference between "falling" and "declining" in the original Gnostic sources, it is apparent that Plotinus has no interest in separating the two, but instead treats them as implying similar absurdities.

4, 2 *does not suffer this*: The world soul "does not suffer this," in the sense that it cannot "decline" from its place in the intelligible world, so that its creative activity in no way compromises its own internal activity of contemplation, as Plotinus has explained at 2, 13–15.

4, 6–7 *We say that . . . its non-decline is*: Plotinus emphasizes the contrast between his view and that of the Gnostics by denying that any falling away from or rupture with intelligible reality could explain the world soul's activity of creating the universe. As he will go on to argue, if the soul is able to create at all, it must be because of its connection with the intelligible world, or, as he puts it, its "non-decline." For this sentence, see the useful comments by Igal (1977, 251), who cites 6, 22; III.8.2, 28; 5, 27 as examples of locutions that are similar to the Greek *neusin . . . tēn poiousan* ("the decline is creative").

4, 7 *<For> if the soul declined*: The sentence explains why the soul's creative activity must be a "non-decline" (see 4, 6–7 above); one thus expects *gar* ("for") in place of *de* ("but"), as accepted by Harder-Beutler-Theiler (1960). Plotinus reasonably assumes that the Gnostics do not literally mean that the soul "declined," that is, tended in a downward spatial direction. He attempts in the following to make sense of the language of "declining" by taking it to imply a kind of forgetfulness on the part of the soul.

4, 8–9 *Where could its . . . the intelligible world*: On the link between creation and contemplation, see III.8.4, 39–43. The argument here, that if the soul is able to produce at all, it cannot have fully declined, relies on the assumption that the soul's creative capacity derives from its contemplation of the intelligibles. At V.8.6, 15–17, we find an explicit argument for this assumption: the world soul could not have arrived at the concepts that would be required to create the universe by reasoning or planning, but must have attained a conception of it from the intelligible world.

4, 10 *did not decline at all*: The Greek word for "at all," *holōs*, could also mean "completely," which would affect the meaning of this sentence. Either Plotinus is stating that the world soul could not have descended *at all* if it is productive of the sensible universe, or that it cannot have descended *completely*. But earlier (see 4, 6–7 above, with further references), he had denied that the world soul descends *simpliciter*, and so the sense of *holōs* as "at all" is preferable. See also the note on 4, 10–11 below.

4, 10–11 *Even if it . . . to see dimly*: I note here the alternative reading *menei* ("remain") in place of *neuei* ("incline"), discussed in Harder-Beutler-Theiler (1960, 423). They rightly point out that it is infelicitous to have *neuei* take on the sense of "inclining (upward)," when it means "declining" in all previous instances. But the overall argument of the passage stays the same on either reading: if the soul were able to create as a result of its decline, it would need to have some memory of intelligible reality. But if it has some memory of intelligible reality, this alone would make it want to return to the intelligibles, which would rule out its supposed decline. Therefore the Gnostics' "creation by descent" narrative is inconsistent. Plotinus' argument is thus dialectical in nature, and does not require that his opponent actually held the view that the soul creates while having a dim memory of the intelligible world, only that if they held it, they would contradict themselves, and if they do not hold it, they have no way of accounting for the soul's decline in non-mythological terms.

4, 13–15 *It would be . . . here below*: "What applies to sculptors" in our world is, according to Plotinus, that they undertake the production of works of art in order to be honored for their skill. The same motivation cannot be transferred to the world soul, presumably because it would mean conceiving of the reality of soul in unduly anthropomorphic terms. See also III.8.2, 6–15, a passage that refutes the idea that nature operates "like wax-makers" (*hoi kēroplastai*).

The idea that the soul creates the world "in order to be honored" (*hina timoito*) has been related to a fragment by the Gnostic Valentinus, reported by Clement of Alexandria at *Stromata* 4.13.9.89.6.2–90.1.4 Stählin-Früchtel-Treu, where a similar phrase occurs (*hina timēthē*): "As much as the image is inferior to the living face, so much is the world inferior to the living Aeon. What is, then, the cause of the image? The majesty of the face, which exhibits the figure to the painter, to be honored (*hina timēthē*) by his name; for the form is not found exactly to the life, but the name supplies what is wanting in the effigy" (tr. Robert–Donaldson). Clement seems to think that Sophia is the portrait-painter, God the "face," and the image Sophia's offspring, the Demiurge. The implication would then be that Sophia creates the Demiurge as a copy of the intelligibles in order to gain honor for this production. Plotinus may conceivably have taken the "image" to be the visible creation, rather than the Demiurge; in any case, he later returns to the idea of creating "in order to be honored" at 11, 21. The precise sense of the Clementine passage is disputed; for discussion, see Stead (1980, 82–86); Pépin (1992, 316–319).

4, 15–17 *Otherwise, if the . . . made this cosmos*: Plotinus had earlier denied that the world soul maintains the universe with the aid of "rational calculation" (*dianoia*), at 2, 14, and will return to the issue later, at 8, 20–21. In the present context, the Gnostics have to explain why the soul set out to create the world, rather than returning to the intelligible world after its fall, if indeed it had preserved any memory of the intelligibles. If it was in order to be honored (see 4, 13–15 above), this kind of creation would be a goal-structured activity, thereby involving rational calculation. But Plotinus denies that rational calculation can ever sufficiently explain the world soul's creation; rather, the answer needs to be sought in its own nature (see also 4, 8–9 above). Cf. V.8.7, 36–44.

4, 17–22 *And when is. . . . up coming here*: On Valentinian Gnostic accounts of creation, the universe is the result of Sophia's illegitimate desire to conceive an offspring. She is expelled from the intelligible world, and, once she repents, will gather the souls of the elect and re-ascend with them, at which point the universe will be destroyed. See Hippolytus, *Refutation of All Heresies* 6.31; Irenaeus, *Against the Heresies*, 1.6.1; 1.7.1.

The present passage constructs a dilemma for this account: either Sophia (whom Plotinus prefers to call "soul" for most of II.9) repents her creation now or she is going to do so in the future. On the first horn of the dilemma, if Sophia repents now, she should also destroy the universe now. The Gnostic argument that she is waiting for the souls of the elect will not do, because souls continue to be reincarnated, rather than becoming pure through their experience of the evil world (on Sophia's gathering the elect before the final conflagration, see Irenaeus *Against the Heresies* 1.7.1; on the idea that the experience of this world is requisite for the purification of souls, common in Gnostic sources, see for example *Zostrianus* (NHC VIII,1) 12.2–7; *Tripartite Tractate* (NHC I,5) 107.22–108.4). How does Plotinus know that souls continue to be reincarnated? Presumably this is simply an empirical fact: given that there is no observable "shortage" of souls to animate bodies, we can assume that a constant number persists. Hence, the Gnostic explanation must be false. On the second horn of the dilemma, if Sophia has not already repented now, she is not going to do so, because she will grow fond of her creation in time. No further support for this half of the argument is offered, but one might supply the thought that producers feel a natural affection for their products, which in some sense reflect their nature and abilities, and thus become an extension of self (see Aristotle, *Nicomachean Ethics* 9.1167b31–1168a3).

See also II.1.4, 30–31: "And we have shown that it is empty to suppose that soul might change its mind, for its direction of the universe is without trouble or harm to it [. . .]" (tr. Armstrong).

4, 22–26 *Nor must we . . . than its image*: At the end of Plato's *Timaeus*, the eponymous speaker sums up the results of his cosmological enquiries by saying that this cosmos is "the greatest, best, most beautiful and most complete" image of the intelligible world (92c7–8). Plotinus remains faithful to this positive evaluation of the cosmos, and argues here and, more explicitly, at 8, 16–29 below, that it is a conceptual mistake to berate an image for falling short of its original. In as much as an image is, by definition, different from, and a representation of, its original, one has to expect that it will fall short in some aspects, as a portrait, for example, will not capture *all* features of a face, only those that can be represented in a given medium. But there are still better and worse images, and the universe is the best image there is of the intelligible world. See also V.8.8, 11–23.

The claim of Plotinus' Gnostic opponents that this universe "has been badly made" (4, 22–23) is included in the alternative, longer title of II.9 listed by Porphyry (*Life of Plotinus* 24.56–57). According to Plotinus, these Gnostics would have taken the evils found in this world (whether these include moral as well as natural evils is not clear from 4, 21–22) as evidence for the evil nature of the Demiurge. Plotinus' own solution to the problem of evil is beyond the scope of this commentary; the two treatises *On Providence* (III.2–3) discuss this issue at length.

4, 27–28 *What other fire . . . in our world*: Fire appears to have played a special role in the cosmology of Plotinus' Gnostics, as being the first element created by the Demiurge. Cf. 11, 27–9; 12, 12–8. The phrase "intelligible fire" translates the Greek *to ekei pur*, which can in some contexts refer to a refined form of fire that makes up the stars (see II.1.4, 11–13). But in its present occurrence, the phrase means the idea or form of fire as it exists in the intelligible world (sometimes called *to noēton pur*, as at IV.4.23, 10). This fire is the cause of the fire in our world, as the following passage, in MacKenna's elegant translation, makes clear: "[T]he cause of fire here is a certain Life of fiery character, the more authentic fire. That transcendent fire being more truly fire will be more veritably alive; the fire absolute possesses life" (VI.7.11, 46–48). See also VI.5.8, 28–35.

4, 28 *Indeed, what other . . . the intelligible earth*: If, as implied here, there can be no intermediary between the intelligible form of earth and our perceptible earth, the Gnostic belief in a "new earth" that serves as the paradigm of our earth without being itself part of the intelligible world cannot be justified. The nature and purpose of the "new earth" will take center stage in the next chapter; see 5, 23–37.

4, 29–31 *What sphere more . . . the intelligible world*: On the spherical (and thus most perfect) shape of the cosmos, see Plato, *Timaeus* 33b. Plotinus here compares the visible sphere of the cosmos with the intelligible world, conceived of as a perfect sphere. The Pre-Socratic philosopher Parmenides had likened the realm of Being to a "well-rounded sphere" (DK B7.43), a view that Plotinus discusses with apparent approval at V.1.8, 18–22.

Chapter 5

The Gnostic opponents exaggerate their own spiritual power, while falsely denigrating the orderliness and intelligence of the sun and the other heavenly bodies, which are immortal beings. They introduce a second soul composed of the elements, and claim that a "new earth" has been created for them.

5, 1–16 *But it is. . . . the mortal soul*: After his impassioned defense of the beauty of the sensible cosmos at the end of Chapter 4, Plotinus now launches an attack against the Gnostics' claim to possessing a spiritual seed that renders them superior even to the heavenly bodies (for this claim, see also 13, 10; 15, 23 below). On their view, the planets will perish in a final conflagration, together with the rest of the universe, while they themselves possess an immortal nature that will allow them to re-ascend to the intelligible world (cf. Irenaeus, *Against the Heresies* 1.6.1). In a passage from Hippolytus (*Refutation of All Heresies* 5.16.1.1–2.1 Marcovich), we find a report about the Peratae, a Gnostic sect who made claims similar to the ones Plotinus criticizes here: "They denominate themselves, however, Peratae, imagining that none of those things existing by generation can escape the determined lot for those things that derive their existence from generation. For if, says (the Peratic), anything be altogether begotten, it also perishes, as also is the opinion of the Sibyl. But we alone, he says, who are conversant with the necessity of generation, and the paths through which man has entered into the world, and who have been accurately instructed (in these matters), we alone are competent to proceed through and pass beyond destruction" (tr. MacMahon). See also Narbonne (2011, 108–111), who discusses this and other relevant passages.

5, 1 *unreasonable*: Inserting *alogon* ("unreasonable") after *alla* ("but"), as proposed by Creuzer and Harder. This improves the grammar of the sentence and explains the *alogos de kai* (". . . is also unreasonable") in 5, 16, where *kai* ("also") naturally suggests that something else has been shown to be unreasonable in what precedes.

5, 8–11 *Nor is it . . . beautiful and pure*: This sentence might be read as saying that for the Gnostics, all men, even the meanest of them, are immortal. In fact, however, we should probably understand "the meanest of men" not to refer to men in general, but to men in so far as they are Gnostics. There is much evidence to support the view that the Gnostics considered themselves to be a select group; see, for example, Irenaeus' report that Valentinus divided mankind into three classes, only one of which is made of a spiritual substance and destined for salvation. See also *Against the Heresies* 1.8.3.

At 5, 8, something needs to be supplied, at least in thought, after *oude* ("nor"), most likely *logon echei* ("it is reasonable"), as pointed out in Harder-Beutler-Theiler (1960, 424).

5, 10–11 *the heaven and the stars up there*: See Plato, *Timaeus* 40b; *Epinomis* 983b–984b; *Laws* 898b–899b for the idea that the heavenly bodies are divine beings. In *Against the Gnostics*, Plotinus does not tire of defending the nobility of the heavens against their detractors (cf. 8, 29–32; 9, 30–31; 16, 9–11.51–55; 18, 30–35). See also IV.8.2, 38–53; V.1.2, 3–4.

5, 12–16 *Seeing the order . . . the mortal soul*: The Greek words *ekei* ("up there") and *entautha* ("here") most likely introduce a contrast between heaven and the stars on the one hand, and our sublunary world on the other, as this translation assumes. On this reading, the passage might appear at odds with Plotinus' repeated assertions that the Gnostics are incapable of recognizing the divinity of the stars (see comment on 5, 1–16 above). But they may well recognize that the stars move harmoniously and with great order, without inferring their divinity from that fact. What Plotinus finds objectionable about their view, then, would be their failure to draw the required inference, whether this failure is due to ignorance of the implication, or plain irrationality.

If the sensible world is as corrupt as the Gnostic opponents claim, they will have to explain why the immortal soul directs its activities toward it, or, in other words, why it has "chosen the worse place," as Plotinus puts it, instead of "the better," i.e., the heavens. His point, more polemical than substantive, is that while the stars (which on his opponents' view have souls of a different, lesser nature than the elect) circle the heavens, the pure souls of the elect toil on the earth below—a topsy-turvy state of affairs that the Gnostics will need to account for.

5, 16–23 *Their surreptitious introduction. . . . say in response*: By the Gnostics' "second soul," we should probably understand a second kind of individual soul, as is required by the wider context of the passage (beginning with the Gnostics' claim in 5, 8 that their [individual] souls and those of the meanest of men are immortal, and continuing to the discussion of the "new earth" at 5, 23–37, clearly the afterlife destination of individual souls). In the background to the Gnostics' two-soul theory stands the idea that the divine principle Sophia is variously affected (with fear, grief, perplexity, and "entreaty" [*deēsis*] or "ignorance" [*agnoia*]) on being expelled from the Pleroma. According to Hippolytus' account of this doctrine, Christ then "rectified" (*diōrthōsato*) her affections (*pathē*), turning them into the material universe (see *Refutation of All Heresies* 6.32.5.2–6.2 Marcovich). The creation of the second soul belongs to this last phase of the process, where Sophia's fear is transformed into a "psychic substance" (*psuchikē ousia*) of a "fiery" (*purōdēs*; 6.32.7.5) nature. A different account of the creation of a second soul by the Demiurge is that offered by Clement of Alexandria in his *Excerpts from Theodotus* 50–51, where we find a distinction between "a divine soul" and a "material soul that is the body of the divine soul" (3.51.2.1–7 Sagnard). This last soul is also described as "earthly and material" (*geōdē kai hulikēn*; 3.50.1.3 Sagnard). See also Epiphanius, *Panarion* 31.19.1–7 (I.410.23–411.12 Holl).

Some Gnostics, then, thought there was a second soul made up of at least one element. Yet scholars have been unable to find a Gnostic source that describes a material soul made up of *all four* elements, which is the view that Plotinus attacks. One is thus faced with the question whether Plotinus is dealing with a small subset of Gnostics, whose doctrines are not fully preserved elsewhere; or whether he misrepresented or misunderstood the actual views of his opponents, as some have suspected, for example Harder-Beutler-Theiler (1960, 424), and Alt (1990, 48). If the latter is the case, Plotinus may perhaps have "translated" the original Gnostic account, which would have mentioned only one element, into familiar Platonic terms. Particularly relevant here is Plato's *Timaeus* (42e), where the Younger Gods are said to borrow from the cosmos portions of "fire and earth and water and air" for the creation of the human body and some unspecified (presumably lower) parts of the human soul. But our evidence on this point allows no firm conclusions.

5, 19–20 *The blending of . . . mixture of both*: In *On Generation and Corruption* 2.3.330a30–b1, Aristotle argues that the elements (earth, water, fire, air) are constituted from combinations of the pairs hot-cold and wet-dry. Plotinus here inverts this explanatory relationship, arguing that the elements combine to produce the qualities of hot/cold and wet/dry.

5, 21 *How then can . . . be from them*: The Greek verb *esti* ("is"), which is to be supplied, can be used to denote identity. Plotinus' rhetorical question is designed to undermine the Gnostic thesis that the soul is identical with the union of the four elements: if the soul just is one and the same thing as the coming together of all four elements, there will be soul as soon as the four elements are conjoined, rather than at some later point. This criticism is difficult to account for, unless one assumes Plotinus' Gnostic source spoke of the creation of a material soul from the elements.

5, 22–23 *When they attribute . . . say in response*: The suggestion that apprehension and will "and countless other things" can result from the combination of elements (the Gnostics' material soul), dismissed out of hand here, is refuted at greater length at IV.7.4, 21–33.

5, 23–37 *Because they do . . . of the world*: A number of Biblical texts refer to the idea of a "new earth," for example Isaiah 65:17 and 66:22 in the Old Testament, and 2 Peter 3:13 and Revelation 21:1 in the New Testament. The same expression, with clear eschatological significance, can also be found in the untitled and anonymous Gnostic text in the Bruce Codex (249.16–21 Schmidt-MacDermot), where the Protogenitor (a demiurgic figure who is also called the Son) is said to have "raised up all the pure matter, and made it a world and an aeon and a city which is called imperishability and Jerusalem" (tr. MacDermot, slightly modified), which is also called "the new earth." It may be identical with the "land of air" that is described as the afterlife destination of souls in the same treatise (263.15–21). See also *Zostrianus* (NHC VIII,1) 5.17–18; 8.10–11. Tardieu (1992, 529) suggests that the anonymous untitled text in the Bruce Codex can be identified with the Apocalypse of Messos to which Porphyry refers in *Life of Plotinus* 16.7. In this case, Plotinus may have had access to it, which would explain his apparent knowledge of the text here. Later in II.9, at 11, 11–12, Plotinus refers to the Gnostics' "alien earth," which appears to be yet another way of referring to the "new earth" of the present passage. Cf. Hippolytus, *Refutation of all Heresies* 6.25 (=6.30.8.4–9.5 Marcovich), describing Sophia's creation of a "heavenly Jerusalem." See also Elsas (1975, 236–237).

Thickening the plot, Plotinus remarks that, according to his opponents, the "new earth" is the *logos tou kosmou* (here, the "rational model of the world"), which he immediately equates with being a "paradigm" (at 5, 26–29). The accuracy of this testimony has been questioned (see, for example, Igal (1982, 501–502n45), but it may be supported by the following passage from *Zostrianus*: "The atmospheric realm came into being by a rational principle, and it incorruptibly manifests generated and perishable things for the sake of the advent of the great judges (that is, stars), lest they experience perception and be enclosed in the creation. But when they came upon it and thereby perceived the works of the world, they condemned its ruler to a perishability that is a pattern for the world, since it is a [substance] and principle of matter, the dark, corrupt [product]" (9.2–15; tr. Turner). There are clearly many difficulties of interpretation that this passage poses, but at least on one reading, it implies that the "atmospheric realm" (that is, the "new earth") contains within it the rational principles (*logoi* in Greek) of sublunary things (this would be the sense in which it can "incorruptibly manifest" perishable things). See also *Zostrianus* 4.20–5.10, for a description of "the luminous cloud," apparently located within the "atmospheric realm," that is reminiscent of the "true earth" in the myth in Plato's *Phaedo* (108d–111c). Note further that the stars, upon encountering the "new earth," condemn its ruler to a perishability "that is a pattern (*tupos*) for the world," which could easily suggest that not only the ruler, but also his realm act as a pattern (or *paradeigma* in Greek) for the sensible world.

5, 26–27 *Why do they . . . that they despise*: If the sensible world is to be despised, according to the views of Plotinus' interlocutors, then its model should share in the blame, and cannot well serve the Gnostics as the afterlife destination to which they must return.

5, 27–37 *Where does this. . . . in their account*: In this concluding argument of the chapter, Plotinus traps his opponents in the following dilemma: either the "paradigm" of the cosmos was created before the cosmos itself, or after it. On the first theory, the paradigm acts as the intelligible model of the sensible world, and logically precedes it, while on the second, it is the afterlife destination of souls, and its creation is consequent upon the destruction of the world. In either case, argues Plotinus, the paradigm serves no purpose; and therefore the hypothesis is untenable.

On the first theory, the creation of the paradigm is subsequent to the "decline" (see comment on 4, 1–15) of its "maker." If the account of the creation of the "alien earth" at 11, 11–14, which talks about "higher beings" that are its "makers," expresses the same idea as the present passage, the "maker" may be identical with Sophia in her higher aspect, which remains in the intelligible world. Plotinus assumes that Sophia has to "decline" in order to produce this paradigm, which would be located outside the intelligible world. It cannot be excluded, however, that Plotinus is reporting two different versions of how the paradigm came to be; see also Alt (1990, 53–54) for further comments.

On the second theory, the paradigm comes into being at what is presumably the end of the world, when matter is taken away to the extent that even the form of the cosmos is destroyed (think of a house losing brick after brick, until it is no longer a house but a mere heap). See also the passage from the anonymous untitled text in the Bruce Codex (249.16–21), quoted above in the comment on 5, 23–37.

5, 29–32 *If the maker . . . have done so]*: This difficult sentence is more ambiguous in the Greek than the present translation might suggest. "The other cosmos" (*kosmon allon*) in 5, 30–31 refers to the "new earth" that the divine "maker" (the higher Sophia) creates before the sensible world (the *kosmos* in 5, 32). The higher Sophia contains "the intelligible *kosmos*" (5, 30–31) within herself, presumably because what creative power she has must ultimately derive from her knowledge of the intelligible world. There are, in other words, three worlds in play here: intelligible, intermediate, and sensible. Plotinus' two rhetorical questions, why the maker should have been eager to create another cosmos (viz. the "new earth") after the intelligible one, and what purpose would be served by this intermediate world, both aim to reduce the Gnostic creation account to absurdity. On Plotinus' view, the soul creates from the necessity of its own nature, not because of some special concern that she acquires at a given moment, and her creation is not aimed at a particular purpose, but simply the by-product of her own inner contemplation. See Commentary on 2, 14.

5, 32–33 *So that the . . . be in vain*: Translations of this passage differ widely, and there is some uncertainty over its precise meaning. Plotinus uses the Greek verb *phulassō* in the middle voice (see e.g. *phulaxasthai* at 5, 36, the aorist infinitive), which often means "to be on one's guard." On this reading, a good translation would be Armstrong's, who writes: "To put the souls on their guard. How could that be? They were not on their guard, so there was no point in its existence." A difficulty for this interpretation is that it needs to explain how the "new earth" can "put" the embodied souls of the elect "on their guard." Perhaps one might suppose that knowledge of their afterlife destination will keep the souls from identifying with their bodies and from attaching value to the material realm. See Schmidt (1900, 39–40) for a similar interpretation.

On an alternative reading, the one adopted here, we should give a passive meaning to the verb *phulassesthai* and its cognates; this passive use is already present in the New Testament, for example in Luke 8:29 and Acts 23:25. In that case, the passage would imply that in some way the "new earth" ensures that the souls "are kept safe," not that it is created in order to keep them "on their guard." How does the "new earth" keep souls safe? It may be that Plotinus is thinking of the Valentinian view according to which the "new earth" is an interim station for elect souls that are awaiting their ascent to the higher spheres (see Clement of Alexandria, *Excerpts from Theodotus* 63–64). As long as the universe continues to exist, these souls "are kept safe" in the intermediate world, in the sense that, while there, they no longer need to engage with the material realm. When Plotinus objects that the intermediate world does not seem to serve any purpose, because it has not in fact kept the souls safe, he is probably referring to the fact that souls continue to be re-incarnated, a point he had already made earlier at 4, 19–22. Cf. *Zostrianus* 4.2–25; 24.21 where the idea that the souls of the elect "are guarded" by certain "glories" has some prominence, but it is not clear from the text how the glories relate to the "new" or "airy earth."

5, 33–36 *If he made . . . undergone it safe*: What is the "experience" that would suffice to keep souls safe? Presumably, it is the experience of evil in the sensible world. Here, as before at 4, 21–22, Plotinus argues that this experience should be sufficient to remind souls that they do not belong to this world, such that they would not be at risk of becoming impure again, and so in no need of being kept safe. Contrary to the Gnostics' view, then, souls should be able to directly ascend to the intelligibles, rather than having to wait in an otiose intermediate realm, if the creation of the "new earth" came after the creation of the sensible world. See also Spanu (2012, 95), who adopts a similar interpretation.

5, 36–37 *But if they . . . in their account*: This sentence marks an important transition in the treatise, which will now turn to a discussion of the Gnostics' terminological innovations and their wider relation to the Greek philosophical tradition. Plotinus has so far argued that the "new earth" cannot have been created either before or after the sensible world. But there remains the possibility that the Gnostics view it as an internal reality rather than a quasi-physical location in the universe, as the argument has hitherto assumed. In a number of dialogues, Plato discussed the theory of recollection, according to which individual souls have an innate knowledge of reality (the world of forms) that can be brought to awareness through enquiry. See *Meno* 80a–86c; *Phaedo* 72e–78b; *Phaedrus* 245c–257b. Plotinus now argues that if the "new earth" were a form present in the soul (what Plotinus would call a rational principle, *logos*), his opponents would endorse a view exactly like Plato's.

Some translators, such as Bréhier, Cilento, and Armstrong, render the concluding question *ti to kainon tou logou*; as "What does their novel doctrine mean?" and not, as here, "What novelty is there in their account?" On the first translation, Plotinus is asking rhetorically what sense can be made of the opponents' theory (the implied answer being "None."); one would need to supply the Greek verb *sēmainei* ("means") here. On the second reading, he asks how the opponents differ from Plato (the implied answer is, "Not at all."); here, *estin* ("is") is to be supplied. This second reading succeeds better in making sense of the transition to Chapter 6, 1–10, where the Gnostics' unacknowledged dependence on Plato is at issue.

Chapter 6

In this chapter, Plotinus offers a general critique of his opponents' relationship with the Greek philosophical tradition.

6, 1–2 *What are we . . . "copies" and "repentances"*: "Sojourns," "copies" and "repentances" are examples of the terminological innovations that had already come under attack in Plotinus' concluding remark at 5, 36–37. All three terms are attested outside of Plotinus' treatise, occurring together only in the Sethian text *Zostrianus* and the anonymous and untitled Gnostic treatise in the Bruce Codex. See *Zostrianus* (NHC VIII,1) 5.17–29; 8.13–16; 12.10–22; 27.15–28.5; 31.6–9 (a badly fragmented passage); 43.12–19; Bruce Codex 263.11–264.6 Schmidt-MacDermot. In the system of *Zostrianus*, there are three different locations outside of the intelligible world (the

Barbelo Aeon) that are inhabited by immortal souls; in ascending order, the Sojourn, the Repentance, and the Self-Generated Aeons (these last are not mentioned by Plotinus). As Turner (2001, 567) puts it, the Sojourn "seems to describe the initial gathering place for disembodied souls in the process of deciding their next incarnation, perhaps in the realm of the fixed stars," citing *Phaedo* 113d–114c and *Phaedrus* 248a–249c as possible Platonic sources of inspiration. The Repentance, on the other hand, derives its name from the character of the souls that inhabit it, whose knowledge (*gnōsis*) is new and who still sin, while more perfect souls inhabit the Self-Generated Aeons. Cf. *Marsanes* (NHC X,1) 2.26–3.17. See also Burns (2014, 96–106). In addition to these three habitats for souls, there are also "copies" (*antitupoi*) of these locations at a lower ontological rank, as the following passage from *Zostrianus* illustrates: "And the inferior [souls] are trained by the Aeonic Copies, which receive a replica of their souls while they are still in the world. After the individual procession of the Aeons, they come into being and they are individually transferred from the copy of the Sojourn to the truly existent Sojourn, from the copy of the Repentance to the truly existent Repentance, [and from the] copy of the Self-generated (Aeons) [to the] truly existent [Self-generated (Aeons)], and so on" (*Zostrianus* [NHC VIII,1] 12.2–18; tr. Turner). The "copies" thus help to explain why Plotinus uses plural forms for the Sojourn and the Repentance; as the passage quoted from *Zostrianus* illustrates, not only is there a real Sojourn, for example, but also a copy of it. These copies would exist below their originals, possibly between the moon and the fixed stars. On the various meanings of *antitupoi* in Gnostic literature, see Puech (1960, 181–182).

It is worth noting at this point that the relation between the "sojourns," "copies" and "repentances" is somewhat unclear in our sources. In the passage from the *Zostrianus* quoted just above, one would naturally think of all three as distinct locations below the intelligible world. But another passage, this time from the anonymous untitled text in the Bruce Codex, suggests a more complex picture, according to which the different realities can be contained within one another. The Lord of the All, in this text, first creates the "airy earth," before moving on to the "Sojourn": "Next (is) the Sojourn. Within this the place of repentance. Within this the copies of *aerodios* [*sc.* the 'airy earth']. Next the sojourning as stranger, the repentance. Within this the self-begotten copies. In that place they are immersed in the name of the self-begotten one who is God over them" (263.20–23; tr. McDermot, slightly modified).

6, 1 *basic elements*: Igal (1981, 148n26) points out—correctly, in my view—that the Greek word *hupostaseis* does not here carry its quasi-technical metaphysical meaning of "realities," as has sometimes been thought; cf. Abramowski

(1983, 8–10). Rather, its meaning is that of "fundamental items" or "basic elements" in the Gnostic "system" under discussion. Cf. Sextus Empiricus, *Outlines of Pyrrhonism* 2.84.13 Mutschmann for this sense, and Lampe (1961), entry "*hupostasis*" I.B.4.d. For a different view, see Tardieu (2013, 432–433), who suggests that *hupostaseis* in the present context is synonymous with "résidences" or "demeures."

6, 2–10 *If they say . . . . and truer contemplation*: Plotinus' use of "if they say" (*ei legousi*) need not indicate that the Gnostics themselves explained the "sojourns," "copies," and "repentances" in terms of "affections" (*pathē*) of the soul, although the passage has sometimes been understood in that way; cf. Abramowski (1983, 8). More likely, Plotinus, for dialectical purposes, imagines how they might give a reasonable account of the meaning of these terms, only to then charge his interlocutors with inventing new words for old concepts. Strikingly, the "repentances" and the "copies" are explained solely in terms of psychology; nothing suggests the intricate geography of salvation that we find in, for example, *Zostrianus*.

The key to understanding the account of the "repentances" and "copies" that Plotinus puts into the Gnostics' mouths lies in his claim that they are plagiarizing Plato's cave analogy. In Plato's *Republic*, the prisoners are physically tied down in a dark cave, where they look at images of reality, and they would not be able to escape to a truer contemplation even if they wanted to (see 514a–515b). It is only the prisoner who is released and forced to go outside the cave who is eventually able to see reality itself (515c–516d). The cave, of course, is only an analogy, and we need to ask what it is that frees us from our bonds and makes us look toward the real beings. Here, I think, is where the "repentances" come in: Plotinus interprets them as "changes of purpose," another meaning of *metanoia*, such that a soul in the state of repenting is not regretting a past misdeed but is undergoing the sort of spiritual transformation that is needed to ascend out of the cave (cf. *metastrophē* at *Republic* 532b7). These "repentances" are "affections" (*pathē*) of the soul, not in the specific sense that they involve some kind of excessive emotion that is misaligned with rational judgments, another meaning *pathē* can take, but only in so far as they involve some change that the soul undergoes when it changes from accepting sensible reality to desiring to transcend it. See also Puech (1960), 189–190 for the meaning of *metanoia*.

Next, Plotinus envisages that his opponents might, as a possible explanation of their "copies," suggest that the soul is affected by images of the intelligibles, while it does not perceive the intelligibles themselves. The relevant sense in which the "copies" are "affections" has now shifted somewhat. It can be illustrated with reference to the faculty of sight: when I perceive an object, my faculty of sight receives the form of the object, and is in this way affected by it. Cf. IV.3.26, 1–9; IV.4.23, 18–28 for passages that suggest Plotinus gives some role to affections in his theory of perception, although he insists that we can perceive the objects of perception themselves, not simply impressions of them (cf. IV.6.1, 28–31). In the Allegory of the cave in Plato's *Republic*, there are different layers of "images of reality" that affect the soul, from the "shadows" thrown by puppets and objects that are passed along a fire inside the cave (515c), to the images that the prisoner is said to perceive outside the cave, when he is first released and cannot bear looking at the sun itself (516a–b). These last images, the closest reflections of intelligible reality, are related to the kind of discursive thinking (*dianoia*) that Plato associates with mathematical reasoning, and which can be transcended by an intuitive grasp of the forms that, unlike mathematics, does not take its starting point from images of reality. On Plato's model, which Plotinus imagines will be adopted by the Gnostics, progress "toward a truer and truer contemplation" consists in moving from more distant images of reality, for example the objects of perception, to truer reflections of their nature, for instance mathematical concepts such as the square itself.

As has been noted by Harder-Beutler-Theiler, Plotinus does not explain what the opponents' corresponding account for the "sojourns" would be, but it may well be that his comment at 6, 8–10 about their knowledge of the cave analogy in Plato's *Republic* (see especially 514a) can close this gap. The Gnostics may have argued that souls in the sublunary world are comparable to prisoners in the cave, so that the "sojourns" refer to their captivity in the body.

6, 3 *these*: With Igal (1982, 503n50), I take "affections of the soul" as the subject, and *tauta* ("these [viz., the repentances]") as predicate. At 6, 5, *touto* ("this") before *kainologountōn* must be supplied. Other translations, such as Armstrong's, take *tauta* as the subject, and "affections of the soul" as predicate.

6, 6 *the ancient Hellenic [tradition]*: Like Dufour (2006, 257n96), I am here supplying *haireseōs* to follow *Hellenikēs*, which occurs in the same line in the preceding clause. Igal (1982, 503) thinks *phonēs* ("language," in the genitive case) should be added in thought, but in the context of the passage, this option has little to commend itself. The Gnostics are characterized as pretending to be unaware that their ideas already occur in Plato and the Greek philosophical tradition; they are not pretending to be ignorant of the Greek language.

6, 10–24 *In general, some we. . . . the creator is*: The chapter reaches its next and central topic, the Gnostic attempts to give credibility to their own doctrines by presenting them as interpretations of Plato. Plotinus focuses on their reading of *Timaeus* 39e, which distinguishes three intellects in that passage, (1) an intellect at rest, (2) an intellect that contemplates, and (3) an intellect that reflects. It may come as a surprise that the unity of the Intellect once more becomes the focus of controversy, given that Plotinus had already dealt with it in Chapter 1 (see Commentary on 1, 19–20). But arguably, he is now viewing it under a different aspect, namely as a misrepresentation of Plato. The view reported here is somewhat different from, but not incompatible with, the earlier divisions of Intellect into two parts; the third intellect that reflects had played no role in the earlier chapter. Plotinus' complaint against his opponents is that although they have given the third intellect a quasi-demiurgic function, they regard the soul as the creative principle of the universe. For the identification of Intellect and the Demiurge in Plotinus, see V.1.8, 5; V.8.7, 23–25; V.9.3, 25–26. Of particular relevance here is the argument in V.8.7, which states that the completeness of the universe could not be the result of planning; the universe is rather a necessary consequence of Intellect's existence, although the activity of souls assists in its formation. Early in his career, and probably under the influence of Platonists such as Numenius who read *Timaeus* 39e in the way he rejects in the present passage, Plotinus himself brings the activity of a lower kind of "intellect" who "intended" or "planned" (*dianoēthē*) into close relationship with the soul, although he stops short of ever identifying the two, since in his view *dianoia* belongs primarily to soul (see III.9.1, 27–36).

6, 12–14 *the judgments and rivers in Hades and the reincarnations*: There are three great myths of judgment in Plato's writings, in the dialogues *Gorgias* (523a–527a), *Phaedo* (107a–115a) and *Republic* (614a–621d). The *Phaedo*'s final myth additionally describes a system of underworld rivers (111d); it is also in this dialogue that we find an argument in support of reincarnation (69e–72d; cf. with *Meno* 81c). If Plotinus here implies that the Gnostics themselves were talking about "rivers in Hades," our surviving sources do not preserve this aspect of their teaching. The most compelling parallel on this point is Numenius, who apparently thought Plato's underground rivers in the *Phaedo* were situated in the heavens, as Proclus reports: "And he [*sc.* Numenius] equates the subterranean rivers with the spheres of the planets, for he draws up both the rivers and Tartarus itself into these spheres" (fr. 35.10 Des Places = *Commentary on the Republic* 2.129.6–8). He also assigns specific locations to the judges in the same fragment; they are situated between heaven and earth, and "send the souls along, some into heaven and some into the region below the earth and the rivers that are there" (fr. 35.3–5 Des Places = *Commentary on the Republic* 2.129.3–4; all translations by Petty). While Numenius does not expressly mention "the judgments," as in the present passage from Plotinus, one might reasonably think that "judgments" happen where the judges are. There is a distinct possibility that the Gnostics turned to his writings in order to map the heavenly locations where the judgment, purification and reincarnation of souls take place. See Orbe (1976, 576–577) for a discussion of this sentence.

6, 16–19 *since he said we . . . in the living being*: Plotinus quotes Plato *Timaeus* 39e, probably from memory, and with only minor variations (but see Kalligas [2014, 384] for a different view). "He" might be referring to either the character Timaeus or to Plato himself. The *Timaeus* passage is quoted in my comment on 1, 19–20.

6, 24–34 *In general, they. . . . the first nature*: Intellect, as the immediate successor of the One, cannot itself be multiple in the way the Gnostics propose, or else the principle that the procession of entities should proceed gradually, fundamental to Plotinus' metaphysics, would be violated. See also his earlier remarks, at 3, 7–12. The complexity of Gnostic accounts of the intelligible world can be illustrated with Irenaeus' report of Valentinus' Aeons, which number no fewer than 30; see Irenaeus, *Against the Heresies*, 1.1.1–3. Such complexity is by no means peculiar to Valentinus; Nag Hammadi texts such as the *Three Steles of Seth*, *Zostrianus*, and *Allogenes* likewise construct complex hierarchies of Aeons and sub-Aeons.

6, 27–28 *while he and other blessed men had not*: Porphyry also reports that the Gnostics accused Plato of not having penetrated "the depth of intelligible substance" (*to bathos tēs noētēs ousias*); see *Life of Plotinus* 16.8–9. Elsewhere,

Plotinus firmly states his belief that blessed and divine men in the past had attained the truth, although some (Plato!) did so more than others; cf. III.7.1, 13–16.

6, 31–34 *what comes after the first*: If a genuine plurality (and not the Gnostics' specious kind at 6, 28–31) has been discovered among intelligible beings, it must be referred to Intellect, which "comes after the first," that is, after the One. For while the One is the principle of all that exists, it does not contain any plurality at all, unlike Intellect, which contains the plurality of the forms.

6, 35–43 *The form of. . . . clearly by Plato*: That Soul is the principle immediately succeeding Intellect, and so the third reality in Plotinus' system, has already been asserted at 1, 15. Although Plotinus is presenting the core tenets of Platonism as a set of propositions arrived at by "divine men" quite generally, there can be little doubt that he has Plato's particular contribution in mind. I list below the most relevant passages from Plato for each doctrine Plotinus mentions.

(1) The immortality of the soul: *Phaedrus* 245c–246a; *Phaedo* 105e6–7

(2) The intelligible world: *Republic* 7.517b

(3) The first god: *Republic* 6.509b

(4) That the soul must flee its association with the body: *Phaedo* 64d2–66a10

(5) That it is separable from the body: *Phaedo* 69e–72d

(6) That it must flee the world of generation to being: *Theaetetus* 176a9–b1

Some items on this list are not obviously distinguishable; one might think, for example, that anyone believing in (1) will surely also believe in (5). But perhaps Plotinus distinguishes them, because belief in (5) does not necessarily imply belief in (1); the soul may be separable from the body without being able to continue existing indefinitely. The relation between (4) and (6), on the other hand, may be described as follows: while (4) tells us how we should live our lives when embodied, (6) explains the larger purpose of living in this way, which, according to the *Theaetetus*, is to "flee hence" (*ekeise pheugein*; 176b1), that is, to the gods, or to "being" (*ousia*), as Plotinus puts it.

6, 35–36 *But these people . . . disparage divine men*: This remark is best viewed as anticipating the larger discussion of the differences between the world soul and individual souls in Chapter 7. While "the differences among souls" could also refer to the differences among individual souls in particular, no apparent purpose would be served by such a dense allusion to a subject never explicitly discussed in the course of the treatise. That said, Plotinus certainly did disagree with the Gnostics about the factors that distinguish different individual (human) souls especially. For him, souls are distinguished by their different relationships with intelligible realities, as he explains at IV.3.6, 28–34, which in turn depend on a whole range of different factors (such as past lives, the kind of body inhabited, character, luck and upbringing; see IV.3.8, 5–10 and IV.3.15, 7–10). In contrast, some Gnostic texts such as *Zostrianus* could seem to offer a simpler picture, according to which human souls are distinguished by their natures, which are not themselves the result of prior factors, and unchangeable. See *Zostrianus* (NHC VIII,1) 26.19–29; *Tripartite Tractate* (NHC I,5) 118.14–119.34, and compare with Irenaeus, *Against the Heresies* 1.6.1–2; 7.1–5. But see the cautionary remarks by Burns (2014, 86–89) against too simplistic a view of Gnostic claims to belong to a "new race" destined for salvation.

6, 41–43 *For they do . . . clearly by Plato*: In so far as the Gnostics agree with the doctrines listed by Plotinus as Platonic (see above 6, 35–41), their views are acceptable. Like Plato, the Gnostics believed in the existence of an intelligible world (the Pleroma or the Barbelo Aeon, for example), even if they conceived of it in the wrong terms (see comments above on 6, 24–34, and on 1, 19–20). They also held the souls of at least the spiritually elect to be immortal, and agreed with Plato that the nature of the body is a hindrance to the soul (a point of agreement which Plotinus mentions later, at 17, 1–4 and 18, 1–3, although he does not endorse the stronger position of the

Gnostics, that the body is something hateful). Given the contempt that they are said to feel for the universe, they would also endorse Plato's claim that we should flee from the world of generation to that of real, that is, intelligible, being; again, it is the extremism with which they blame the evils of the world that sets them apart from Plotinus.

6, 43–52 *We bear no. . . . than these men*: In the background of this passage stand the "culture wars," as Burns (2014, 8–31) calls them, of the Second Sophistic. The status of Greek culture and its system of education (*paideia*; cf. Plotinus' own use of *pepaideumenōs eirētai* at 6, 54) was gradually being challenged by intellectuals who made use of fictitious or real "Oriental" sources of wisdom in order to give authority to their own views. A telling example for this trend is the Platonist Numenius, who famously asked: "What is Plato but a Moses speaking Greek (*attikizōn*)?" (fr. 8.11 Des Places). The Gnostics were fully involved in this wrestling match over cultural authority, attacking Greek wisdom and promoting instead apocalypses claimed to derive from Jewish or other "Oriental" sages (but in fact most likely to be pseudo-epigraphical). The term "Greek" at 6, 44 thus carries a cultural, not a geographical meaning, as Kalligas (2014, 386) points out. Signs of this conflict over cultural authority are visible in Porphyry, *Life of Plotinus* 16.8–9.14–18.

6, 52–62 *For what was. . . . the particular souls*: Plotinus' catalogue of "unbefitting additions" that the Gnostics have added onto the teaching of the ancients provides the material for much of the rest of this treatise, as pointed out by Harder-Beutler-Theiler (1960, 427). They are subsequently taken up in the following order:

1. Absolute generations and destructions (7, 1–2; 8, 2–5)
2. Blaming the soul's presence in the body (7, 2–4, Chapters 17–18)
3. Blaming the soul's presence in the universe (7, 4–7)
4. The affections of the world soul and of individual souls (7, 7–39)
5. Censure of the universe (Chapters 8–9, 13, 16)
6. The equation of the Demiurge and the soul (11, 14–19)

It must be said, however that we are here given only the sketchiest of agendas. Chapters 10–12 and 14–15 bear a tenuous relation at most to the topics above. Nor does (1), the subject of absolute generations and destructions, continue to be of much relevance to the discussion; the same is true for (6).

6, 55 *the deception that prevails among men*: At first sight, the reference to "deception" (*apatē*) prevailing among men expresses a general pessimism about the epistemic abilities or achievements of Plotinus' fellow men. But this has not prevented scholars from suspecting that the passage targets a particular type of (in Plotinus' eyes) deception, namely Christianity; see for example Schmidt (1900, 83).

6, 58 *absolute generations and destructions*: The adjective *panteleis* (absolute) could be read as qualifying only "destructions." If it were so read, one would need to explain what Plotinus finds objectionable about the "generations" that the Gnostics are said to introduce. Perhaps we could, on this reading, take him to mean "generations" (viz. processes of coming-into-being) that occur temporally in the intelligible world. But the simpler alternative will be to have *panteleis* qualify both "generations" and "destructions." "Absolute," in this case, means the creation of the universe from nothing (or perhaps from some pre-existing chaos in which matter is not yet distinguished), on the one hand, and the destruction of the universe at the end of time on the other. The qualification "absolute" is necessary to make clear that the unobjectionable admission of "generations" and "destructions" *into* the sensible universe is not at issue. Cf. 3, 12–15, with Commentary; V.8.12, 20–26.

Chapter 7

Plotinus investigates the differences between individual souls and the world soul.

7, 1–2 *We have said . . . the intelligibles exist*: A reference back to 3, 11–12, and perhaps to 4, 18–22. See V.8.12, 15–25, where Plotinus defends the perpetuity of the cosmos on the grounds that it shares, *qua* natural image, the eternity belonging to its original (the intelligible cosmos), as long as that original exists. See also II.3.18, 17, where he describes the cosmos as "an image that is always being made" (*eikōn aei eikonizomenos*).

7, 2–4 *Further, it has . . . for the soul*: See Plato's *Phaedo* 67a; cf. 65a–d, and *Laws* 828d4–5. Plotinus himself refers to Plato's view that the soul's communion with the body "fetters" it (cf. *Phaedo* 67d) at IV.8.1, 29–31. At IV.8.2, 42–49, he gives two reasons why "communion with the body" (*koinōnia pros sōma*) may be irksome to soul, either because it presents an obstacle to thinking, or because it fills up the soul with pleasures, desires, and fears. Importantly, however, neither of these reasons is applicable to the world soul or the soul of the stars: "neither of these misfortunes can befall a soul which has never deeply penetrated into the body, is not a slave but a sovereign ruling a body of such an order as to have no need and no shortcoming and therefore to give ground for neither desire nor fear" (IV.8.2, 44–49; tr. MacKenna).

7, 4–8 *But to conceive. . . . individual souls are*: It is a mistake to infer from the difficulties that individual souls experience in the world that the world soul suffers the same; such reasoning commits the "fallacy of composition." As Plotinus points out with his example of potters or coppersmiths (whom he regards with evident contempt), what is true of one group of citizens—that they have an unruly disposition, say—need not be true for the city as a whole, which may be well governed overall. His task in this chapter is to explain how the relation between the world soul and the universe is fundamentally different from that between the individual soul and its body. See also III.2.3, 11–22 for a similar kind of argument.

The fall of Sophia has already been discussed in Chapter 4; now, the question at issue is whether her presence in the universe in some sense places her in an unnatural, regrettable state. Cf. IV.8.2, 24–26, which may be viewed against this background of anti-Gnostic polemic: "For it is in no way an evil for soul to give body the power of well-being and existence, because not all providential care taken over an inferior stops the carer from remaining in the best possible state" (tr. Fleet).

7, 9–18 *Beside the other. . . . it in turn*: Individual souls animate bodies that are already formed by the world soul.

In that sense we are "tied down" already at the moment of birth, when the soul enters the body. Cf. 18, 14–17 below, and IV.3.6, 10–15. The language of "binding" and "being bound" illustrates the philosophical point that the activity of the world soul, which is firmly directed toward the intelligible world, remains unimpeded by its providential care for the world's body, since it does not actively interfere in or deliberate about particular events in the cosmos, given that the world's body is complete and self-sufficient. Individual souls, on the other hand, are much more closely involved in the sustenance of their bodies, which, unlike the world's body, are partial and deficient. Cf. IV.8.2, 32–33.

7, 9–10 *countless times elsewhere*: "Countless times" is, in this case, no exaggeration; the most relevant treatises are IV.8 (especially Chapters 2–3), and IV.3.1–18, where the differences between world soul and individual souls are discussed at length.

7, 15 *unaffected*: See 7, 18–22 for the denial that the world soul can receive any "affection" (*pathēma*) from the body; it is therefore "unaffected" (*apathēs*).

7, 15–18 *The part of . . . it in turn*: Not much weight should be given to the talk of "parts" here, since the world soul does not strictly speaking have any distinct parts (see also 2, 11, where it is described as "the soul that is not a part"). But it is all the same true that Plotinus distinguishes different aspects in its activity, such that its higher form remains at rest and contemplates intelligible nature, while another, lower "form of soul" (*eidos psuchēs*), equivalent to nature as a whole, perpetually receives "reason-principles" (*logoi*) from the higher soul that become instilled into matter. Cf. II.3.18, 13–16.

7, 18–22 *Because in general. . . . its own life*: In this complex passage, we are to think of the body of the universe as "existing in" the soul of the world. While the body of the universe is "affected" by the world soul, as can be observed from the rotation of the heavens, for example, who derive their motion from the soul, it does not in turn affect the world soul, which remains strictly aloof in its activity of contemplation. In the grafting metaphor, the tree represents the world soul, and the shoot the cosmos. Whatever happens to the cosmos, which comes to "life," so to speak, when it is present in soul, will not affect the world soul. Grafting was a common practice in ancient agriculture (see, for instance, Virgil, *Georgics* 2.69–82), so that it comes as no surprise to find similar metaphors in other writers, such as St. Paul in Romans 11:24 and Clement of Alexandria, *Excerpts from Theodotus* 56.4.

7, 22–27 *In fact, when. . . . the intelligible world*: In order to drive home his point that the world soul is "unaffected," Plotinus offers a thought-experiment in two stages. He first asks what would happen to "universal fire" (*to holon pur*) if the "fire within you" (*to en soi pur*) were quenched, drawing inspiration from Plato's *Philebus* 29b–c, where Socrates presents a similar argument to his interlocutor Protarchus. Like Plotinus, Socrates distinguishes between "the fire in us" (*to pur par'hēmin*) and the fire in the universe (*to pur en tōi panti*). By the "fire in us," Socrates means that part of fire that, along with the other elements, constitutes an individual body, while "the fire in the universe" seems to refer to the totality of fire taken collectively. Just as Plotinus takes it as obvious that the universal fire is not affected by the existence or non-existence of any one particular fire, so Socrates asks rhetorically: "Is the fire in the universe generated, nourished, and ruled by the fire that belongs to us, or is not quite the reverse, that your heat and mine, and that in every animal, owe all this to the cosmic fire?" (29c5–8; tr. Frede).

The second stage in Plotinus' thought-experiment transfers the lesson from the *Philebus* to the world soul, arguing that the same relation obtains between world soul and universal fire as between universal and particular fire, such that the destruction of universal fire would not affect the world soul, but only the constitution (*sustasis*) of its body. See also II.1.4, 32–33.

But while the influence of the *Philebus* on the present passage cannot be denied, one might wonder whether Plotinus' choice of fire may be deliberate, given the important role that it plays in the cosmology of his opponents. Perhaps his point is that they must recognize, on their own principles, that the greater whole is unaffected by the destruction of some of its parts (for evidence that fire could be viewed as a universal principle by the Gnostics, see Hippolytus' report of Simon Magus, who is said to have believed that fire is "the principle" [*archē*] of the universe, at *Refutation of All Heresies* 6.9.3.3–4 Marcovich). And so just as the universal fire, on their view, will survive the quenching of any one individual fire, so they should agree that the world soul would survive the disappearance of universal fire, in order to retain a consistent position.

7, 27–32 *For the constitution. . . . of soul wanted*: The military metaphor of the world soul ordering all things to remain in their allotted places captures an important aspect of its activity. Plato, in the *Phaedrus*, describes the soul as "governing the whole universe" (*Phaedrus* 246c1–2), which Plotinus takes to imply that the world soul oversees the causal network of antecedent conditions and consequences in the world (cf. II.3.16, 23–27). In contrast to the body of the universe, which cannot disintegrate into anything outside of itself because it already contains everything (cf. II.1.1, 12–13), our individual bodies (for example) are in constant flux, losing part of their substance and being replenished by nourishment daily (cf. II.1.8, 22–27). In Plotinus' metaphor, these bodies are like ranks in an army ready to flee from the enemy; they require extra encouragement to keep in their places, beyond the arrangement of troops put in place by their general (the world soul). Analogously, individual bodies require constant attention for their maintenance, a task that falls to individual souls who "by a secondary bond" (*desmōi deuterōi*; see 7, 30) ensure their preservation as far as possible. See also II.1.3, 23–26. The distinction between the "primary bond," that is, the arrangement of the whole universe put in place by the world soul, and the "secondary bond" that arises from the activity of individual souls, can be viewed as an interpretation of Plato's *Timaeus*, where the Demiurge, after creating the world soul and the planets with "indissoluble bonds" (43a2), delegates the creation of particular living beings to his subordinates, the Younger Gods, who create bodies out of elements with "copious rivets, invisible on account of their smallness" (43a3).

7, 33–39 *If some of. . . . anything from them*: The misfortunes that individual creatures encounter do not imply that the universe is poorly arranged; it is rather due to a misalignment between the parts, as when a small animal is swept away by the natural motion of a river, or, as in the present example, a turtle trampled by a troupe of dancers. As Plotinus explains at IV.4.32, 44–52, the changing fortunes, for better or worse, of the parts are a precondition for the unimpeded life of the universe, which cannot privilege the parts over the arrangement of the whole.

Chapter 8

The universe preserves a likeness of intelligible reality; it is thus eternal, beautiful and good. The stars are good evidence for this, and it is absurd of the opponents to boast that they themselves are nobler.

8, 1–5 *To ask "why. . . . cause of creation*: Asking "why did the soul create the universe" amounts to asking "why does the soul exist," because it is in its nature to create. Plotinus thus rejects any attempt to explain the creation of the universe by appealing to the fall of a divine principle or a deliberate decision of the Demiurge to imitate a higher reality. It is interesting to note that the question "why did the Demiurge create?" might be taken to imply that the soul is identical with the Demiurge, a title which Plotinus elsewhere reserves for Intellect alone. But he may here be pointing out only the absurdity of his opponents' question, without actually endorsing their identification.

8, 3 *perpetuity*: "Perpetuity" translates the Greek *to aei*, which describes an everlasting duration of time, rather than a timeless eternity, for which *to aiōion* is the customary term. To say that an entity existing everlastingly in both past and future directions of time has a beginning is a contradictory proposition, and rejected by Plotinus for that reason. His argument is *ad homines*, however:

the question "why did the soul create this cosmos" could be understood non-temporally, so as to mean "why is the soul such that it always brings about the cosmos?" But Plotinus does not consider this possibility; the most charitable explanation for this oversight would be that his sources compelled him to read their account as implying a temporal beginning of creation.

If one assumes that the creation of the cosmos takes place at a moment in time, it seems that there must have been a time when the creator underwent a change from not intending to create the universe to having that same intention, which leads us to Plotinus' second objection to asking "why did the soul create?" One might wish to counter his objection by saying that the creator may always have had the very same intention of creating the universe at one particular moment of time. But even in that case the actual activity of creation implies a change, in the creator, from an earlier state of not creating—a possibility dismissed here without further argument.

8, 3–4 *turning from one thing to the next*: The activity of "turning" (*trepesthai*) from one thing to the next belongs particularly to the faculty of "rational calculation" (*dianoia*). Plotinus often contrasts this kind of planning activity with the creative power of the world soul; see 2, 14; 4, 15–17 above, and IV.4.10, 13–15.

8, 10–16 *If in fact . . . the intelligible gods*: How should the contrast between the life of particular living things and that of the cosmos be understood? One might think that Plotinus is here suggesting that the temporally limited and changing life possessed by individual living things (with periods of growth and decline, for example) is life in its lowest development, in contrast with the "continuous" (8, 14) and always fully developed life of the cosmos. Particular living things thus possess life "inarticulately" in the sense that their lives fall short of the fuller development of life in the cosmos. See Aristotle, *History of Animals* 579a24 for this sense of the word *adiarthrōtos.* See also III.8.9, 36–37 where Plotinus argues that Intellect must contain all the forms "with exactness (*akribōs*) and not roughly," or else it would possess them only "imperfectly and *adiarthrōtōs.*" The contrast between "exactness" and "indistinctness" overlaps at least partially with that between "full articulation" and "inarticulateness," which may explain *enarges* ("distinct") at 8, 14.

8, 15–16 *image of the intelligible gods*: Plato, *Timaeus* 37c6–7 talks about the cosmos as an "image of the eternal gods," and Plotinus seems to have this passage in mind, equating "eternal" with "intelligible." Cf. *Epinomis* 983e–984b.

8, 16–19 *But if the. . . . able to possess*: For a similar defense of the cosmos, as the most beautiful image of the intelligible world, see already 4, 22–26 above. Plotinus gives two reasons why the world is as good a likeness of the intelligible world as there can be: first, because it is the necessary consequence of Intellect's internal activity (see comment on 8, 22–23 below), its existence is also necessary; the universe therefore imitates Intellect's timeless being with its own eternal existence. Second, our cosmos is the first imitation of the intelligible world, and will thus best display its salient features, such as beauty and order; the Gnostic idea of a "new earth" or paradigm of the sensible world (the "other cosmos" at 8, 26.28) that is a more perfect imitation of the intelligible world is implicitly rejected as absurd here. See also III.2.2, 8–18; V.8.8, 22–23.

Unlike Plotinus, who, in the tradition of Plato's *Timaeus* (see Commentary on 8, 15–16 above), stresses the closeness of the relation between intelligible reality and its perceptible manifestation (the cosmos), some Gnostic writings emphasize the deficiency of the visible likenesses of intelligible reality; cf., for example, the following passage from the Valentinian *Tripartite Tractate* (NHC I,5): "Like the Pleromas are the things which came into being from the arrogant thought, which are their (the Pleromas') likenesses, copies, shadows, and phantasms, lacking reason and the light, these which belong to the vain thought, since they are not products of anything. Therefore, their end will be like their beginning: from that which did not exist (they are) to return once again to that which will not be" (78.28–79.4; tr. Attridge-Mueller).

8, 20–21 *not by rational calculation or artifice*: That the world soul produces the visible universe by rational calculation and planning, in the manner of craftsmen or indeed Plato's own Demiurge (on a literal reading of the *Timaeus*), is also denied at 2, 14; 4, 15–17 of this treatise; see Commentary on these passages.

8, 22–23 *the activity of the intelligible world must be double*: The doctrine of "double activity," which states that each entity possesses an internal activity by which it constitutes itself, and an external manifestation of that activity which produces a lower reality, here establishes the point that the generation of the cosmos is necessarily linked to the activity of the intelligibles, rather than the result of some tragic rupture in the process of emanation, as the Gnostics would have it. See also Commentary on 3, 7–12.

8, 24–25 *most powerless thing of all*: The "most powerless" entity of all would be matter, the extreme end (*to eschaton*) of the process of emanation. See 8, 21 above, and I.8.7, 21–23; II.5.5, 11–19; III.2.2, 9–10.

8, 25 *marvelous power*: See VI.2.3, 24. Plotinus had already alluded to the "marvelous power" of the world soul, which derives from its contemplation of the Intellect, at 2, 15; see also II.1.4, 15–16.

8, 29–30 *Indeed the whole . . . to the sky*: Plato's *Timaeus* is a useful point of reference here. At 30d–31a, Timaeus describes how the Demiurge, intending to make the cosmos most like its intelligible model, ensured that it contains all living creatures. The diversity of forms in the intelligible world, in other words, is reflected in the diversity of living beings in the sensible world. See also III.2.3, 20–25.

8, 30–32 *But why are . . . around in order*: Plato's *Timaeus* 39d–e already describes the creation of the stars in terms that suggest their closeness to the divine model that they are said to imitate. See also my comment on 5, 10–11, with further references to the divinity of the stars in Plotinus.

8, 32–39 *Why would they. . . . lost his mind*: The thought that the stars have virtues, and the subsequent argument in favor of it, are worthy of comment. Plotinus argues (i), that the stars have no evil tendencies, such as dispositions to pursue inappropriate sources of pleasure, for example, which they would need to overcome with the sort of virtues practiced by members of a social community, e.g. temperance; and (ii), that the stars have no bodies, so that they do not require a different kind of virtue, namely the kind of "purificatory" virtue that is necessary for dissociating oneself from any "communion" with the body. This distinction between two kinds of virtue is explained at length in I.2. One might object to this argument that Plotinus does not prove that the stars have virtues, but rather the opposite, that they have no need for any virtues at all, since there is no domain of activity in which they could meaningfully be said to exercise virtuous conduct. But Plotinus is ready to recognize virtues surpassing those of the ordinary and the purificatory kinds, namely virtues that arise in the soul once purified, and that can be described in terms of contemplation of the intelligibles and impassivity toward the body. Presumably these virtues of the purified soul are also the virtues that the stars display to a superlative degree. See I.2.6, 23–26.

8, 36 *eternal leisure*: See V.8.3, 18–4, 4 for the idea that the heavenly bodies are "at leisure," in so far as they participate in the contemplation of Intellect.

8, 38 *the stars*: Note that the Greek phrase *ta ekei* (literally, "the things up there") is ambiguous. Plotinus could be referring either to the stars, as this translation assumes, or to the intelligibles, as Dufour (2006, 262n150) thinks. The context of the passage (8, 29–39) suggests that the Gnostic denigration of the visible universe, and particularly the stars, is at issue here; hence the expression *ta ekei* probably refers to the latter. See also 5, 1–16.

8, 39–46 *For if the souls. . . . on the intelligibles*: If the Gnostic opponents resent the presence of their souls in the universe, they face a dilemma: they must have descended into it either willingly or unwillingly. If they have descended against their will, they cannot claim that their souls are superior to the universe and the world soul that it animates. For in that case the world soul would have forced them to come down, and so it would have been in command, and so better than the Gnostics' souls (cf. 8, 41–42: "In souls, the ruling part is better"). See 10, 19–26 for the view that individual souls descended as "members of Sophia," which could be taken to imply that individual souls descended against their will because the divine principle Sophia, of which they are a part, in her turn declined from the intelligible world. Alternatively, if the opponents descended willingly into the visible world, then there is nothing that can stop them from leaving it again if they do not like it, by way of suicide (implied by the Greek verb *apallattesthai* ["depart"] at 8, 43). This casual attitude to suicide sits somewhat uncomfortably with what Plotinus says elsewhere, where he seems to think that suicide can be justifiable only in extreme circumstances, such as falling into the hand of enemies (I.4.7, 31), or feeling the approach of insanity (I.9, 11–15). But given the polemical context of the present passage, we should not expect to find Plotinus' considered view on the subject here. See O'Brien (1993, 80–81) for a discussion of 8, 39–43. See also *Zostrianus* (NHC VIII,1) 3.23–28 where the narrator recounts his attempted suicide.

Chapter 9

This chapter defends the view that the order of the cosmos is just against the Gnostics, and turns to attacking their notion of a special providence.

9, 1 *wealth and poverty*: The personification of wealth and poverty, as entities that can be "censured," owes something to Plato's *Symposium* 203b–e, where love is described as the child of wealth and poverty. As Plotinus makes clear, what someone wishing to cast blame on the arrangement of the universe will decry is "the unfair distribution" (*to ouk ison*, at 8, 1–2) of material goods.

9, 4–5 *have the advantage . . . have the better over . . .* : "Have the advantage" and "have the better over" translate the difficult Greek expression *pleon echein*, which has a range of meanings, chiefly (i) "getting more than one's fair share"; (ii) "getting the better over someone"; or (iii) generally, "gaining some advantage" (see Liddell Scott Jones, entry for *pleonekte-ō* A.2). At 9, 4, no object is specified in the Greek, making sense (iii) most relevant here; at 9, 5, where there is an object ("private citizens"), sense (ii) is intended.

9, 6–11 *Rather, the wise. . . . who are better*: Plotinus distinguishes three different ways of life. There is, (1) the life of the sage, and (2) the more human life, which subdivides into two, (2a) the life characteristic of the man who pursues ordinary virtue, and (2b) that typical of the common crowd. These ways of life are distinguished according to the dominant end that is pursued therein. Plotinus does not imply that the sage, for example, could not engage in the activities of the man of "ordinary virtue," only that it will not be the activity around which his or her life will be primarily organized. The division of lives grounds the claim that a lack of material goods such as wealth and honors cannot and should not bring the wise person to berate the state of the universe or to feel envy toward those more successful in their acquisition. Since these material goods are not things of intrinsic value, they do not properly fall under the concern of the wise man seeking to separate his soul from the body as far as possible in this life and to contemplate the intelligibles. Cf. V.9.1 for a similar threefold division. Many Gnostic writings divide mankind likewise; see for example, Irenaeus, *Against the Heresies* 1.6.1–2; 1.7.5; *Tripartite Tractate* (NHC I,5) 118.14–119.34; Clement of Alexandria, *Excerpts from Theodotus* 54–57, and the useful comparative table in Kalligas (2014, 390). See also Plato, *Gorgias* 500c–d, where the life of philosophy is contrasted with that of rhetoric and politics.

One question of interest here is the sense in which the middle class in this threefold division, the men of ordinary virtue, "share in some good" (*metischei agathou tinos*). The thought might be that since virtue itself is a good, possessing virtue in some degree (although not in the same degree as the wise man) means having a share of the good that is virtue. Less likely, but not impossible, would be to think that "ordinarily" virtuous men "share in some good" in the sense that they are involved in the life of a social and political community, which could be seen as good to the extent that it displays an order and rationality that is more fully apparent at higher levels of reality.

The relative contempt in which manual labor is held by Plotinus, as an activity with little or no intrinsic value, but rather instrumental for the production of goods that are needed by the superior two classes, is undeniably unpleasant, but consistent with other passages in the *Enneads*, e.g. at 7, 5–6; III.8.4, 45–47.

9, 11–17 *If someone commits. . . . citizen in it*: Now the discussion shifts to the problem of "moral evil," which, Plotinus argues, cannot be taken as evidence for the imperfection of the universe. In his view, moral weakness is explicable in terms of some bad condition of the soul; to make this point, he alludes to a fragment from Heraclitus, according to which "a man when he is drunk is led by a beardless youth, stumbling and not knowing where he goes" (DK B117). As such, the responsibility lies squarely with those who neglect their souls (who are "like beardless children," presumably in the sense that their judgment is immature), and not with the universe.

The comparison of the world with a gymnasium with winners and losers at 9, 14–17 might seem to have troubling implications. It could suggest a degree of fatalism, to the effect that we each have a role assigned to us in the world, as either winners or losers, with no power to change our lot. But the passage need not be read in this way: of course, the losers in the gymnasium may eventually decide to train hard and so in turn become winners, and, conversely, the winners may become complacent and become losers. Nothing in the passage implies that people cannot change from one group to the other. But the analogy could still be thought of as countenancing a bizarrely competitive view of the world, where people are either winners or losers, rather than, say, engaged in co-operative enterprises such as families and cities. To address this concern, we need to ask what the real equivalent in our world is to the winners and losers in the gymnasium. One might think that the analogy is between athletes in the gymnasium and virtuous and vicious people in our world. In that case, Plotinus would simply be saying that it is up to us whether we train ourselves to be moral "winners," that is, whether we develop virtuous dispositions and pure souls, or whether we slack off and become vicious. On this reading, the fact that it is up to us to take on either role does not entitle us to cast blame upon the order of the universe, since we alone are ultimately to blame for any shortcomings within ourselves. Understood in this way, the "competitive" element of the analogy is extraneous, and introduced merely to bring home the notion of virtue as something that can be trained and exercised. Cf. III.2.8, 16–26.

9, 15–16 *wronged . . . murdered*: Plotinus is now directly addressing his Gnostic interlocutors, arguing that the evils of the world should be of no concern to them if they believe that their souls are immortal. Note the sarcastic tone at 9, 16: those who wish to escape from this world should, on the strength of their convictions, be grateful if someone else dispatches them from it.

9, 17 *nothing compels you*: The same point, that suicide always remains as an option for those convinced, like Plotinus' Gnostics, that they ought to remove themselves from this world, was made before at 8, 43.

9, 17–26 *Moreover, it is. . . . concerning divine matters*: Just as there are punishments and judgments in cities, so there is a cosmic justice that assigns different circumstances of life to souls depending on their actions in past incarnations. As Plotinus argues in III.2.13, 3–11, "a man, once a ruler, will be made a slave because he abused his power and because the fall is to his future good. Those that have money will be made poor—and to the good poverty is no hindrance. Those that have unjustly killed, are killed in turn, unjustly as regards the murderer but justly as regards the victim, and those that are to suffer are thrown into the path of those that administer the merited treatment" (tr. MacKenna). But while the specific circumstances of one's life, e.g. the social station into which one is born, and even how one dies, are all part of the fate that one is accorded depending on one's previous life, it is still up to the individual to act virtuously or viciously within the limits of destiny. The Platonic background to this idea is especially the Myth of Er in *Republic* 10.614d–621d. See also Plotinus' discussion of providence in III.2–3.

Notice that the claim "it is agreed" at 9, 17 introduces a degree of ambiguity into the passage. Is Plotinus claiming that belief in judgments and punishments belongs to the common ground that Gnostics and Platonists share? In that case, the concluding remark, at 9, 25–26, that "anyone ignorant of this is very reckless and boorish about divine matters" cannot well be directed against the Gnostics, but would be a general reflection aimed at no one in particular. Alternatively, if "it is agreed" at 9, 17 were to mean "it is agreed among all sensible people," not including the Gnostics, the biting concluding remark at 9, 25–26 could be directed at Plotinus' opponents. See also 9, 46 for a similar allegation of "boorishness" (*agroikia*), this time clearly directed at the Gnostic opponents.

9, 22 *"easily be acquitted"*: Plotinus is here quoting an unnamed poet who was apparently writing in the Ionian dialect of Greek (cf. *rhēidiōs* for Attic *rhadiōs*). Some scholars have suggested that a verse by Theognis (*Elegies* 1034: "Not easily shall mortal man escape the destined gifts of the gods" [tr. J. M. Edmonds]) may be Plotinus' inspiration here. See Cilento (1971, 247).

9, 26–35 *No, one must. . . . multitude of gods*: The Gnostic claim to forming a kind of spiritual elite is commonly attacked in the heresiological literature; especially instructive here is Irenaeus' report in *Against the Heresies* 1.6.4: "they highly exalt themselves, and claim to be perfect, and the elect seed. For they declare that we simply receive grace for use, wherefore also it will again be taken away from us; but that they themselves have grace as their own special possession, which has descended from above by means of an unspeakable and indescribable conjunction; and on this account more will be given them" (tr. Roberts-Rambaut). Plotinus attacks this claim on the grounds that someone committed to it "is no longer excellent" (9, 28–29), a remark that can be related to his later claim that the good man will be "well disposed" (*eumenōs echei*) toward all men, at 9, 45. Plotinus seems to be saying that concern for others, and their attainment of goodness, is in some way inextricably bound up with the wise man's own goodness. Conversely, denial of other people's ability to become good would be the kind of selfishness that negates any claim one can have to being good oneself, perhaps because it is the result of some irrational impulse which exaggerates one's own individual potential, at the expense of recognizing it in others. Against the Gnostics' pretension to having a special spiritual nature, Plotinus sets his own vision of a gradual and continuous ascent in goodness, from human beings to good daemons (intermediate beings between humans and gods, referred to also at 17, 33–34; cf. Porphyry, *On Abstinence* 2.38.6–24), to the stars that look up to the intelligible world (9, 30–31; identified as gods earlier, at 8, 30–32), to the world soul ("the ruler of the universe," after Plato's *Phaedrus* 246e4), the intelligible gods, and finally the "great king" in the intelligible world (9, 34). "The great king," the summit of the ascent, may refer to either the One, or the upper reaches of the intelligible world, as Roloff (1970, 184–185) and Alt (1990, 28n89) think. A comparison with other passages where Plotinus uses a similar description (I.8.2, 7–9; V.1.8, 1–2; V.5.3, 6–24; VI.7.42, 8–14; VI.8.9, 18–21) makes it likely that the "great king" describes the One here too.

9, 35 *displayed*: Reading *endeiknumenon* ("displayed") with M and C, in place of *endeiknumenous*, to agree with *to mega autou* ("his greatness").

9, 35–45 *The task of. . . . origin from him*: This apparent rejection of monotheism raises interesting questions of interpretation. At first sight, Plotinus appears to forestall a possible misinterpretation of the ascent to the "great king" that he has just described. We are meant to understand that the first principle has the power to bring a multiplicity of all gods into existence, even though at the level of the One these gods are not yet differentiated. It does not follow from this that the divine is simply one, since the intelligible entities and visible gods that follow from the One are real beings. But what is the relevance of this argument in the present anti-Gnostic context? After all, the Gnostics have earlier been charged with precisely the opposite tendency, creating superfluous divisions in the intelligible world rather than unifying them into a single divine being. Some scholars suggest that Plotinus now has his sights on Judaeo-Christian monotheism, and not specifically the Gnostics; see Dufour (2006, 264n170), and Armstrong (1973, 6), who thinks Plotinus attacks "the monotheism of the 'jealous god,' separated by an unbridgeable gulf from his creation, guarding his divinity as an unique prerogative which it is blasphemy and idolatry to attribute to any other being." But such a sudden shift of target would itself stand in need of explanation. It is more likely that Plotinus focuses on the Gnostics' contempt for the cosmos and the stars. While the Gnostics wish to remove the stars and the cosmos from the sphere of divine influence, and focus on the differences between them and their first principle (see 9, 42–43), Plotinus reminds us that these differences are natural, and that the power of the One manifests itself in the plurality of gods. The relevant sense in which the Gnostics reduce the divine to a unity is by making it a single "pneumatic" substance, such that anything is divine if and only if it shares in that substance. Against this view, Plotinus insists that the divine can take multiple forms, and that the procession of divinities from the first principle is continuous. See Spanu (2012, 149), with whom I am in broad agreement here.

9, 41 *announce through oracles*: By "oracles," we should probably think of the signs (*sēmeia*) of future events that the stars display to humans, as Plotinus explains in a later chapter (13, 20–25).

9, 45 *all <gods>*: I accept Kirchhoff's insertion *<kai tous theous> kai anthropous* ("all <gods> and . . . men").

9, 45–52 *Next I reply. . . . removed from Intellect*: In Plato's *Theaetetus* 176c1–2, Socrates famously claims that we should flee from this world, and that this flight is itself "becoming like god as far as one can" (*homoiōsis theōi kata to dunaton*). The important qualification "as far as one can" limits the scope of reasonable ambition to what is attainable for human nature; Plotinus argues that the Gnostics overstep this limit. He implies that what motivates their claim to spiritual supremacy is not a conviction arrived at by reasoning, but an irrational presumption. As he puts it, "to think that one is above Intellect is already to be removed from It." This may be, first, because it is a false belief, and so cannot fall within the remit of Intellect, who, as an ideal knower, only thinks what is true. But, compatibly with this account, one might also think that the adoption of the false belief is to be explained in terms of some emotional appeal that the belief exerts, e.g. by flattering one's own view about one's place in the universe. As such the process of belief-formation is unreliable and does not inevitably lead to truth, unlike the way an ideal knower would infallibly be related to the objects of knowledge.

9, 45 *a noble person should ascend*: The Greek word *semnon* ("holy," "august" or "noble") could be taken to qualify *metron*, "measure," at 9, 46, but I have followed HS$_2$ in taking it as a masculine accusative ("a noble person . . ."), which seems to give a better sense here.

9, 52–64 *But stupid people. . . . a great number>*: On the alleged presumption of the Gnostics, see the comment on 9, 26–35 above. What is objectionable about the two speeches that Plotinus lays into his opponents' mouths, at 9, 53–54 and 56–59, is that they encourage their listeners to think of themselves as superior to other people and even to the gods. Cf. Irenaeus, *Against the Heresies* 2.30.2.

9, 56–57 *a child of god*: The Platonist Celsus reportedly caricatured the speech-making of inspired prophets in terms similar to Plotinus' own portrayal of the Gnostics, as Kalligas (2014, 393) notes: "[Many] are accustomed to say, each for himself 'I am God; I am the Son of God'; or, 'I am the Divine Spirit; I have come because the world is perishing, and you, O men, are perishing for your iniquities. But I wish to save you, and you shall see me returning again with heavenly power'" (Origen, *Against Celsus* 7.9.10–14 Borret; tr. Crombie).

9, 59 *without making any effort*: Compare Clement of Alexandria's complaints about unnamed Gnostics: "For there are some who cannot bear at all to listen to those who exhort them to turn to the truth; and they attempt to trifle, pouring out blasphemies against the truth, claiming for themselves the knowledge of the greatest things in the universe, without having learned, or inquired, or made any effort (*ouden ponēsantes*), or discovered the consecutive train of ideas—whom one should pity rather than hate for such perversity" (*Stromata* 7.16.103.1.1–2.1 Stählin-Früchtel-Treu; tr. Wilson).

9, 59 *<when>*: Reading *hotan* for *eita*, as proposed by Harder-Beutler-Theiler (1960, 430), and reading a period after *alloi* at 9, 60 rather than a question mark.

9, 59–60 *join the chorus*: Although the idea that others will "join the chorus" (*sunepēchōsin*) may be understood metaphorically, Dufour (2006, 265n179) rightly points out that certain Gnostic rites involve phrases spoken by bystanders, and not only the initiator and the initiand. Cf. Irenaeus, *Against the Heresies* 1.21.3.

9, 60–64 *It is as. . . . a great number>*: The Greek text at this point is difficult, and has been emended in a number of different ways. This translation reads *ti an, ei chiliopēchus* *einai nomizoi, tous <d'> allous pentapēches einai akouoi; monon de phantazoito hōs ta chilia arithmos megas*, accepting Kirchhoff's <*d'*> and ignoring the other changes proposed in the *Addenda* to HS_2, which do not improve the sense of the passage. If one were to accept their changes, the result would be the following alternative translation: "It is as if, in a group of people who do not know how to count, one man without the knowledge of counting had heard that he is a thousand cubits tall, and imagines only that one thousand cubits is a large number. What would happen except that he would think that he was a thousand cubits tall, but that the others are five cubits tall?"

How should we understand the analogy? The deluded person (assigned a male gender by Plotinus, and referred to as such in the following) is said to "imagine," and so to entertain in his thought the belief, that (i) 1,000 cubits is a large number, and, together with (ii) the conviction that he is 1,000 cubits tall, and the others five cubits, infers the belief (iii) that he must be much taller than those around him. According to Plotinus, the Gnostic is in a similar situation. (a) He entertains the belief that possessing a special kind of knowledge will elevate anyone above humans and gods; (b) that he possesses such special knowledge, and others do not; so as to arrive at (c), the belief that he must be of a nature far superior to other people. Two points in particular are worth noting about this analogy. First, the deluded person does not have a grasp of measurements and therefore lacks a full understanding of the content of all three beliefs that involve reference to measures, that is, (i)–(iii). Analogously, Plotinus seems to imply that the Gnostics are similarly ignorant with regard to their beliefs (a)–(c), since, presumably, they lack any understanding of what makes a person "superior," and what real knowledge consists in. Second, notice how the analogy explains that the beliefs of the deluded person are arrived at "by hearsay," that is, as something that is uncritically accepted, rather than being the product of some kind of reasoning from prior beliefs. Presumably, this "hearsay" is equivalent to the Gnostics' writings and revelations, which, Plotinus suggests, will be accepted equally uncritically by their followers. If one puts these last two points together, that the Gnostics do not, strictly speaking, understand what they are saying, and that they have blindly accepted a set of beliefs, one may feel that Plotinus is hardly being charitable toward his opponents. This fact ties in with the larger question of the purpose and nature of Plotinus' debate with the Gnostics in the present treatise (see Commentary on 10, 7–11). For a distant ancestor of the counting analogy, see Plato, *Republic* 426d–e.

9, 64–69 *Next, if god. . . . at you either*: If God can have a special concern for a particular class of embodied human beings in the universe (cf. Clement of Alexandria, *Excerpts from Theodotus* 74–75), nothing prevents him from directing his attention elsewhere, and from having a more general concern for the universe at large. If God has no such general concern for the universe, on the other hand, there is no reason why he should be concerned with the Gnostics either. So on either horn of the dilemma, it is inconsistent to believe that God's providence extends to only a part of the universe, and not the whole.

9, 67–68 *Yet why, when . . . which you exist*: What is here translated as "looking beyond" (*exō blepein*) is often rendered as "looking outside." But this latter alternative obscures Plotinus' train of thought. His point is that if God cares providentially for the Gnostics, he is already "looking" outside himself, and so there is nothing preventing him from looking "beyond" (another sense of *exō*) what he is currently "looking" at, or concerned with. And so there is no good reason why God could not also turn his attention to the universe that the Gnostics inhabit.

9, 70 *But they have no need for god*: Plotinus is here imagining a retort that someone with sympathies for the Gnostics (perhaps one of those "friends" that are mentioned below, at 10, 3–5) might make. If the Gnostics do not have any need for God at all, including His providential concern, Plotinus' argument at 9, 64–69 becomes irrelevant.

9, 70–75 *Yet the cosmos. . . . at the universe*: Cf. 9, 1–5 above. See I.2.5, 9–11 for the notion that a soul that has become purified will accept pain "meekly" (*praōs*), that is to say, without excessive emotional reactions to it; as well as I.4.7, 8–42. See also *Laws* 903c for the idea that one must "look at the universe," not one's own preferences, at 9, 75.

9, 75–79 *A man who . . . to himself alone*: For the thesis that everything aims at contemplation, see III.8.1, 1–8. See also the comment on 9, 45–52 for the Gnostic claim to be uniquely able to reach the intelligible world.

9, 79 *does not give*: As Harder-Beutler-Theiler (1960, 431) point out, reading *didōsi* ("gives") in place of the participle *didous* ("giving") would give the sentence a much-needed main verb.

9, 80–83 *But even though. . . . in fact have*: Compare this passage with 9, 60–64 and 5, 1–16 above.

It seems likely to me that the Gnostics are still the subject of the sentence; I am therefore maintaining the reading *polla* ("many things"). If one accepted the change to *polloi* ("many people") proposed in the *Addenda* to HS_2, the sentence would read: "But even though there are many people who know that they do not possess these things . . . ."

Chapter 10

In this chapter, Plotinus admits that he has no hope of persuading the Gnostics, but is writing for his close followers. Instead of writing a comprehensive critique of their views, he focuses on their account of creation.

10, 1–3 *Therefore, if one . . . of their arguments*: In light of the preceding chapters, we are probably to understand that each remaining Gnostic doctrine, if examined carefully in the way Plotinus has done before, will turn out to be either (i) the result of introducing superfluous distinctions, (ii) an attempt to disguise traditional Hellenic wisdom under new terminology, (iii) simply incoherent, as involving some element of self-contradiction, or (iv) delusional, in the way discussed in Chapter 9 above (especially 9, 26–64).

10, 3–5 *[But we will . . . not know how*: Mock-refusal to criticize one's opponents out of a feeling of "respect" or "reverence" (*aidōs*) is something of a literary *topos*; it is famously used in Plato's *Republic*, where Socrates expresses his misgivings about confronting Homer (595b9–10). Cf. 14, 44–45 below, where Plotinus suggests that a harsh polemical tone would be inappropriate. And despite his apparent promise not to pursue the examination of Gnostic beliefs any further, this is precisely what Plotinus will go on to do for the remaining chapters, although he selects their (in his view) most egregious errors rather than attempting a systematic refutation. See Edwards (1989, 230), who suggests that "there is more rhetoric here than sentiment." The supplement "[But we will not do this,]" is needed to make sense of *gar* ("since") after *aidōs* at 10, 3.

10, 5–7 *They, however, do . . . to be true*: "They" is most naturally taken to refer back to the "friends" at 10, 3 toward whom Plotinus feels a certain respect, a respect which is rather tempered by the robustness of his criticisms. The "friends" are a distinct group from the students, whom Plotinus hopes to dissuade from Gnostic doctrines; the subsequent lines (10, 7–11) suggest that some interaction between the two would have taken place, and can be read as evidence that Gnostic sympathizers attended his seminars. Porphyry, describing Plotinus' school, makes a distinction between casual listeners (*akroatai*) and more intimate disciples (*zēlōtai*) that is relevant here; the "students" (*gnōrimoi*) in the present passage presumably belong to the latter group. See *Life of Plotinus* 7.1–2. Cf. Igal (1981, 139–140).

10, 7–11 *But in what . . . not trouble them*: This passage, and especially Plotinus' remark that he sees no hope of persuading the Gnostics themselves, but is rather addressing his students, carries great importance for understanding the target audience of this treatise and its overall purpose. His aim is not to win over the Gnostic "friends" whom he regards as well nigh incorrigible, but to show to his students the superiority of his own teachings. The claim that certain Gnostic teachers were incapable of producing arguments for their beliefs is, unsurprisingly, echoed in the heresiological literature; see, for example, Irenaeus, *Against the Heresies* 3.15.2, who describes the conduct of Valentinian teachers thus: "And if any one of their auditors do indeed demand explanations, or start objections to them, they affirm that he is one not capable of receiving the truth, and not having from above the seed [derived] from their Mother; and thus really give him no reply, but simply declare that he is of the intermediate regions, that is, belongs to psychic natures" (tr. Roberts-Rambaut, slightly modified).

10, 12–14 *There is another . . . and divine men*: What is this "other way" in which someone can defend "the doctrines of ancient and divine men"? Most likely, Plotinus has in mind the kind of direct and large-scale polemical attacks that he delegated to his students, and which are lost to us. Our main evidence on this point comes from a passage in Porphyry's *Life of Plotinus* 16.9–18: "Therefore, having himself produced many refutations in his seminars, and having written the book which we have entitled *Against the Gnostics*, Plotinus left it to us to pronounce on what remained. Amelius reached a total of forty books in his response to the book called *Zostrianus*, while I Porphyry have produced numerous refutations of the book of

Zoroaster, proving the book to be entirely spurious and recent, a fabrication of those who upheld this heresy to make it seem that the doctrines which they had chosen to acclaim were those of the ancient Zoroaster" (tr. Edwards).

10, 14–18 *So let us. . . . call it absurdity*: Although Plotinus has just refused to undertake a comprehensive refutation of the Gnostics, he evidently does not consider the case against them closed at this point. What is most surprising is not that he continues the discussion, however, but rather that he takes up a doctrine that has already been extensively discussed in Chapter 4, namely the fall of Sophia. In my comment at 4, 1–15, I have already argued that there is no fundamental incompatibility between the two accounts. While the account in Chapter 4 is sketchy about the details of Sophia's creation, the later discussion, from here on until the end of Chapter 12, spells out the process of creation in considerably more detail. We will never know for sure why Plotinus felt he needed to return to the issue, but part of the reason must surely be that he takes this particular Gnostic doctrine as "surpassing" all others "in absurdity" (10, 18). Arguably (and argument is needed, as Plotinus nowhere makes this explicit), the Gnostic doctrine of creation is reduced to the height of absurdity at 12, 34–35, where the responsibility for the evil in this world must be referred back to the intelligibles. If Plotinus viewed this (for him untenable) result as the logical conclusion of the Gnostics' illumination of matter, he may have considered the issue important enough to deal with it more extensively here than in Chapter 4. Moreover, the view that the soul shapes or "illuminates" matter is not far removed from Plotinus' own position, which may partly explain why he here revisits the topic. On the illumination of matter by soul, see for example I.8.14, 38–39. It is connected to the fall of the soul in the same treatise (14, 40–48). See also I.1.12, 21–28 on the same subject, and the lucid discussion by Rist (1967, Chapter 9).

10, 19–26 *They say that. . . . be in matter*: This second account of the decline of Sophia differs from the version in Chapter 4 in some important respects. First, Plotinus acknowledges that a distinction between soul and Sophia may need to be drawn, although he subsequently continues to talk about soul only. A second important difference between the present account of Sophia's fall and the one in Chapter 4 is that individual souls, as "members of Sophia," are now conceptually distinct from the soul or Sophia. Third, the reference to an "image" (*eidōlon*) created in matter at 10, 26 appears to refer to the creation of a lower Sophia, who will in turn go on to create the Demiurge—an aspect omitted from the simpler presentation of Sophia's decline in Chapter 4. This lower Sophia, identified with the sinful Intention (*Enthymēsis*) of the higher Sophia in the Pleroma, is sometimes also referred to as Achamoth (after the Hebrew word for wisdom, *hokmah*), as in Irenaeus' report at *Against the Heresies* 1.4.1: "The Intention of that

Sophia who dwells above, which they also term Achamoth, being removed from the Pleroma together with her passion, they relate to have, as a matter of course, become violently excited in those places of darkness and vacuity [to which she had been banished]. For she was excluded from light and the Pleroma, and was without form or figure, like an untimely birth, because she had received nothing [from a male parent]" (tr. Roberts-Rambaut). See *(First) Apocalypse of James* (NHC V,3) 34.1–36.6 for the distinction between the two Sophias, and also *Gospel of the Egyptians* (NHC III, 2) 57.1, where a "material" (*hulikē*) Sophia is mentioned, though with no suggestion that she has been produced by a higher Sophia, as in the present passage. Finally, note that the soul that has declined is the direct creator of the cosmos in the earlier account in Chapter 4 (see 4, 2.6.8–9), while the Demiurge and his mother are said to be the creators of the universe in the present passage (10, 19–11,14).

One way of explaining the apparent discrepancies between these two accounts is suggested by Narbonne (2013, 418), who thinks that they present different versions of the Gnostic myth of Sophia's (that is, the world soul's) fall. On his view, Plotinus first discusses a simpler, Valentinian account in Chapter 4, before turning to the more elaborate Sethian creation account in Chapters 10–11. But a simpler, and I think preferable, explanation can be given: in the dialectical context of Chapter 4, the details of the

Gnostic creation account can be put to one side. Here, the controversy centers on the claims that the universe is perishable and will ultimately be destroyed, and that the soul is the ultimate instigator of this botched creation. As a result, Plotinus "telescopes" distinctions in his opponents' account that he will later make explicit, when it is important for his polemical purposes to separate soul's illumination of matter, which brings about a lower soul that in turn creates the Demiurge, from the Demiurge' own creation of the cosmos.

One great difficulty with this second account of Sophia's decline is that it seems to ascribe two beliefs to the Gnostics that cannot easily be reconciled: (i) The soul, which is related to, if not identical with, Sophia declines, while other individual souls follow her by descending (10, 19–23); (ii) The soul, for whose sake the individual souls descended, did not descend, that is, did not decline (10, 24–25). Plainly, one and the same soul cannot both decline and not decline at the same time, and so (i) and (ii) cannot be true together. It might be argued that this apparent inconsistency ought to be accepted as evidence that the Gnostics contradicted themselves, or that, at any rate, Plotinus thought they did. But in Chapter 10, a mere six lines separate the assertion of the soul's decline (at 10, 19) from the denial of the same (10, 25)—yet what Plotinus goes on to criticize about this account is not its glaring inconsistency, but a subtler tension between the Gnostics' view that the soul "declines" but does not "descend" (at 11, 1–6, on which see the comment below). If a better explanation of this remarkable oversight on Plotinus' part can be offered, it is surely to be preferred.

In my view, the difficulty can be resolved if one ignores the problematic phrase *hoion mē neusai* ("that is, did not decline") at 10, 25, which may well be a gloss by a later editor. Someone persuaded by Plotinus' reasoning at the beginning of Chapter 11, that denying the soul's descent implies denying its decline also, would naturally, but mistakenly, have explicated "descended" with "declined." Once the problematic phrase is excised, the picture Plotinus presents is internally consistent: the "decline" of Sophia, understood as its turning toward and illumination of matter, brings with it the "descent" of individual souls, that is, their taking on human bodies. But compare Dufour (2006, 268n200) for a different view, according to which the confusion in Plotinus' account may be due to syncretism between Valentinian and Sethian Gnostic beliefs. See also Igal (1982, 517n107).

The several stages in the Gnostic creation account that Plotinus discusses can be illustrated as follows:

(1) Pre-existing, unformed "darkness"

(2) The higher Sophia "declines" and illuminates the "darkness"

(3) The lower Sophia comes into being as an image in the "darkness"

(4) The lower Sophia produces the Demiurge as an image in matter

(5) The lower Sophia ascends to the "alien earth" and abandons the Demiurge

(6) The Demiurge creates the cosmos

Cf. Spanu (2012, 166), to whom I am indebted here. Plotinus' account of Gnostic beliefs, as it is presented here, can be usefully compared to *Zostrianus* (NHC VIII,1) 9.17–10.20, where much the same sequence of events is narrated. See the commentary in Barry (2000, 510–514).

10, 22 *"members of Sophia"*: Cf. Ephesians 5:30, where St. Paul describes the faithful as "members" (*melē*) of Christ's body. In the case of the Gnostics, the idea of "being a member" of Sophia is perhaps to be explained in terms of the pneumatic nature of their souls, which are made of the same element as Sophia herself. Cf. also the fragment from a Gnostic hymn in the *First Book of Jeu*, 79.7–82.26 Schmidt-MacDermot, a text to which Kalligas (2014, 396) draws attention. See also Rudolph (1980, 121–131).

Note that there is a possible ambiguity in the verb *sugkatelēluthenai* at 10, 22 ("descend together"). It could mean that all the souls descend together with one another, or that they descend together with Sophia. But at 10, 25, Plotinus suggests that Sophia does not in fact descend, so that we should probably think of individual souls jointly descending.

10, 25–26 *<the darkness>*: Reading *to skotos* in place of *tōi skotōi*, with Heigl and Kirchhoff; an accusative object seems to be required, as at 11, 1–2. Without this change, Plotinus would be saying that, on the Gnostic view, the soul was shining *in* the darkness. But, on the Gnostic view, the salient point is rather that the soul is doing something *to* the darkness, namely illuminating it, which then results in the production of an image in matter. In the next chapter, the "darkness" is quite clearly identified with matter (11, 14–5), so that we can perhaps assume that it refers to "matter" here also.

10, 26–33 *Next they fabricate. . . . kinds of reproaches*: The first image that is created in matter is the lower Sophia, which is brought forth by the higher Sophia that declines. The distinction between higher and lower Sophia is not generally made explicit in Plotinus' presentation, a fact that adds to it an extra layer of complexity. It is likely that the lower Sophia in turn produces the Demiurge, who goes on to create the visible universe, which would explain why Plotinus refers to the lower Sophia as the Demiurge's "mother" (e.g. at 10, 31; 12, 3.9–10).

The precise status of the "image of the image" (*tou eidōlou eidōlon,* 10, 27) in this account of creation is difficult to determine. A comparison with *Zostrianus* (NHC VIII,1) 10.4–5, where the Coptic has the same Greek term *eidōlon,* suggests that Plotinus is here quoting directly from some version of this text. In *Zostrianus,* the Demiurge appears to be distinct from "the image of the image," since he is said to create through or with it. Many scholars assume, however, that Plotinus takes the Gnostic Demiurge to be identical with the "image of the image"; see e.g. Igal (1982, 518n109); Pasquier (2006, 658); Burns (2014, 68).

10, 27–28 *matter or materiality*: Plotinus sees an instance of the alleged Gnostic tendency to introduce new and superfluous terminology in the employment of the word "materiality" (*hulotēs*) (see also 6, 5 above). But as Alt (1990, 51n161) points out, one Hermetic text defines "materiality" as the "actuality of matter" (*hulēs energeia*) (*Hermetic Corpus* 12.22=22.9 Nock-Festugière). The Gnostic opponents may well have attempted to draw a distinction along similar lines, between unformed matter and matter that has been shaped by a divine power, in which case Plotinus' comment would be more than a little uncharitable.

10, 31 *separated from his mother*: The Demiurge's mother is the lower Sophia. His separation from her can be understood in two senses, as pointed out by Igal (1982, 518n111): according to the Valentinians, the lower Sophia inhabits the so-called "intermediate place," which may be identical with the "new" or "alien earth," so that the Demiurge would be spatially separated from her. See Irenaeus, *Against the Heresies* 1.7.1, and cf. the Sethian view reported by Irenaeus, *Against the Heresies* 1.29: "But they relate that a mighty power carried him [*sc.* the Demiurge] away from his mother [*sc.* Sophia], and that he settled far away from her in the lower regions, and formed the firmament of heaven, in which also they affirm that he dwells" (tr. Roberts-Rambaut). But the Demiurge is also "separated" from his mother because of his ignorance, since he imagines himself alone to be the creator, when in fact he acts together with the creative power of Sophia. See Irenaeus *Against the Heresies* 1.5.3.

10, 32 *to the status of the lowest images*: The phrase *helkousi ap' eschata eidōla* ("they drag down [*sc.* the cosmos] to the status of the lowest images") is difficult to interpret, but Plotinus' thought may be that on the Gnostic account, the universe will be at a third remove from reality, since it is produced by an image of an image. It will thus be comparable in ontological status to the picture of a chair, which is an imitation of the real chair that the painter sees, which is itself in some metaphysical sense the imitation of an ideal chair. Cf. Plato, *Republic* 10.597e–598c.

10, 32–33 *the composer of this treatise . . . all kinds of reproaches*: On the reading of the Greek text favored here, the verb *loidorēsētai* is construed as intransitive and in the middle voice, such that the phrase *hina sphodra loidorēsētai ho touto grapsas* would refer to the writer of the particular Gnostic tract that Plotinus has been using as his source (some version of *Zostrianus*). MacKenna's translation, "Such is the blasphemy of one of their writers," captures this reading well. It is rather peculiar that Plotinus, who does not single out any of his opponents anywhere else in the treatise, should at this point feel compelled to point out that he takes inspiration from a particular source. But this is what the text suggests.

On a different interpretation, put forward by Pépin (1992, 316–318), *loidorēsētai* is to be understood as passive in meaning, and *touto* as referring back to a "picture." *Graphein* is then to be translated as "sketching" or "painting," just as the verb *diazōgraphein* ("to paint") is used in Plato's *Timaeus* to describe the creative activity of the Demiurge (55c2). The translation would then read: "So far as for the author of this picture to be laden with violent reproaches" (Pépin (1992, 318). However, like Kalligas (2014, 396), with whom I am here in agreement, I find it difficult to believe that *touto* should refer to the universe understood as a "picture."

Chapter 11

Two views come under attack in this chapter: (1) That the soul began the process of creation by illuminating a pre-existing darkness; and (2), that the creative image resulting from this illumination is a substance or a "conception."

11, 1–6 *We reply first. . . . it once near*: Having outlined the Gnostic view of the fall of Sophia and the generation of the Demiurge in the final paragraphs of the preceding chapter, Plotinus now examines how the soul's "decline" can be understood in relation to the illumination of matter that is supposed to result from it. He presents what is effectively a dilemma: if, on the one hand, the soul both has the power to "illuminate" the darkness by sending out light and does not "descend," as his opponents apparently grant (see 11, 25), then it becomes difficult to see what meaning can be given to its "decline." Alternatively, "declining" might mean that the Soul moves spatially next to what it illuminates, a position that he does not explicitly argue against here, either because he thinks that it is obviously absurd that an immaterial entity should move "spatially" (*topikōs*), or perhaps because he has attacked a similar view elsewhere. For this last possibility, compare VI.5.8 [23], 10–22 [13–15 omitted]: "Note, however, that when we sometimes speak of the Ideas illuminating Matter this is not to suggest the mode in which material light pours down on a material object . . . We do not mean that the Idea, locally separate, shows itself in Matter like a reflection in water; the Matter touches the Idea at every point, though not in a physical contact, and, by dint of neighborhood—nothing to keep them apart—is able to absorb thence all that lies within its capacity, the Idea itself not penetrating, not approaching, the Matter, but remaining within itself" (tr. MacKenna, slightly modified). See also I.1.12, 23–28 for a discussion of how the soul's illumination of matter can be linked to the notion of a "decline."

The phrase "perhaps the darkness lay somewhere in the lower world" suggests that the "darkness" (that is, matter) existed before it came to be illuminated, presumably in an unformed, chaotic state. A variant of this view can also be found, for example, in the Nag Hammadi treatise *On the Origin of the World* (NHC II,5) 97.24–98.7. Note, however, that Plotinus' language suggests a degree of hesitation on his part, as the repetition of *pou* ("perhaps"; "somewhere") shows.

11, 6–8 *But if the . . . powerful than it*: If the notion of a "decline" does not explain the soul's illumination of matter, the alternative proposal that Soul illuminates "while remaining with itself" and "without purposely contributing" anything to the illumination faces a difficulty of its own. For in that case, the intelligible realities should be able to illuminate the lower realms even more than the Soul. What is objectionable in the Gnostics' view, for Plotinus, is that they attribute responsibility for matter's illumination to soul alone (the higher Sophia), without extending it to intelligible reality more generally. The present passage thus anticipates a line of argument developed more fully at 12, 30–44. Cf. 2, 15–17 above.

11, 8–11 *And if the . . . production of images*: "The rational design" (*logismos*) of the cosmos is identified with the "alien earth" (*hē xenē gē*) immediately below (11, 11–12). "Alien" in this context does not have any negative connotations, but is probably to be understood as "alien to this visible world," as Puech (1960, 189) points out. At 5, 24–27, different terminology refers to the same place, which also acts as the ideal model of the sensible world: "the new earth" (*hē kainē gē*), "the rational model of the world" (*ho logos tou kosmou*) and "the paradigm of the world" (*to paradeigma tou kosmou*). Cf. V.8.4, 15, where Plotinus dismisses the idea that anything could be present in the intelligible world "as if in a strange land" (*ep'allotrias hoion gēs*).

By "soul," Plotinus has in mind the Gnostics' higher Sophia. He adds an important detail to the creation account so far discussed: Sophia's illumination of matter is in some way (the Greek phrase *tōi logismon labein* ["by grasping its rational design"] could support a variety of interpretations) made possible by her grasp of the rational model of the cosmos. But if Sophia has cognitive access to the paradigm of this universe, Plotinus objects, why does she need to attend the "production of images" (*hē tōn eidōlōn genesis*), that is, the creation of her proxy agents lower Sophia and the Demiurge who are images created from the illumination of matter? Why should she not be able to create without intermediaries?

11, 9 *the soul*: I read *autē* in place of *autēi*, with R and J, making "the soul" the subject of the sentence.

11, 11–14 *Next, did the . . . makers to decline*: Plotinus continues his examination of the soul's illumination into the darkness. The dialectic of the chapter so far has taken its point of departure from the idea that the soul may illuminate the darkness without descending, "while remaining by itself" (11, 6). According to the account Plotinus is considering now, the (lower) soul or Sophia may have created the cosmos as a by-product of her understanding of its rational model. He objects that this explanation is vitiated by the fact that the creators of the paradigm, namely the higher soul or Sophia, have "declined," that is, turned to a lower reality, in order to create it. By parity of reasoning, if the lower soul creates the cosmos as a result of its contemplation of the paradigm, it will likewise be led to "decline." That the creation of the paradigm is consequent upon the decline of its "maker" (or, as here, "makers"; perhaps Plotinus is still unsure whether soul and

Sophia are the same, as at 10, 21, which would explain the plural) was already touched upon at 5, 27–37.

This translation reads a question mark at the end of the sentence, not a period.

11, 14–17 *Next, how could. . . . joined to him*: Two separate points are made in this passage. First, how could matter, once the higher Sophia has illuminated it, bring forth "psychic images," in other words the lower Sophia and perhaps also the Demiurge? For the meaning of "psychic images," see Hippolytus, *Refutation of All Heresies* 6.32.7.7–8.1 Marcovich, who reports a Valentinian view according to which the Demiurge is "psychic" (*psuchikos*), that is to say, made from a psychic substance. The lower Sophia is usually said to have a pneumatic, not a psychic substance; cf. Irenaeus, *Against the Heresies* 1.2.4 (=1.1.3.24–27 Harvey); Epiphanius, *Panarion* 31.18.2. Perhaps some confusion on Plotinus' part must be suspected on this point. Second, Sophia would have no need for matter if she wanted to produce "psychic images," and, if she were to produce them, they would not become oblivious of their creator like the Gnostics' Demiurge, but rather follow the soul and stay attached to her by some natural affinity that Plotinus does not further describe.

11, 17–26 *Next, is this. . . . to the "conception"*: The "image" in question here is the lower Sophia. Although much of the passage is ambiguous, the rhetorical question later at

11, 23–24 ("What *further* need was there to introduce a maker . . .") suggests that up to this point the Demiurge has not been discussed. Moreover, at 10, 25–26 only the lower Sophia is explicitly said to be the result of the illumination of the darkness. Finally, and most importantly, a number of Gnostic sources support the notion that the lower Sophia is a "conception" (*ennoēma*), while the same cannot be said for the alternative, that the Demiurge is a "conception." Most likely, *ennoēma* is a variant of *enthumēsis*, another word for "conception" or "thought" that can be applied to the lower Sophia, as Bouillet (1857, 289n2) had already argued. See Irenaeus *Against the Heresies* 1.2.4; 1.4.1; 2.18.2–4. See also Schmidt (1900, 41–42), who adopts the same interpretation. For a different view, see e.g. Dufour (2012, 270n212) and Kalligas (2014, 397), who think that the Demiurge is the "image." See the Commentary on 12, 2–3 on this issue, and 12, 9–16, where various forms of *enthumeisthai* cluster together. In some reports of Gnostic views, we find the lower Sophia described as both a pneumatic "substance" and a "conception"; see, for instance, the Valentinian account at Irenaeus, *Against the Heresies* 1.2.4 (=1.1.3.24–27 Harvey). This might explain why Plotinus asks whether his opponents think of the lower Sophia as a "substance" or a "conception"; he will go on to argue that either option implies absurd consequences for the Gnostics' creation account.

The argument against the first half of his question, whether the image is a substance, begins by asking whether the lower Sophia has the same faculties as the higher Sophia, including a rational soul. In that case, of course, the two cannot be distinguished in so far as their suitability to create the Demiurge, and through him the cosmos, is concerned. But if the lower Sophia is a worse product, she must lack the rational faculties, and so be either a plant-like or "generative" (animal) soul, according to a division of soul-powers that goes back to Aristotle (cf. *On the Soul* 432b10–11, and 413b24–27 for the difference of the rational soul from these lower forms). In that case, the lower Sophia qua lesser soul could not be said to be motivated by a desire for honor, which presupposes a degree of rationality that is presumably absent in plants and animals (at least in Plotinus' view). Other complex motivations, such as arrogance or recklessness (*tolma*), or intellectual activities such as creating "through imagination" (*dia phantasias*) or "rational planning" (*logizesthai*), should be equally unavailable to her. For the combination of "arrogance and recklessness," see Clement of Alexandria, *Stromata* 4.13.90; for "recklessness" (*tolma*) alone, see Irenaeus, *Against the Heresies* 1.1.2.19 Harvey; 1.29; Epiphanius, *Panarion* 31.17.4; *Apocryphon of John* (NHC III,1) 14.9–15.2. At times, Plotinus himself invokes "recklessness" (*tolma*) as a cause for the soul's descent into bodies; see V.1.1, 3–10. For the idea at 11, 21 that the soul created the world "in order to be honored," see the comment below at 4, 13–15. Plotinus denies that the world is the result of "rational planning" (*dianoia*) at 2, 14 and 8, 20–21, two passages that can be compared with the notion of "calculating" (*logizesthai*) in the present passage. On creation "through imagination" (*dia phantasias*), compare this passage from *Zostrianus*, describing the Demiurge: "Because there was within her [*sc.* Sophia] no pure, original image, either pre-existing in him or that had already come to be through him, he used his imagination and fashioned the remainder, for the image belonging to Sophia is always corrupt [and] deceptive" (10.10–17; tr. Turner).

On the alternative supposition, that the lower Sophia is a "conception," the Demiurge has no further role to play. We can only guess what Plotinus' argument for this conclusion would have been; the Greek text at this point does not spell out all the requisite premises. One attempt to reconstruct his line of thinking could proceed as follows. First, assume that the "conception" takes its name from the higher Sophia, from which it becomes separated (I take this to be the answer to Plotinus' rhetorical question at 11, 25). If the "conception" were powerless to create, it could not be an "image" of its more powerful cause, the higher Sophia; therefore, one must also grant it the power of creating. And if one does grant it that power, the Demiurge becomes superfluous. In order to support this reading, one has to assume that the question at 11, 25–26

where the lower Sophia is said to have created Christ "by her memory of better things" (*kata tēn gnōmēn tōn kreittonōn*). Cf. 4, 8–9 above.

Note how the meaning of the "image" seems to have shifted. Whereas before the term referred to the lower Sophia (see the comment on 11, 17–23), it now includes the Demiurge as well. Only a few lines later, at 12, 9–10, the meaning of the "image" will shift once more, to refer specifically to the Demiurge, but not his "mother," the lower Sophia. Such confusion of terms demands an explanation. One likely scenario is that Plotinus himself was uncertain about the roles played, respectively, by the lower Sophia and the Demiurge in the process of creating the universe. Some Gnostic sources suggest that the lower Sophia acts through the Demiurge, while others seem to show the Demiurge as an independent actor who creates in order to be honored and produces one thing after the next. Cf. Irenaeus, *Against the Heresies* 1.5.3; 1.17.1, and see Schmidt (1900, 42). A modern analogy with Plotinus' use of "image" might be someone talking about "the college," which could in some contexts refer to staff members ("the college elected its new President"), in others to students ("the college with the greatest success in the league tables"), and in others to both ("the friendliest college on campus"). See also the remarks by Alt (1990, 57).

12, 3–12 *Next, is it. . . . comes to be*: Plotinus points to an apparent inconsistency in the Gnostics' account: on the one hand, the Gnostics, as true souls, are supposed to be ontologically superior to the Demiurge and his mother, who are themselves only images, and material images at that. Yet the Demiurge and his mother are apparently able to do what only few of the elect souls are capable of, namely to preserve a memory of the intelligible world. So the same entities appear as both inferior to the Gnostics and as superior to them.

12, 5–7 *Scarcely one or . . . some other time*: Plotinus may be thinking of visionary ascents by select individuals, who communicate their experiences to others. Both *Zostrianus* and *Allogenes* employ this conceit.

12, 5 *as true souls*: With the claim that the Gnostics enter the world as "true souls," one is most likely to understand that they view themselves as possessing a "pneumatic" or "perfect" (*teleios*) nature, different from lesser souls who are made of a psychic or material substance. Cf. Irenaeus, *Against the Heresies* 1.5.1–2, who reports that psychic and material souls were first formed as "images" (*eikones*) by the lower Sophia (Achamoth), and then "distinguished" (*diakrinanta*) into two kinds of substances by the Demiurge. This account might explain the contrast between "true souls" and "images of souls" (*eidōla psuchōn*, at 12, 4) in the present passage.

12, 7–12 *And is it . . . comes to be*: This translation follows Heigl's punctuation, which treats *ē kai tēn mētera* ("or its mother") as parenthetical. Grammatically, "the mother" could also be the object that the "image" thinks of, but this translation prefers to consider both "the mother" and the "image" as the subject for *enthumēthēnai* ("think"), and only "the intelligibles" (*ekeina*) as object. Nothing in the text suggests that the Demiurge contemplates his mother. The qualification "a material image" (*eidōlon hulikon*) is to be attributed to the "image," which here refers primarily to the Demiurge, although in fact his mother, the lower Sophia, is an "image in matter" too (see 10, 25–26). Kirchhoff's reading of <*ek*> ("from"), in place of the second *kai* ("and"), at 12, 11, is indispensable; the text should read: *kai kosmou labein ennoian* <*ek*> *kosmou ekeinou* ("and derive a conception of this cosmos <from> the intelligible world").

12, 13–23 *So for what. . . . intelligible world too*: Two modes of production are contrasted here: (i) that characteristic of crafts, where for example a blade might be produced in isolation from the knife-handle, and (ii) that of nature, where the coming into being of a child, for instance, does not proceed with an arm first, and then a leg, etc., but with the generation of the whole child in the form of an embryo. This generation of the whole child takes place through the sketching of an "imprint" (*tupos*, a Gnostic term of art, but here used in its ordinary sense) of the living being onto the menstrual fluid, which is the receptacle of the imprint. On this account, menstrual fluid and sperm (the carrier of the imprint) stand to each other as matter to form. Plotinus considers this latter, natural form of production to be prior to craft production, and therefore argues that the creation of the universe has to begin, not with a part, such as fire, but with the whole, which would necessarily include all the elements. Therefore the notion that fire is the first element created by the Demiurge is absurd, because it assimilates the creation of the universe to the wrong mode of production. On the alleged priority of fire, see above 11, 28–29. Cf. Turner (2006, 575n5), who suggests the "unconsuming and indestructible fire" around the Kalyptos Aeon at *Zostrianus* 116.16–24 as a point of reference. See also II.3.16, 6–13; V.8.7, 36–44.

12, 16 *in its thinking*: In the space of a few lines, from 12, 9–16, Plotinus uses the noun "thinking" (*enthumēsis*) and cognate verbal forms (*enthumēthēnai, enthumēstheis*) six times. More than indifference to prose style may be at play here, given that the Gnostics themselves called their lower Sophia *Enthumēsis*. By punning on their terminology, Plotinus emphasizes what he perceives as the absurdity of the Gnostic view that a material image can engage in "thinking" about the intelligible world from the moment of its creation, and that "thinking" one thing after the next can provide an explanatory model for the process of creating the world.

12, 18 *the crafts are posterior to nature and the cosmos*: The principle that the crafts imitate nature, and are therefore posterior to it, can be found in Aristotle, for example *Physics* 2.194a21–22, where it occurs as the antecedent of a conditional. See also V.8.2, 1–6.

12, 23–25 *But perhaps they . . . in this way*: This comment is best understood as sarcastic, rather than as seriously revealing the true intention behind the Gnostic creation account: settling the Demiurge with the task of imprinting the whole of the cosmos in matter, which he is unable to do because he has never contemplated the intelligible model that he needs to imprint, would at least allow the Gnostics to give some creative role to their own, superior souls, which were mentioned before in this chapter, at 12, 4.

12, 25 *<this image>*: This translation reads *ekeino* in place of *ekeinos*. Throughout the passage, the reference is to the image; the sudden change to a masculine singular subject, as implied by *ekeinos*, seems difficult to defend here.

12, 25–30 *Further, to determine . . . the best principles*: In other words, the high degree of rationality that is exhibited in the regular movement of the heavens cannot be accounted for by a power as imperfect as that of the

Gnostics' Demiurge or his mother, the lower Sophia, who are mere "images."

12, 30–39 *Why in fact.... the primary causes*: According to the Gnostics, as Plotinus understands them, Sophia's fall is both a temporal event and the consequence of some blameworthy state of mind on her part. The following is an attempt to make the progress of the argument clear: (I) if the creation of the universe is in accordance with nature, then it must always have been in accordance with nature. If it has always been in accordance with nature, however, the universe does not exist because of some temporary condition of the soul, but rather according to a necessity rooted in the nature of the intelligible causes themselves. (II) If the creation takes place contrary to the soul's nature, and what is contrary to nature is evil, then (a) evil must already exist in the intelligible world. In that case, (b) evil will exist prior to the universe, which implies that (c) the cosmos cannot be the cause of evil, but that (d) evil must be the cause of the cosmos. Thus if (a)–(d) are true, it follows that the cosmos cannot introduce evil into the soul, and that it must rather be the case that soul, *qua* intelligible cause, introduces evil into the cosmos. On this argument too, then, the responsibility for the creation of the universe lies with the intelligible causes, and the source for any evils or imperfections in the visible world must be referred back to them. See I.8.3, 1–6, where this possibility is rejected. See also O'Brien (1993, 81–82), whose analysis of the passage I am here following.

12, 38 *the creation of the world*: Some translations read Heigl's *to kakon* ("evil"), in place of *ton kosmon* ("the world"). But HS_2 are probably right in maintaining *ton kosmon*, despite the complaint by Harder-Beutler-Theiler (1960) that it is "nonsensical" (*unsinnig*) (432). Plotinus has stated at the outset of his discussion that he aims to show how the Gnostics must admit the true causes of the cosmos (12, 32), and this is what he claims to have accomplished at 12, 37.

12, 39–44 *And if this. . . . the primary causes*: Matter is here identified with the darkness that the soul illuminates. The discussion of this illumination, for example at 10, 25–26 and 11, 1–2 clearly presupposes that the darkness already exists before it is being illuminated. Some Gnostic descent narratives similarly presuppose the pre-existence of darkness, for example the Nag Hammadi treatise *Trimorphic Protennoia*, where the divine Protennoia describes how she "[descended to the] midst of the underworld" and "shone [down upon] the darkness" ([NHC XIII,1)] 36.4–5; tr. Turner). In many Gnostic descent narratives (*Zostrianus*, *Apocryphon of John*), matter is the result of some action taken by a divine principle, but not the cause of that principle's decline, which makes Plotinus' comment at 12, 42–43 puzzling. But in some Gnostic sources, the darkness plays a more active role, for example in the Sethian *Paraphrase of Shem*, where the "stirring" of the darkness frightens Spirit and so causes it to look down (see [NHC VII,1] 2.19–28). See O'Brien (1993, 82–86) for a detailed discussion of this passage.

12, 39 *matter, from which [the world] would come forth*: The Greek text does not specify what it is that comes forth from matter, but "the world" is the most likely candidate, unless one accepts that the subject is in fact "evil," on an alternative reading of the Greek discussed in the note on 12, 38. On the translation provided here, the Greek would effectively have to read as follows: *ei de dē, kai hē hulē hothen phaneiē* [sc. *ho kosmos*] [sc. *anapheresthai dei epi ta prōta*]. This sentence has been discussed in detail by Ferroni (2013), who suggests a different construction of the Greek, reading *ei de dē* [sc. *ta prōta*] *kai hē hulē hothen* [sc. *esti/ēn*] *phaneiē;* ("And what if the primary beings appear to be the place from where also matter emerged"?).

12, 44 *in the compelling arguments before*: See 12, 30–2.37 above. A different translation for this sentence is offered by Igal, who renders it: "y esto equivale a una forzosidad antecedente" ("and this amounts to an antecedent necessity").

Chapter 13

This chapter criticizes the opponents' views on the nature of the stars and evil.

13, 2–6 *This is because . . . of all things*: The opening of the chapter recalls the succession of entities, already discussed at 1, 11–16, from the One to Intellect and the realm of forms, to the world soul and individual souls, and finally to "the extreme points" (*ta eschata*, at 13, 5), that is to say, to bodily nature (cf. I.8.4, 1–5) and, at the ultimate remove from goodness, matter (cf. 8, 21, and see Commentary on 8, 24–25). The language of "first, second and third" takes its inspiration from a passage in the pseudo-Platonic *Second Letter* (312e), which is quoted in the comment on 1, 19–20. Plotinus returns to the order in which entities proceed from the One in order to show that the universe is the natural outcome of a necessary process, rather than something evil. He returns to the flawed conception of evil that underlies the Gnostics' censure of the cosmos at the end of the chapter, at 13, 25–33.

13, 6–18 *One should oneself. . . . its major parts*: Having argued that one must "meekly" (*praōs*) accept the nature of things in their varying gradations of goodness, Plotinus exhorts his readers to "rush toward the first principles" and to put an end to the "tragedy of terrors" (13, 7) that in their view takes place in the spheres of heaven. How do these exhortations connect with the argument of the previous lines? One possibility would be to think that "rushing toward the first principles" stands for the mental activity of referring things in the sensible world to their intelligible causes; it is not, in other words, a pious encouragement to "flee hence," but should be read metaphorically. Once one has grasped the first principles of the universe, one should then stop talking about "the tragedy of terrors" in the heavenly spheres, because any suggestion that they exercise some evil tyranny over souls is incompatible with a true understanding of their causes. The "tragedy of terrors," in this context, may describe the obstacles that individual souls encounter in their ascent through the heavens, which they must overcome through seals, passwords and addresses, as a report of Ophite doctrine by Celsus, in Origen's *Against Celsus* 6.31 illustrates. Cf. the Nag Hammadi treatise *(First) Apocalypse of James*, where Jesus advises his brother in the following terms: "James, behold, I shall reveal to you your redemption. When [you] are seized, and you undergo these sufferings, a multitude will arm themselves against you that <they> may seize you. And, in particular, three of them will seize you—they who sit (there) as toll collectors. Not only do they demand toll, but they also take away souls by theft. When you come into their power, one of them who is their guard will say to you, 'Who are you or where are you from?' You are to say to him, 'I am a son, and I am from the Father.' He will say to you, 'What sort of son are you, and to what father do you belong?' You are to say to him, 'I am from the Pre-existent Father, and a son in the Pre-existent One'" (NHC V,3) 32.29–33.24; tr. Schroedel). Cf. also Irenaeus, *Against the Heresies* 1.21.5, who adds to his similar account: "When the companions of the Demiurge hear these words, they are greatly agitated, and upbraid their origin and the race of their mother" (tr. Robertson-Rambaut). The lamentations and regret of Sophia are likewise derided as a "melodrama" (*tragōidia*) by Epiphanius, *Panarion* 31.17.1 (=1.410.28 Holl), a passage to which Harder-Beutler-Theiler (1960) draw attention (see their note ad loc.). Cf. Epiphanius, *Panarion* 31.8.1 (=1.398.6 Holl), and see also Rudolph (1980, 172–180).

13, 8 *"make all things gentle"*: A reminiscence of Pindar, *Olympian* 1.30–33: "Grace, who fashions all gentle things for men, confers esteem and often contrives to make believable the unbelievable" (tr. Svarlien). As Kalligas (2014, 401) points out, the context in which the original verse occurs (note the phrase "make believable the unbelievable") adds an element of irony to the quotation.

13, 9–12 *What is really. . . . and the earth*: That some Gnostics viewed the influence of the stars as potentially threatening can be seen from Clement of Alexandria, *Excerpts from Theodotus* 69–72. But it is somewhat surprising that Plotinus' Gnostics are here said to fear the stars because of their fiery bodies, and parallels to this effect in other Gnostic writings are hard to come by. Alt (1990, 31) suggests that Plotinus is mistaken in thinking that the fiery bodies of the stars make the Gnostics afraid of them, rather than the powers (sometimes called Archons) that govern them and that can hinder the soul's ascent into the higher regions. But the disappointing truth may simply be that any sources that might reflect similar views to those of Plotinus' opponents have been lost. Note that II.1.4, 11–13, where Plotinus insists that the heavenly fire is "equable and gentle" (*homalon kai ēremaion*), may tacitly engage with the Gnostics' claim that the heavenly spheres are something to be afraid of.

13, 10 *educated and refined knowledge*: Once more, Plotinus contrasts the "educated and refined knowledge" (*pepaideumenē kai emmelēs gnōsis*) of the philosopher with the Gnostic claim to the possession of a special "knowledge" (*gnōsis*) derived from revelation and available only to a select group. See the comment on 6, 43–52 above, and also 9, 35–36.

13, 15 *they co-operate and collaborate*: Cf. II.3.8, 6–8; II.3.10, 7–10.

13, 18–20 *If men are . . . order and arrangement*: The view that the planetary rulers or Archons establish something of a tyranny over the universe can be related to a number of Gnostic sources, for example the *Apocryphon of John*. In this text, the Archons are said to establish the rule of Fate (*heimarmenē* in Greek) "with measures and times and moments," imprisoning the gods of heaven, the angels, daemons, and men ([NHC II,1] 28.21–31).

13, 20–25 *We <must> consider . . . dispositions of souls*: In his detailed discussion of "whether stars are causes" (II.3), Plotinus, like the Stoics before him, grounds the ability of the heavenly bodies to act as signs of future events in the general connectedness of the universe (what he calls its "one common breath of life," *sumpnoia mia*, at II.3.7, 17–18). But if the stars are able not only to signal future events, but also to influence them, the threat of astrological determinism immediately arises: just how much of the future do they control? In II.3.10–15, the stars are given some limited influence; they may have the power to affect one's bodily constitution for better or worse, for example, without being able to overturn one's nature completely (cf. II.3.13, 38–47). But the soul in its best part is separate in its activities from outside influences and thus immune to any power the stars may exert. Plotinus' answer to the Gnostics, then, is that they exaggerate the power of the stars to influence events in the universe when they talk about a "tyranny" imposed by the heavenly rulers. Cf. III.1.10, 4–15; III.2.10, 12–19; IV.4.39, 1–5. See also III.4.6, 47–60 on the interaction between universal fate and the "dispositions" (*diatheseis*, at 13, 25) of individual souls.

13, 21 *<must>*: Accepting Bréhier's insertion of *dei* ("must") before *nomizein* ("consider").

13, 25–33 *And again, one. . . . Intellect to another*: In this complex paragraph, Plotinus sets out to refute an argument against the good order of the cosmos that his Gnostic opponents might put forward. Their argument infers from the observation that not all men are good the conclusion that the universe is imperfect, since, the argument supposes, in a perfect universe everyone would be good. For this interpretation, one must supply in thought "the nature of the universe" at 13, 26; the same phrase, "censuring the nature of the universe" occurs in the introduction to the chapter, at 13, 1. The remark "since this is not possible [*sc.* that all men be good]" at 13, 26 probably expresses Plotinus' own view; cf. III.2.4, 28–44.

Against this argument, Plotinus can point out that it is a mistake to demand the same kind of goodness in the sensible world as exists in the intelligibles. If things in this world fall short of the greater perfection there, this happens in accordance with their nature—which is partly self-determined, and partly subject to outside influence—and therefore cannot count as evidence that the universe is badly made. Cf. III.3.3, 1–18. If one accepted the Gnostics' reasoning, on the other hand, one would be forced to allow the existence of evil in the intelligible world also, since in the succession of entities from the One there is a gradual

their views on the powers of magic, which have particularly troubling implications (hence the *malista*), since they undermine the impassibility of the intelligibles, making them instead subject to the utterances and actions of mere mortals.

14, 2–9 *For when they. . . . the realities beyond*: The key to understanding Plotinus' disapproval of the practices that he describes lies in the notion of "exercising a magical power over the realities beyond" (14, 6–7), that is to say, over the Soul as well as the realities above Soul. In an earlier treatise, Plotinus is quite ready to accept the efficacy of magic, explaining that its power is based ultimately in the cosmic sympathy that holds together the different parts of the universe (IV.4 [28] 40, 1–9). The intelligibles, including individual souls in their highest, intellectual aspect, are not subject to this universal sympathy connecting the parts, however, and herein lies the reason for Plotinus' disapproval of the Gnostics' real or alleged practices. For the philosopher's immunity from magical practices, as far as the rational part of his soul is concerned, see IV.4.43–4. This last point is given vivid illustration in Porphyry's story of how a certain Olympius was hoisted by his own petard, when his attempts to cast evil spells upon Plotinus backfired because of the latter's mighty soul (*Life of Plotinus* 10.1–13). For a good discussion of the evidence for magical practices such as "chants, sounds, breathings" and "hissings of the voice," see Spanu

(2013, 9–14). He points out that the "hissings of the voice" in 14, 7 seem to have been an established part of magical ritual, as parallels in the *Greek Magical Papyri* show (cf. 4.561; 7.769; 13.602 Preisendanz). Cf. Irenaeus' report of the Gnostic Basilides, who is said to have practiced "images, incantations, invocations, and every other kind of curious art" (*Against the Heresies* 1.24.5), as well as his accounts of Simon (1.23.4) and Carpocrates (1.25.3). Cf. also *Allogenes* (NHC XI,3) 53.36–37; *Zostrianus* (NHC VIII,1) 127.1–2. See also Brisson (2013) for the magical practices of the Gnostics.

A question worth raising here is the extent to which we can trust Plotinus' report that the Gnostics attempted to influence by magic, not only those powers under the sway of the evil Demiurge, like the Archons and the stars, but also the higher intelligible powers. It seems clear from a number of texts that knowing the true name of a divine principle was associated with the possession of a mystical power; for example, in the *Gospel of the Egyptians* (NHC III,2) 44.1–9, we find the name of the Father, "an invisible symbol," as IEOUEAO, with each vowel repeated twenty-two times. But the larger issue on which any assessment of the veracity of Plotinus' report depends, namely whether examples such as the above ought to be regarded as attempts to influence the divine or rather as expressions of devotion that presuppose no causal power inherent in the names and words, is unfortunately not one that can sensibly be pursued in this commentary. The reader may wish to consult the texts collected in Chapter 3 of Meyer and Smith (1999). For a skeptical view of Plotinus' report, see for example Alt (1990, 33). See also Turner (2001, 609–613) for a useful comparison of three Gnostic prayers with possible "theurgical significance," from *Zostrianus* (NHC VIII,1) 86.13–23; 88.9–22; 51.24–52.8), *Allogenes* (NHC XI,3) 54.6–37, and *Three Steles of Seth* (NHC VII.5) 126.5–13 respectively.

14, 9 *<By the same means>*: Reading *hois* in place of *hoi*, with A and Q. Alternatively, one might read *hoiois*, with Armstrong, who translates: "by the sort of statements."

14, 9–11 *If they do. . . . from the incorporeals*: What is holy about the intelligible realities, we are to understand, is the fact that they are unchanging and unaffected by anything we may or may not do. Belief in the efficacy of magic, Plotinus argues, undermines the transcendence and changelessness of these realities. See IV.4.42, 19–23, and IV.4.43–44 more generally. The Stoics considered the human voice to be corporeal (see Diogenes Laertius, *Lives of the Philosophers* 7.55), and Plotinus seems to accept their view here. See also Iamblichus, *On the Mysteries* 1.15.25–31 des Places, a passage which suggests that Porphyry raised the same objection against theurgy as Plotinus does against Gnostic magic here: "And if it seems to you [*sc.* Porphyry] incredible that the incorporeal should hear a voice, and that what we utter in prayer should have need of a further sense-organ, and specifically of ears, you are deliberately forgetting the facility of the primary causes for knowing and comprehending within themselves all that is inferior to them" (tr. Clarke-Dillon-Hershbell).

14, 11–13 *When they say . . . like the philosophers*: "Regimen" translates the Greek word *diaita*, which can mean "way of living" quite generally. But since Plotinus is here talking about the prevention of diseases in particular, he may well have the medical sense of *diaita* in mind, as involving a specific regimen that promotes the well-being of the body, and takes into account factors such as diet, exercise, and climate. See, for example, the Hippocratic treatises *On Regimen in Health* and *On Regimen* I–III for an illustration of this sense. "The philosophers" in this passage seem to be, in the first instance, the physicians, with whom Plotinus is here and in the following forging an alliance against the Gnostics. Three doctors (Paulinus, Eustochus, and Zesthus) are known to have belonged to Plotinus' close circle, which may go some way toward explaining his medical interest here and elsewhere in the *Ennead* (see for example, IV.3.23, 9–21). Cf. Porphyry, *Life of Plotinus* 7.5–12.17–21.

14, 13–23 *But in fact. . . . be a cure*: The beliefs that, first, daemons cause diseases, and second, that exorcising them via magic spells can be a cure, were widely held in antiquity. Christian spells meant to exorcise daemons can be found in Meyer and Smith (1999, 43–44; 336). For the link between daemons and diseases, see for example Origen, *Against Celsus* 1.68; Macarius, *Apocriticus* 2.10. It is interesting to compare Plotinus' response to these spurious exorcisms, and his explanation of disease and healing in the terms of Hippocratic medicine, with Origen, who rejects naturalistic medicine in favor of daemonology; cf. *Commentary on Matthew* 13. 6. See also Iamblichus, *On the Mysteries* 2.6.18–20. Many of the remedies Plotinus here lists where already familiar to Plato; cf. *Republic* 406d.

14, 17–18 *those with real understanding*: The Greek phrase *tous eu phronountas* could be rendered with "sensible people," in which case it would imply that Plotinus viewed the majority of his contemporaries as accepting that diseases had natural causes. But it is likely that *tous eu phronountas* has a more restricted application, referring to "those with real understanding" of the human body, namely the philosophers (including natural philosophers and physicians; cf. 14, 13).

14, 23–27 *Was the daemon. . . . happened to him*: Two arguments against the causal role of daemons in bringing about diseases can be derived from the cures employed by doctors in Plotinus' time. First, why does fasting result in a cure, if the illness that gets cured is brought about by a daemon? It must be, Plotinus offers with a heavy dose of sarcasm, because the hungry demon has wasted away through lack of sustenance. Second, when a cure is effected, what happens to the daemon? Does he leave at once, or remain inside? If the daemon remains inside the body after the cure, his presence cannot by itself be sufficient to account for disease, since an apparently healthy person could in this case carry daemons. If the daemon leaves at once, what happens to him as the result of the cure that compels him to depart?

In line 25, read a question mark after *tēkesthai*, not a comma.

14, 27–28 *The disease nourished him*: We have here another instance where Plotinus imagines or anticipates what a Gnostic might respond to his objections. The idea that daemons, as quasi-material beings, derive their sustenance from the fumes of sacrifices, for example, is not uncommon in ancient texts, but it is difficult to find evidence for the claim that they feed on diseases specifically. On the sustenance of daemons quite generally, see for example Origen, *Against Celsus* 7.35.4; 8.30.2–4; Psellus, *On the Activity of Daemons* p. 15 Boissonade. Plotinus' point here is that the daemon cannot be one and the same thing as the disease, if the daemon at the same time derives its sustenance from it.

14, 29–36 *Next, if the. . . . recalled their daemons*: Building on the interim conclusion that the daemon is different from the disease (see 14, 27–28), Plotinus goes on to examine the idea that a demon is the sufficient cause of disease. If the daemon can cause disease in the body without any of the physical causes of disease being present in the body, anyone possessed by a demon will be sick as long as the demon is present—a position that is presumably contradicted by the fact that people convalesce without undergoing exorcisms. But if, on the other hand, the daemon is supposed to cause disease in conjunction with the physical causes, two problems result. First, if the physical causes of fever will alone be sufficient to produce fever, adding the daemon as an additional cause of the disease is superfluous. And second, the coincidence of physical causes of disease and the presence of daemons seems to imply the absurd notion that the daemon somehow acts as the assistant of whatever physical cause underlies the disease.

14, 34–36 *But in fact . . . recalled their daemons*: Plotinus offers something of a justification for his discussion of curative exorcisms; he may be aware that he is digressing from his main theme, that of the Gnostics' proclaimed power over the intelligibles. What unites the discussions of magic and daemons is no more than the eagerness of the opponents to appear as powerful and holy men (cf. 4, 9–10 and 4, 15–16). Thus, when Plotinus claims that "it has become clear how and why they [sc. *Gnostics*] make these claims," we are probably meant to infer that they do so arrogantly and mistakenly, and for the sake of deceiving credulous people.

14, 36–37 *read their books*: The exhortation of Plotinus to his readers to go and read the Gnostics' books, as is implied by the Greek verb *anaginōskousin*, suggests that they were readily available. Porphyry's list of Gnostic books in circulation at Rome supports this view; see *Life of Plotinus* 16.3–7 and Introduction, pp. 16–17.

14, 45 *it would <not> be appropriate*: With a final remark, Plotinus stops himself from pursuing the discussion in the same aggressive tone, and offers the following reason for doing so (reading HS_2's text without changes): "It would be appropriate for us to talk about them [*sc.* the Gnostics] in this way." The logic here is most obscure, and I submit that Mueller was right to insert a negation (*ouk*) after *hēmin*. If this textual change is accepted, the chapter echoes Plotinus' earlier reluctance to attack the Gnostics in too aggressive a manner. He realizes that the comparison of the two schools, with sharp lines drawn between Platonists and Gnostics, holiness and arrogance, reason and presumption, does not square well with the "certain respect" he claims to feel for his opponents at 10, 3 above. Therefore, one need not suppose that this last sentence originally signaled the end of the treatise, and that the subsequent chapters, covering the Gnostics' attitude to ethics (15), providence (16) and the physical world in general (17–18), were later additions.

Chapter 15

The effect of the Gnostics' teachings on moral conduct is pernicious. The absence of any serious inquiry into ethics in their writings reflects their indifference to virtue and the fine.

15, 1–3 *This point in . . . it in contempt*: What effect the Gnostics' beliefs about the creation of the sensible world and their place within it had on their conduct is a question that continues to be of interest to scholars to this day. Traditionally, it has been thought that Gnostic ethics fall into one of two extremes, directed either toward asceticism, a consequence of the view that the material world, including the body, is evil, and that the best preparation for escape from the Demiurge's creation consists in detachment from this earthly realm; or toward libertinism, that is, behavior that transgresses societal conventions and norms, as a revolt against the human moral order that is ultimately founded in the "tyranny" of the Demiurge and his pawns, the lower Archons governing the stars (see comment on 13, 18–20 above). For this dichotomy, see, for instance, Jonas (2001, 274): "Opposite as the two types of conduct [*sc.* libertinism and asceticism] are, they yet were in the gnostic case of the same root, and the same basic argument supports them both. The one repudiates allegiance to nature through excess, the other, through abstention." See also Puech (1960, 186–187).

Our evidence that the Gnostics embraced sensual pleasures or made no distinction between right and wrong comes almost entirely from hostile sources. These include important reports by heresiologists on the conduct of the Valentinians (see Irenaeus *Against the Heresies* 1.6.2–4), as well as on a number of other Gnostic sects, such as the Simoneans, Basilideans, and Carpocratians. See Williams (1999, 164–184) for a discussion of this evidence, who also points to the remains of Epiphanes' *On Righteousness* preserved in Clement of Alexandria, *Stromata* 3.6.1–9.3 as possible direct evidence for libertinism, but ultimately remains doubtful about their Gnostic credentials (186). Note also Porphyry *On Abstinence* 1.42.1–24, where unnamed "Barbarians," possibly Gnostics, justify their indulgence in animal foods by way of their spiritual *largesse,* which is able to absorb all manner of defilements. In texts written by the Gnostics themselves, there is no compelling evidence for a tendency toward libertinism; if anything, the evidence from many Nag Hammadi writings points toward spiritual withdrawal, if not asceticism. Cf. *Authentic Teaching* (NHC VI,3) 30.6–25: "The adversary spies on us, lying in wait for us like a fisherman, wishing to seize us, rejoicing that he might swallow us. For he places many foods before our eyes, (things) which belong to this world. He wishes to make us desire one of them and to taste only a little, so that he may seize us with his hidden poison and bring us out of freedom and take us into slavery. For whenever he catches us with a single food, it is indeed necessary for us to desire the rest. Finally, then, such things become the food of death" (tr. MacRae). See also e.g. *Testimony of Truth* (NHC IX,3) 29.26–31.15; *Zostrianus* (NHC VIII,2) 44.1–22; Irenaeus, *Against the Heresies* 1.24.2.

All this is to say that Plotinus' report in this chapter should be read with a good measure of skepticism. He himself grudgingly acknowledges that not all Gnostics display the wanton behavior that would be consonant with their doctrines, as he construes them, at 15, 20–21 below. In this context, it is also worth pointing out that he will later, in Chapter 17, accuse the Gnostics of being insensitive to the beauties in this world, and deriving their hatred for the body from a mistaken reading of Plato, attitudes which do not obviously square well with abandonment to the senses. Cf. 17, 1–4; 18, 1–2. But we need not go as far as to think that Plotinus is contradicting himself. Rather, the tension between the two accounts reveals a subtlety in his argument: his point is that the exhortations to flee the body do not yield usable guides for conduct, and, in the Gnostics' case, do not restrain any tendency toward licentiousness they may have (cf. the sneers at 17, 28–29; 30–31). Theoretical asceticism and decadence in practice are not incompatible, in other words, but, claims Plotinus, go hand in hand where the Gnostics are concerned. Cf., however, Williams (1999, 178–179) for a different view.

15, 4–10 *There are two. . . . pleasure and enjoyment*: This classification of philosophy into two opposing schools on the "goal" (*telos*), that is to say, the end toward which all action is in some sense directed, and rationally ought to be directed, conveniently ignores the possibility that *both* pleasure and virtue could serve as the end of actions; cf. Cicero, *Academica* 2.131. Behind it stands a polemical purpose, which explains the degree of misrepresentation that is evident here. The Gnostics are portrayed as even more disreputable a sect than the one founded by the most disreputable philosopher among the Greeks, namely Epicurus. Epicurus' philosophy is classed with the school that pursues "bodily pleasure" as a goal—a consequence, Plotinus implies, of his denial of providence. The thought seems to be that, convinced of the absence of a divine justice bestowing punishments and rewards in this life and the next, Epicurus thought it reasonable to pursue enjoyment rather than virtue. Cf. Atticus' critique of Aristotle, in Eusebius, *Preparation of the Gospel* 15.5.4.1–5.1 Mras: "For every one who is human and constrained by human desires, if he despise the gods and think they are nothing to him, inasmuch as in life he dwells far away from them, and after death exists no more, will come prepared to gratify his lusts" (tr. Gifford). There is no question that Epicurus denied any active involvement of the gods in the affairs of the universe, and "did away" with providence as Plotinus understands it here. See, for example, Diogenes Laertius, *Lives of the Philosophers* 10.139 for this doctrine. Much more problematic, however, is the claim that Epicurus set up *bodily* pleasure as a goal. In clear contradiction with Plotinus' report, Epicurus himself states that "when we say that pleasure is the end, we do not mean the pleasures of the dissipated and those that consist in having a good time, [. . .], but freedom from pain in the body and from disturbance in the soul" (*Letter to Menoeceus* 131.8–12; tr. LS). But, in Plotinus' defense, Epicurus at times exaggerated the role of physical pleasures in his ethical teachings, perhaps to shock his readers or for polemical purposes, as the following statement illustrates: "The beginning and the root of all good is the pleasure of the stomach; even wisdom and culture must be referred to this" (Athenaeus, *Deipnosophistae* 546F=fr. 409 Usener).

Plotinus, on the other hand, unsurprisingly groups his own school with those who pursue "virtue" (perhaps one must understand the Stoics as included in this group too) and "the fine" (*to kalon*). The Greek term *to kalon* can have both moral and aesthetic meaning; it may be used to describe actions undertaken for the common good on the one hand, as a comparison with Aristotle's *Nicomachean Ethics* shows (see for example, 1168a33–34; 1169a8–11.31–32.34–36), but is also associated with notions of order and harmony (a well-made product, for example, can be said to be *kalon*). For Aristotle, *to kalon* is particularly connected with the exercise of virtue, so much so that he can claim that the brave person, for example, acts "for the sake of the fine" (1115b12; 1116b2–3). For a good survey of the meanings of *to kalon* in Aristotle, see Irwin (2010). In this chapter, Plotinus, following Aristotle's usage, talks about the fine in the sense of pursuing, or being motivated to pursue, morally admirable actions ("choosing the fine" at 15, 6; "going in pursuit of the fine" at 15, 23; "heeding the fine" at 15, 25), but also uses the term in a more general sense (cf. "seeing anything fine in this world" at 15, 14; "for them, nothing in this world is fine," at 15, 21), probably referring to anything worthy of admiration.

For a different classification of philosophies in Plotinus, see V.9.1, which is usefully compared with the dichotomy in the present passage by Cornea (2013, 467–470). He makes the interesting suggestion that Plotinus "may have intended to symbolically rally against the Gnostics all the suitable 'Greek' philosophers, i.e. Platonists, Peripatetics, and Stoics, because all of them, no matter how different they were, at least accepted Providence [. . .]." (473).

15, 7 *elsewhere*: The two connected claims made here, first, that the desire for virtue "depends" on god, and second, that it can be referred back to him, are explained in more detail in treatise I.2 “On virtues.” As Plotinus argues there, virtue depends on god in the sense that virtues in this world depend for their existence on participation in the order and harmony in the intelligible world (cf. I.2.1, 13–15.46–47). These virtues can also be referred back to god, that is to say, Intellect, because they have as their goal the desire to become like god, and are thus intrinsically directed toward him (I.2.1, 3–5; I.2.3, 19–22).

15, 7 *<how>* Reading Volkmann's *pōs* (“how”) in place of *hōs* (“as”).

15, 10–11 *Yet this doctrine . . . and providence itself*: Unlike Epicurus, who only denies the existence of providence and any deities that exercise providential care for the universe, the Gnostics consider the order imposed upon the world by the Demiurge a “tyranny” that does not aim at the good of the whole universe and shows no signs of justice in the way it assigns good or bad fortunes (see 9, 1–26 and 13, 18–20). But although the Gnostics view the cosmic order in stark terms, they reserve for themselves alone a special kind of providence that presumably does not depend on the Demiurge; cf. 9, 52–69. Thus, in Plotinus' eyes, they both slander the providential order that actually exists and introduce a new form of providence that is nonsensical. Cf. also III.2.1, 5–10, where Plotinus probably engages with a Gnostic argument against providence, and note the reference to an "evil creator" (as in the extended title of II.9) at 1, 9 of that treatise.

15, 10 *insolent*: The Greek word *neanikōteros*, here translated as "insolent," occurs notably at Plato, *Gorgias* 509a.

15, 10–11 *the master of providence and providence itself*: As Gerson (1998, 34) points out, the "master of providence" is the One, which is superior to, and the causal origin of, the providential order that is strictly speaking administered by Intellect (that is, "providence itself"). See IV.4.9, 1–5.

15, 15–17 *This doctrine also . . . a man wise*: Plotinus here implicitly accepts that virtue is the result of nature, habit *and* reason. The nature of virtue, and whether it comes about by nature, training or teaching, or in some other way, is a traditional one in Greek ethics, and occurs most famously at the opening of Plato's *Meno* (70a). The repetition of "temperance" (*to te sōphronein*) at 15, 15 looks to be a textual error, perhaps a marginal gloss that was wrongly copied into the manuscript. HS_2 rightly suggest excising it.

15, 20–21 *unless someone in their group is superior*: Only those among the Gnostics who are naturally endowed with virtuous qualities such as temperance and courage would be able to resist the harmful effects of their own doctrines—a sarcastic comment on Plotinus' part, but perhaps also an implicit recognition that the Gnostics under attack were not known to exhibit the licentious conduct and selfishness here attributed to them. Natural virtues are imperfect, in that they require the virtue of wisdom for their full development, which has a more universal grasp of right action; cf. I.3.6, 16–24. The distinction between natural and full virtues of character goes back to Aristotle, *Nicomachean Ethics* 1144b1–17.

15, 21–22 *For them, nothing . . . pursue one day*: Most likely, what the Gnostics will ultimately go on to pursue is their re-integration into the Pleroma. They only attain this goal after their deaths, when their souls ascend to the "new earth" (5, 24–25), a place intermediate between this world and the intelligible one, where they gather until the end of days, when all the elect will be restored to their place of origin.

15, 22–26 *However, those who. . . . toward the intelligibles*: Note that the phrase "those who already have the knowledge (*gnōsis*)" (*tous ēdē egnōkotas*) at 15, 22–23 is perhaps the closest Plotinus comes to referring to his opponents as "Gnostics." "Knowledge" in this context means the esoteric knowledge that is revealed by the divine and that is instrumental for achieving salvation. For this sense of "knowledge," see for example *Gospel of Truth* (NHC I,3) 21.4–22.20; *Gospel of Philip* (NHC II,3) 77.16–30; Clement of Alexandria, *Excerpts from Theodotus* 78. Cf. Rudolph (1980, 115–116). Plotinus argues that the Gnostics, who claim to possess a special knowledge and to derive from a divine nature, should also have gone and "heeded the fine" in this world. As he makes clear, this includes not only contemplative activity but also performing actions that in some way create greater order or "set right" (*katorthoun*) things in this world, whether this extends only to one's own conduct, or, more likely, also to improving the lives of others and that of one's community. From the highly qualified way in which the argument is presented, in an unreal past tense, we are clearly meant to infer that, since the Gnostics have not in fact made any positive difference in this world that they despise, their claim to issue from a divine nature is also undermined.

15, 27–34 *The fact that. . . . or purifies it*: Several of the five points regarding virtue listed here—(1) The definition of virtue; (2) The parts of virtue; (3) How virtue is acquired; (4) How virtue is preserved; (5) How one takes care of the soul or purifies it—are addressed in treatise I.2 "On virtues," namely (1) I.2.2, 10–11, (2) I.2.3, 11–19; I.2.6, 11–27, and (5) I.2.5, 2–21. Plotinus' views on the remaining points have to be inferred to some extent, but the notion of purification (*katharsis*) will be crucial to both the acquisition and the preservation of virtue; see I.2.5, 1–21; I.2.7, 8–10; I.6.6, 1–17. His polemic against the Gnostics is also, at the same time, an opportunity to present the merits of his own school. The same is true for the complaint, at 15, 34, that the Gnostics do not teach how to look toward god. Apart from the cultivation of the virtues of character and intellect, Plotinus gives a prominent role to the study of dialectics in the soul's ascent, as he explains in I.3.

One might at first thought be sympathetic to Plotinus' critique here: someone able to identify the goal of life who is ignorant of the principles of human action cannot well guide anyone toward the goal who is not already inclined toward it. But if the Gnostics had thought seriously about the foundations of ethics, we might expect that this activity would have left some trace in writing. However, the inference at 15, 27–28 from "the Gnostics did not write about virtue" to "the Gnostics did not care about virtue" is surely very problematic. One can easily imagine that some of the rules of conduct that may have governed life in Gnostic communities would have been transmitted orally, as Alt (1990, 35) points out.

15, 32–40 *Saying "Look to. . . . a mere name*: Plotinus insists on the necessity of cultivating the "lower" virtues of character, such as moderation and courage, before the higher virtues of the soul and especially its intellectual part can be perfected. For this reason, he regards as obviously absurd the question in the subsequent lines whether one could be "looking toward god" while at the same time being unable to control one's emotions and appetites. Cf. I.2.7, 10–12; I.3.6, 16–17. Proclus quotes the conclusion of this chapter (14, 38–40) in his *Commentary On the Timaeus*: "But the word 'God' without virtue is a mere name, as

Plotinus says, and the many use it not with wisdom but randomly" (1.369.22–25).

15, 34 Reading *kai pōs* with Volkmann, in place of *pōs kai.*

Chapter 16

The cosmos cannot be separated from the intelligible world; contempt for the former implies ignorance of the latter. The opponents' mistaken notion of providence reveals their confusion.

16, 1–2 *the gods and other fine things within it:* "The gods within the cosmos" are the stars, whose purity and immortality (both traditional attributes of divinity) were touched upon earlier at 5, 8–11. See also 8, 29–34.

16, 2–5 *Every wicked man . . . that very act:* This translation does not adopt Kirchhoff's deletion of *pas kakos* ("every wicked man") at 16, 4, which is accepted in HS_2, but instead reads Heigl's conjecture *pagkakos* ("completely wicked"). If *pas kakos* were excised, and not emended as suggested here, the translation would read: "It is likely that every wicked man would have despised the gods at an earlier time, and if he did not despise them before, even if he was not wicked in all other respects, he would have become so by the very act of despising them." On either translation, Plotinus is implying, first, that the origin of wickedness will in most cases be contempt for the gods; and second, that contempt for the gods is sufficient for transforming an ordinarily wicked person (presumably someone who has some moral qualms about some things) into a perfectly wicked person. The optative *an kataphronēseien* indicates that Plotinus is making a statement he considers not to be true absolutely, but as conjecture. In Plato's *Laws*, the Athenian Stranger presents much the same claim in order to justify legislation against atheism: "No one who believes in gods as the law directs ever voluntarily commits an unholy act or lets any lawless word pass his lips" (885b; tr. Saunders). If people do in fact commit lawless or unholy acts, the Stranger continues, it is because they believe either that the gods do not exist, or that they are indifferent to human affairs, or that they can be swayed by prayers and sacrifices. See also SVF III.660.

It is worth noting that some translations have tried to give a clearer sense to what is here translated as "at an earlier time" (*pro tou*). Dufour thus translates *pro tou* as "before," and expects the supplement "despising the world" to follow, presumably in light of 16, 1, while Spanu has "before (the disciples' doctrine was established)." I take it that *pro tou* here is used to mean something like "before he did whatever it is that turned him into a wicked character."

16, 5–7 *Further, their supposed . . . from anything else*: Underlying Plotinus' argument here is that the universe forms a whole with interconnected parts that are in various ways responsive to one another. A vivid illustration of this idea is given at IV.4.41, 1–9, a passage already pointed out by Cilento (1971, 267), which discusses the efficacy of prayer.

The Gnostics place themselves outside of this cosmic sympathy (*sumpatheia*), Plotinus argues, by claiming that they alone have a special kinship with the intelligible gods. This point is taken up by the Greek word *asumpathēs* (16, 6), translated as "cut off from anything else" here. It is worth recalling, in this context, that some Gnostic sects like the Valentinians posit a principle called Horos ("Limit") that separates the intelligible from the visible world. This, in Plotinus' view, would be further evidence that the Gnostics place the intelligible word in isolation from the rest of the universe, unlike Plato, who in passages like *Symposium* 211c–d and *Phaedrus* 250e–252c insists on the possibility of gradual ascent from one to the other. See comment on 3, 18–20 above.

16, 7–9 *also welcomes anything that is their kin*: The thought that like is dear to like is a traditional one in Greek philosophy. See, for example, Homer, *Odyssey* 17.218; Plato, *Gorgias* 510b; *Laws* 716c–d.

16, 9 *every soul is a child of Father Intellect*: Intellect is described as the "father" of individual souls in a number of places in the *Enneads*, for example at V.1.1, 2; V.1.2, 37; V.1.3, 14. Because Soul as an hypostasis is the result of Intellect's external activity, the analogy of a father bringing a child into being is apt, especially if one adds the idea that a child's rationality is less developed than that of the father, just as Soul's own activity of discursive thinking is only an imperfect reflection of the rationality in Intellect. Igal (1981, 144) makes the valuable suggestion that the claim that "every soul is a child of Father Intellect" can be read as a polemical rejection of the Gnostic distinction between pneumatic, psychic, and material souls. See notes on 2, 6 and 12, 5 above.

16, 10–11 *much more connected to the intelligibles*: For the special connection between the stars and the intelligibles, see IV.3.17, 1–12.

16, 14 *do not know the intelligibles except in speech*: Since the Gnostics despise both the visible universe as a whole, and the stars in particular, they cannot truly understand the intelligibles. If they did understand them, they would also be able to grasp how their nature is reflected in the sensible world, for example in the rationality that makes the universe a well-regulated and ordered whole, and in the regular motion of the stars. HS_2 delete *hoti* ("that"), but it seems necessary here; as Dufour (2006, 277n276) points out, *lekteon* ("we must say") or something to this effect must be understood to govern the sentence.

16, 14–27 *Otherwise how can. . . . what succeeds him*: In Chapter 15, 10–11, the Gnostics' doctrine of providence had already come under attack, but only in passing. It now becomes the focus of a sustained argument designed to show that the idea of providence extended only to a select group of people (cf. the claim that "god only looks after them" at 16–17) is inconsistent. The form of the argument is that of a dilemma: either god directs his care toward the Gnostics, in which case he will direct it toward the whole cosmos. Or he does not direct it toward the whole cosmos, in which case he will also not direct it toward the Gnostics. Behind this argument stands a more general thesis that the divine is omnipresent because it is incorporeal, and therefore not limited by space, which Plotinus defends in VI.4–5. On the conception of providence in the Platonizing Sethian texts from Nag Hammadi, see also Burns (2014, 89–93). See also 9, 64–69 for a parallel argument.

16, 27–30 *But whether some . . . going to be*: The cosmos "receives something" from the intelligible world through the intermediary of the world soul, who brings life to the cosmos and arranges its order. Since the intelligibles exist forever and cannot withhold the emanation of their power, which is a necessary consequence of their nature as well as a reflection of their intrinsic goodness, the cosmos will never be deprived of divine influence; in this sense it is never going to be "abandoned" (*apoleipetai*). See 3, 5–15 above.

16, 28 *or whatever else it is you want*: With this remark, Plotinus implicitly recognizes that the Gnostic conception of divine care for the salvation of elect souls does not overlap with the meaning of providence as it would be used by Stoic and Platonic philosophers, who agree on its general and universal applicability. Cf. e.g. Cicero, *On the Nature of the Gods*, 2.78–80; 164; Alcinous, *Handbook of Platonism* 26.1–2; Pseudo-Plutarch, *On Fate* 572F. Some Gnostic sources demote this kind of universal connection between causes and their effects in the visible world to the status of "fate," a malevolent tyranny, while they preserve the notion of "providence" to the saving action of higher powers. For this sense of a special providence, see Valentinus fr. 2, in Clement of Alexandria, *Stromata* 2.20.114.4.1–6.5 Stählin-Früchtel-Treu: "For the many spirits dwelling in the heart do not allow it to become pure: rather each of them performs its own acts, polluting it in various ways with improper desires. And in my opinion the heart experiences something like what happens in an inn. For the latter is full of holes and dug up and often filled with dung by indecent guests who have no consideration (*pronoia*) for the place, since it does not belong to them. Just so, a heart too is impure by being the habitation of many daemons, until it is cared for (*mechri mē pronoias* *tugchanei*). But when the Father, who alone is good, visits the heart, he makes it holy and fills it with light. And so a person who has such a heart is called blessed (*makarizetai*), for that person will see God" (tr. Wilson).

16, 30–32 *For providence deals. . . . intelligence show this*: The text does not specify what the world soul is participating in, but the context makes it likely that it is providence, understood in its highest aspect, which is Intellect (see III.2.1, 21–26, where Plotinus suggests that providence in the universe has its source in Intellect). The operation of providence is compared to a general laying down battle orders at III.3.2, 3–15, illustrating the point that particular events fall under a more universal plan laid down in advance. See also III.2.17, 18–53.

16, 39 *he does not even see this universe*: "This universe" translates the Greek word *touton* (lit. "this"), which could also stand for "the intelligible cosmos." But given Plotinus' overall argument, that ignorance about the reflections of intelligible reality in the sensible world implies ignorance about intelligible reality itself, the former option is preferable.

16, 39–48 *Indeed, could there. . . . to the intelligibles*: The relation of the musician, the lover and the mathematician to intelligible reality is also discussed in I.3.1–3. It is striking that Plotinus includes painting among the arts whose products can trigger recollection of intelligible reality, given that Plato presents a powerful case against the "imitative" arts of dramatic poetry and painting at *Republic* 598a–c; 603a. According to Plato, painting copies the appearance of reality, that is, visible objects, rather than reality itself, which encompasses intelligible forms. By doing so, painting along with all other imitative arts appeals to the non-rational part of the soul, which takes pleasure in seeing multifarious shapes and is unable to discriminate the appearance of beauty (as it is represented in a painting, say) from the reality of beauty. In some passages, Plotinus comes closer to this Platonic devaluation of art; cf. IV.3.10, 17–19; III.8.5, 6–10. But against this must be set other passages suggesting that artists do not in fact represent mere appearances of intelligible reality, but rather imitate that reality directly, which would thus render their productions immune from Plato's strictures in Book 10 of the *Republic*. See the famous discussion of the sculptor Phidias at V.8.1, 32–41.

16, 43–44 *the same things in the same way*: This ambiguous phrase supports two interpretations, depending on how one understands "in the same way" (*homoiōs*). On one reading, the contrast is with the experts in geometry, who, in ideal conditions, do see the same things, for example equilateral triangles, in the same way, as equilateral triangles. One and the same depiction of Richard III, on the other hand, will invoke loathing in one person and admiration in another, such that aesthetic experience contains a subjective element that Plotinus here recognizes. On an alternative reading, the point is that people who look at paintings have a different experience from the experts in music and geometry, but not necessarily different from one another. While the musician and the geometer already have some grasp of intelligible reality, and thus take pleasure in perceiving manifestations of that reality, the ordinary admirer of a portrait does not have a prior understanding of the world of forms. Thus, people looking at beautiful pictures are "bewildered" (*thorubountai*) and brought to recollection when they realize that the beauty they perceive is already present in their thoughts, that is to say, in the reflections of the forms (*logoi*) that their souls contain.

16, 47–48 *the same affection that moves lovers*: Cf. Plato, *Phaedrus* 251a1–252b1. See also I.6.7, 12–19.

16, 49 *well represented*: The manuscript reading *memigmenon*, which suggests that beauty is here thought of as being "mixed in" well with the face of a person represented in an artwork, has struck many scholars as insupportable, and Creuzer's conjecture *memimēmenon* ("represented"), also adopted in this translation, restores good sense to the passage. Cf. Plato's *Phaedrus*, where Socrates describes the effect a god-like face that is a "good representation" (*eu memimēmenon*) of beauty can have on its beholder (251a3).

16, 52–53 *the form that becomes apparent in the stars*: "The form that becomes apparent" in the stars may specifically refer to the signs of the Zodiac, as Dufour (2006n286) notes. Cf. IV.4.35, 42–56, where the influence that certain configurations of stars have on the sublunary world is discussed.

Chapter 17

Plotinus defends the beauty of the cosmos.

17, 3 *the kinds of obstacles*: The body is said to be an "obstacle" (*empodion*) for the acquisition of wisdom at *Phaedo* 65a10. Note that Plotinus assumes that his opponents could have derived their contempt for the world from a mistaken reading of Plato, which underlines the strong Platonic influence on the Gnostics. Although he does not deny that Plato, in the *Phaedo* and elsewhere (see comment on 17, 3–4 below), makes comments suggesting that the soul's embodiment is an undesirable state, Plotinus balances this view with passages from the *Timaeus* (especially *Timaeus* 29a–e; 30d; 34a–b) that emphasize the necessity of the soul's embodiment for the completeness and perfection of the sensible universe, in so far as individual souls shape and animate particular bodies, which in turn make this world a "beautiful image" of the intelligible world. On this complex issue, see IV.8, particularly IV.8.1, 28–50; 5, 1–16, and the relevant notes in Fleet (2012). Cf. 6, 59–60; 7, 2–4 above. For the body as an "impediment" to thinking, see also IV.3.19, 24–27.

17, 3–4 *that every bodily nature is worse than the soul*: No single Platonic passage is the source for the principle that "every bodily nature is worse than the soul." At IV.8.1, 28–36 Plotinus catalogues some of the main evidence for his view that "Plato holds the whole of the sensible world in low esteem," and includes references to Plato's *Phaedo* (66b–67b; 82e2), *Gorgias* (493a2–3), *Republic* (515c) and *Phaedrus* (246c–d; 248c).

17, 4–21 *they ought to. . . . make it beautiful*: In this extended thought experiment, the Gnostics are invited to embark on a process of removing the cosmos' mass in thought, a process that is designed to reveal the intelligible nature underlying the visible universe. What the Gnostics are supposed to discover is first the intelligible sphere (see comment on 4, 29–31), in other words the realm of Being and the forms (including the form of the cosmos itself), which acts as the perfect model for the cosmos. Next, they are to envision how individual souls transform the greatness of power in the intelligible world into three-dimensional corporeal extension (the Demiurge is thought to do the same by the Marcosians; cf. Irenaeus, *Against the Heresies* 1.17.2). The result of the souls' activity is a visible sphere that has a mass, and which is set in motion by the world soul (on this last point, see II.2.1, 6–11.14–19.39–51). Now Plotinus leaves his interlocutors a choice: they can either think of the visible sphere as being already in motion, which gives them a correct idea about the world soul, because the visible universe always depends on it, or they can think of the visible sphere as static, which will presumably impress on them how great a power is required to move it. Either way, they will grasp something true about the world soul. If they pick the first option, however, they have to understand that the world soul is not tied to the world's body to such an extent that it will be affected by it. Instead, the relation is strictly asymmetric: the world soul gives its power, and receives nothing in return. The purpose of this thought experiment becomes clear in the last lines, at 17, 18–21. Once one has attained a conception of how the world soul is able to bring the body of the universe into motion, one must also grant that it has the power to make the visible world as beautiful as possible, by passing on the beauty that it perceives in the intelligible world to the visible realm. And once this is granted, the Gnostics' contempt for this world is shown to lack any foundation in reasoning.

Several assumptions are required in order to read the thought experiment in the way sketched out above, which owes a debt to Dufour (2006). First, one needs to assume that "this sphere" at 17, 11 does not refer to the intelligible sphere, as, for example, Harder-Beutler-Theiler

(1960, 437) and Alt (1990, 38) think, but rather to the product of the individual souls' activity (*to genomenon* at 17, 8), that is, the visible universe conceived of as a sphere (for this conceit, cf. IV.3.17, 16). One further needs to assume that "the power of god" at 17, 12 means "the power of the world soul." Finally, I take the subject of the genitive absolute *dioikousēs* ("governing") to be "the power of god," and not, as is grammatically possible, "this sphere" at 17, 11. This last point, incidentally, provides a strong argument in favor of the interpretation proposed here. On the alternative reading (taking "this sphere" to mean the intelligible sphere, and making it the subject of *dioikousēs*), the intelligible sphere must be thought of as resting "because it is not yet governing anything else," as though the activity of governing something else would somehow set the intelligible world into motion, surely an intolerable hypothesis in Plotinus' eyes. Cf. V.8.9, 1–14; VI.4.7, 22–39 for two similar thought experiments.

17, 7 *<and>*: This translation adopts the reading *kai to noēton* in place of *kata to noēton,* with Kirchhoff *et al.* Some object for *eis diastasin proagagousas* ("leading . . . into extension") seems to be required here, such as *to noēton,* which at the same time acts as the indirect object for *megethos dousas* ("giving magnitude"). Without this textual change, one might translate, with Armstrong: "souls in their order which without bodies give magnitude and advance to dimension according to the intelligible pattern."

But it is not easy to make sense of the idea that souls are "advancing to dimension": the souls may produce matter and physical stuff, but they themselves do not change their own nature by becoming extended, physical things, as the phrase very nearly suggests. An alternative, adopted by Bréhier (1924, 135) would be to retain *kata to noēton,* and to understand "the universe" as the object of the souls' activity, such that the souls would give magnitude to the universe and lead it into extension according to an intelligible pattern. See Spanu (2012, 200) for a discussion of this sentence.

17, 8–9 *<what has come into being>*: Reading *to genomenon tōi amerei tōi tou paradeigmatos* in place of *tou genomenou tōi amerei to tou paradeigmatos,* as suggested by Harder-Beutler-Theiler (1960). Without this change, a possible translation would be "such that [the greatness] of the model equals in power the indivisible greatness of what has come into being." But this reading gets the thought of the passage back to front: souls make the visible world like intelligible reality; they do not assimilate the intelligible model to the world of generation.

17, 9–10 *For greatness there . . . here in mass*: For a discussion of the interrelation between power in the intelligible world and mass in the sensible world, see Spanu (2014). The word for "mass," *onkos,* describes matter under the aspect of its extension in three dimensions, as Plotinus explains at II.4.11, 25–43.

17, 12 *the beginning, middle and end*: Compare Plato *Laws* 715e7–716a2, where the Athenian Stranger imagines giving the following address: "Men, according to the ancient story, there is a god who holds in his hands the beginning and end and middle of all things, and straight he marches in the cycle of nature" (tr. Saunders).

17, 15 *placed a body inside the soul*: Although one can, in a loose sense, talk about the soul's presence to the body, strictly speaking the soul is omnipresent, and therefore cannot be "placed" anywhere in particular. For this reason, Plotinus talks instead of body being placed inside the soul, as already Plato does in the *Timaeus* (36d–e). Cf. III.7.11, 33–35; IV.3.22; VI.4.1, 3–8; 2, 39–43; 4, 26–34.

17, 16 *the soul does not undergo any affection*: The point that the world soul remains unaffected by the material universe has been argued for at 7, 8–22.

17, 21–31 *This very beauty. . . . a bad state*>: Having argued that an understanding of intelligible reality will lead one to appreciate that beauty in the sensible world is the natural result of the ungrudging nature of the divine, Plotinus now explores why the Gnostics' souls are not, as he says, "moved" by perceptible beauty. There is a hint of puzzlement, and also irritation, in this passage. Even though Plotinus considers the possibility that contempt for beauty may be grounded in indifference to worldly matters, he immediately rejects this position as absurd, since he has already argued that perceptible beauty is a reflection of that higher reality with which the Gnostics would certainly claim to be concerned. Cf. 16, 48–56. In a biting aside, he recommends that the Gnostics should extend their contempt for the world to pretty boys and women "so that they do not yield to licentiousness"— the implication, of course, is that they have already very much yielded. The final arrow directed at them targets their psychological duplicity: whatever pride they take in their indifference to worldly beauty is no more than an after-effect of their former depravity (see my comment on 17, 31 on the Greek text).

17, 25 *The primary beings*: These are the intelligibles, as sketched out in Chapters 1–3 of this treatise.

17, 28 *<too>*: Inserting *kai* after *an poioien tou* would improve this sentence; it may have dropped out because of the *kai* after *paisi*. The thought here is that contempt for the world at large should also include contempt for the passions that bind one to it, and so by extension for the "objects" that arouse such passions.

17, 31 *<when they were in a bad state>*: Kirchhoff's conjecture *kakōs diatethentes*, in place of *kai pōs diatithentes*, greatly improves the sense, and is accepted by this translation. If this text were accepted, Plotinus would be implying that the Gnostics, before turning against visible beauty, were drawn to it in excess. This sense is well captured in MacKenna's translation: "[T]heirs is the perverse pride of despising what was once admired." For the same imputation, see 18, 13–14.

Maintaining HS_2's text would give something like Armstrong's "and what sort of a way of managing is that?" or, as suggested by HS, "and how are they dividing up [the beautiful and the ugly] (*quomodo distribuentes* [sc. *pulchrum et turpe*])?" Neither of these alternatives has much relevance to Plotinus' argument in the passage.

17, 32–48 *Next, we should. . . . reaching the goal*: The description of the ascent from beauty in "partial and perceptible" things owes a debt to Plato's *Symposium* (especially 210a–211b). Although perceptible things may participate in beauty, their participation is imperfect compared to that of purer beings, for example the good daemons referred to earlier at 9, 30, whose beauty is given as an example (see also the comment on 17, 34). Their imperfect participation means that perceptible things may be beautiful in some respects but not in others, or beautiful on the outside, but not inside. When such conflicting appearances present themselves, however, we should, according to Plotinus' argument here, give priority to internal beauty over external appearances.

The contrast between inside and outside in this passage requires some further explanation. From the one example that Plotinus himself gives, that of seeing beautiful people who are ugly inside, it is likely that the contrast will include the difference between outward appearance and moral character, such that a vicious person, for example, would be "ugly inside." On this interpretation, Plotinus would be making the striking claim that a wicked person, say a tyrant, will at most possess a false appearance of beauty, but not true outward beauty. Here one may wish to protest: surely an attractive tyrant genuinely has the physical features that make him or her attractive, so in what sense can one say that these present a "false appearance"? As long as the appearance presents the outward features that a person really has, it should be called a "true appearance." One way of responding to this complaint would be to say that a pleasing outward appearance is a false appearance of beauty, not in the sense that it represents features that are not genuinely there (the tyrant may really have a symmetrical face, for example), but in the sense that the appearance is intrinsically defeasible, that is to say, that further observation of the tyrant would eventually show ugly features as well. The judgment "This person looks beautiful," when applied to a vicious person, is thus more liable to turn out false than when applied to a virtuous one. I take this to be the force of the comment made at 17, 44–45 ("I think he has not really seen them"), where

Plotinus appears to suggest that on close enough observation, the attractive tyrant will turn to be ugly. But having denied that someone can be internally ugly and outwardly beautiful, Plotinus makes an important concession: it may be that the ugliness is something "acquired" (*epiktēton*) by those who have an essentially beautiful nature—an "accretion," in other words, as *epiktēton* is translated here. One might think of someone who by nature has a generally virtuous disposition, but who through the influence of his friends develops a love of gossip, say. In this case, the "beautiful nature" is not totally corrupted, but it is lessened by the addition of the desire for titillating news. In a case like this, Plotinus says, it is conceivable that one can genuinely "see" the outward beauty of the person while also recognizing the element of internal ugliness.

Within the wider argument of this chapter, the discussion of "partial" beauties serves to create a contrast with the world soul, where there can be no conflict between inner and outer beauty; cf. 17, 48–56 below. On the perception of beauty, see I.6.3, 9–16.

17, 34 *the beauty of daemons*: Such claims about daemons may seem strange to us, but it should be remembered that Plotinus himself was not averse to the magical practices *en vogue* in his time, if his biographer Porphyry is to be believed. The latter reports that Plotinus "readily" (*hetoimōs*) agreed to attend a conjuration of his personal daemon when an Egyptian magician came to Rome. The apparition, however, was no ordinary daemon, but a god-like one; cf. *Life of Plotinus* 10.15–25. On the beautiful appearances of daemons, see also I.6.7, 19–21.

17, 36 *the intelligible beauty is extraordinary*: See Plato, *Republic* 509a6; *Symposium* 218e2.

17, 37 *proceeding from them toward the intelligibles*: The ascent toward beauty described here is reminiscent of Plato's *Symposium*, where perceptible beauty has a similar role of leading the soul upward to intelligible beauty. Cf. *Symposium* 210a–212c.

17, 45 *he has not [really] seen them*: The person deluded by exterior beauty may have made a mistake or not *really* seen the object of his admiration for what it is, but he surely must have perceived it in order to say anything about it; hence some qualification of "seen" should be understood.

17, 45–46 *he <wrongly> takes <them> to be beautiful*: I am here following Bury's proposal (1945, 53) to read *allōs . . . <tou>tous kallous* in place of *allous . . . tous kallous*. As Bury points out, the intended sense of the passage is that those who are blinded by exterior beauty mistakenly hold a belief of the form "This and such is beautiful"; one thus expects an adverbial construction. Armstrong, who does not make the textual changes proposed by Bury, translates: "[. . .] if anyone is going to say that he has seen people who are really beautiful but are ugly within, I think that he has not really seen them, but thinks that beautiful people are other than who they are."

17, 47–48 *there are many obstacles to reaching the goal*: Most importantly, the body poses an obstacle to the activity of contemplation; see 17, 3 above. But other influences such as upbringing and one's social environment may also present obstacles toward the attainment of one's "goal" (*telos*), that is to say, the perfection of one's nature, which, for Plotinus, will require the acquisition of virtue.

17, 48–56 *But what was. . . . bad attaching itself*: In order to defend the beauty of the universe, Plotinus rules out two distinct explanations of how it might be thought of as imperfectly beautiful: (i) because of some imperfection internal to it, or (ii) because of some outside "accretion." Option (i) is dismissed because supposing that the universe is internally imperfect might invite the comparison with a child that has not yet reached the full development of its capacities. This possibility Plotinus rejects as absurd, presumably on the grounds that, for all of its infinite past existence, the universe was as well made as it could have been, such that no process of development could lead to its more perfect realization. Option (ii) subdivides into two: the accretion would have to somehow attach itself to (a) the body or (b) the soul of the universe. But (a) is impossible, because the universe is the totality of all bodily things by definition, and has been made so as to contain a plenitude of beings in imitation of the fullness of its intelligible paradigm. So, we are to infer, there is no bodily thing outside of it that could corrupt its body. Alternative (b), that the soul of the universe becomes corrupted by an outside cause, is dismissed rather swiftly, as being difficult to imagine. The argument for rejecting this option may be that only something non-physical could "attach" itself to the soul, but since evil does not have existence in the intelligibles, nothing bad could come to the soul from there.

17, 49–50 *those beings to which nature has not granted perfection from the beginning*: These are human souls, which may choose to become evil, even though their "goal" (*telos*), or the fullest and best development of their characteristic capacities, above all reason, is to become virtuous.

17, 54 *The universe contained everything*: See Plato *Timaeus* 32c–33d.

Chapter 18

The body is no obstacle to contemplation.

18, 1–14 *But perhaps they. . . . of the stones*: In his opening move, Plotinus considers a possible explanation for the Gnostics' contempt for the body. They may separate themselves from the rest of the universe and despise perceptible beauties in order to put a distance between themselves and the body, and so perhaps to lead a purer life. This strategy, however, is refuted with the analogy of the two residents, one of whom admires the skill of the architect, while the other rails against the construction. *Pace* Roloff (1970, 221–222), Plotinus does not mean the house inhabited by the two residents to stand for the visible world in general; rather, it is analogous to the bodies which individual souls inhabit, as 18, 14–17 ("As long as we have bodies, we must stay in the houses built by our good sister soul . . .") makes quite clear. In Plotinus' eyes, the wise man will bear whatever necessities he encounters (cf. 9, 72–75), including the necessity of being embodied, and is able to live in the body without being disturbed by its influence.

Note how Plotinus, at 18, 13–14, insinuates once again that the Gnostics are psychologically duplicitous, openly despising what they cherish in secret. Cf. 17, 28–29.31.

In line 13, I read *<pros>poieitai* ("pretends") in place of *poieitai* ("makes," "renders," "represents"), as suggested already by Dodds (1922, 94).

18, 14–35 *As long as. . . . from the beginning*: In this important section of the treatise, Plotinus presents his own vision of the relation between body and soul. He argues that it is both possible and desirable to live in the body in much the same way as the world soul is present to the body of the universe, and as the stars are present to the heavenly bodies. Concretely, this means being unaffected—or, as he puts it here, using the language of Plato's *Phaedrus* (25d7), being "immune to blows" (*aplēktos*)—by pleasures and pains, and strengthening our ability to endure misfortunes through virtue. He clearly envisages that this attitude can be developed more fully over time, as the reference to being prepared in "nature and pursuits" suggests (18, 34–5). The problem how the soul can remain "unaffected" even though it has desires and feels emotions in virtue of its kinship with the body is explored in greater depth in III.6; in this treatise, Plotinus explains that "affections" (*pathēmata*) are caused by outside impressions (*phantasmata*), which can present a given object as, for example, fearful or desirable to the soul. The task of philosophy is to "purify" the soul, that is to say, to direct it toward its own activity of contemplation, rather than having it pay attention to images from the sensible world presented to it through its affective faculty. See particularly III.6.3, 27–35; 5, 2–19.

18, 14–17 *As long as . . . creating without toil*: "The good sister soul" (cf. IV.3.6, 13 for the expression) is the world soul, whose creative activity has been discussed earlier in the treatise; see Commentary on 2, 14 for a collection of references. See also IV.8.8, 14–15 for the world soul's ability to order the universe "without toil." Note that Plotinus' claim that "we must" (*dei*) remain in our bodies seems to imply a rejection of suicide. On this question, see also the note on 8, 39–46 above. The world soul creates our bodies (the "houses" that she is said to build here) before they become animated, as was explained earlier at 7, 10–11.

18, 17–20 *Or do they . . . the world "brothers*: See also 5, 8–11 for a similar reproach, that the Gnostics exalt the "meanest of men" but exclude the stars from sharing in immortality. Evidence that some Gnostics called one another "brothers" and "sisters" can be found, for example, in Epiphanius' *Panarion* (e.g. 31.21, 6; 32.4, 8; 33.3, 1). See also Puech (1960, 180–181).

18, 20 *"with their raving mouth"*: See Heraclitus, fragment B92. The full fragment, from Plutarch, *On the Pythian Responses* 397A, reads: "The Sibyl with raving mouth, uttering mirthless, unadorned, unperformed sayings, reaches a thousand years with her voice because of the god" (tr. Graham). While Heraclitus may have regarded the Sibyl's oracular pronouncements as an apt analogy for the hidden Logos that rules all things, Plotinus quotes the fragment in order to emphasize the irrationality of the Gnostics' utterances.

18, 20–24 *It is right . . . of the universe*: The "beings" referred to are the stars, who are able to inhabit their bodies without suffering any disturbance to their contemplation. Their impassivity to outside influences is thus very close to that of the world soul. Plotinus' point here is that the Gnostics would be better off to call the stars their brothers rather than the base people he thinks they associate with.

18, 24–26 *This consists in . . . something painful occurs*: The language of "coming up against" (*krouein*) and "assailing" (*prospiptousin*) echoes that of Plato's *Timaeus* (43b7–c1), where the character Timaeus explains that some perceptions can arise from a creature's body "colliding" (*proskrouein*) with fire, air, or water. But Plotinus is not here interested in the physical process of sense perception, but rather in the evaluative attitude one displays toward pleasure and the appearances that perception presents.

18, 35 *this is possible from the beginning*: There is, in other words, no development that the world soul or the stars undergo in order to reach perfection. See also 17, 52 above for this point.

18, 35–40.46–48 *Their contemplation certainly. . . . whole lifeless universe*: For the Gnostics' alleged elitism, cf. 5, 1–11; 9, 26–28.43–64.75–83; 16, 5–7. Instead of bringing still further arguments against the Gnostics' claim to spiritual superiority, Plotinus offers something of a diagnosis of their error. For some reason, the passage has become disjointed: the phrase *Dia touto gar* ("It is because") at 18, 46 explains why the Gnostics are ignorant of the proper meaning of "outside," and completes the argument of 18, 38–40. I am thus transposing lines 46–48 to come after 18, 40. This change not only restores Plotinus' argument, but also results in a much more satisfying conclusion to the treatise; anyone will agree that 18, 49 ("because they do not see that their soul comes from outside") is an odd note to end on, especially after the rhetorical flourish of 18, 40–46.

What, then, is the source of the Gnostics' error, according to Plotinus? He thinks that when they talk about death as "departing from here" (*exelthein*; the verb contains the Greek word *ex*, "from," "out of," which is in turn related to the word *exō*, "out," "outside"), they mean removing themselves from this universe, most likely by ascending through the planetary spheres. Since the stars remain in their place and cannot "depart" from the universe in the same way, the Gnostics view them as inferior to themselves. The mistake, argues Plotinus, is to think that the soul can "depart" at all so as to be "outside" (*exō*) the universe in a spatial sense. Because it is an incorporeal entity that has no location in space, the soul is always already "outside" the visible universe. Consequently, the extent to which the stars are able to engage in contemplation of the intelligibles ("to look at what is outside," as Plotinus puts it) in no way depends on their ability to spatially depart from the universe to some higher sphere. They are able to contemplate because their souls are related to purer bodies that do not suffer from the same affections (such as pleasures, desires, and fears) that disturb human contemplation (cf. IV.8.2, 14–26). For Plotinus' view on the sense in which the intelligibles are "outside" the sensible world, see V.1.10, 6–9. Cf. also V.8.4, 15–18; V.8.10, 40–45, where Plotinus describes the spiritual ascent in terms of an interior vision rather than a departure "outside," as the Gnostics would have it, and see Hadot (1999, 220).

18, 38 *<that>*: Accepting Creuzer's conjecture *<tois> aei* here, to correspond to *tois* ("they [*sc.* the stars]" in the dative case) at 18, 37.

18, 39–40 *"takes care of the whole lifeless universe"*: For Plotinus, the world soul takes care of the "lifeless universe" (Plato, *Phaedrus* 246b6) by remaining in the intelligible world, and passing on the power that it receives from there to the universe, as was explained at 2, 10–18.

18, 48 *their soul*: Grammatically, *autōn* ("their") could refer back to the Gnostics, as Spanu (2012, 51) takes it, and not, as I have assumed above (Commentary 18, 35–40.46–48), to the stars. Plotinus' argument would then be that, since the Gnostics hold a mistaken belief about how soul is present to them, they also hold a mistaken belief about the ability of the stars to contemplate.

A note about the singular "soul": although one would perhaps expect the plural "souls" here, Plotinus elsewhere argues that all souls are in some sense one, so that one soul can be present to many bodies at once. Cf. IV.3.5, 14–18; IV.9.2, 24–8.

18, 40–46 *Therefore, it is . . . these stand still*: Arguably, Plotinus' life is an illustration that it is possible to purify oneself from love of the body; as the very first sentence of Porphyry's *Life of Plotinus* impresses on the reader, "Plotinus the philosopher, who was our contemporary, seemed to be ashamed of being in a body" (1.1–2). Porphyry further emphasizes the degree to which Plotinus was able to help others (rather than denying them the ability to pursue higher things, as the Gnostics are frequently alleged to do, as for example at 18, 35–36) while at the same time directing his attention toward the intellect (9.17).

In the final comments, Plotinus returns once more to defending the divinity of the stars. He charges the Gnostics with being under the spell of a deception, like those who mistakenly judge that the stars stand still even though they are moving (cf. Cleomedes, *On the Circular Motions of the Celestial Bodies* 130. 15, as pointed by out by Harder-Beutler-Theiler [1960], for a similar illusion in the case of the sun). Presumably, the analogous mistake of the Gnostics is to focus on the bodily nature of the stars, which is the focus of their censure, while ignoring that the order and harmony in which the stars move suggest that they are endowed with a greater than human intelligence.

Select Bibliography

I. Ancient Authors

(a) Classical and Patristic

ALCINOUS: Dillon, J. 1993. *Alcinous: The Handbook of Platonism*. Oxford: Clarendon Press.

ARISTOTLE: Ross, W. D. 1924. *Aristotle: Metaphysics*. 2 vols. Oxford: Oxford University Press.

CLEMENT OF ALEXANDRIA: Sagnard, F. M. 1948. *Clement d'Alexandrie. Extraits de Théodote*. Paris: Cerf.

DIOGENES LAERTIUS: Hicks, R. D., trans. 1925. *Lives of the Eminent Philosophers*. 2 vols. Cambridge, MA: Harvard University Press.

EPIPHANIUS: Holl, K. 1915–1933. *Epiphanius, Bände 1–3: Ancoratus und Panarion*. 3 vols. Leipzig: Hinrichs.

HIPPOLYTUS: Marcovich, M. 1986. Hippolytus. *Refutatio omnium haeresium*. Berlin: De Gruyter.

IAMBLICHUS: Clarke, E., J. M. Dillon and J. P. Hershbell. 2000. *Iamblichus: On the Mysteries*. Atlanta: Society for Biblical Literature.

IRENAEUS: Harvey, W. W. 1857. *Adversus Haereses*. 2 vols. Cambridge: Cambridge University Press.

NUMENIUS: Des Places, E. 1973. *Numénius: Les fragments*. Paris: Les Belles Lettres.

ORIGEN: Borret, M. 1967–1969. *Origène. Contre Celse*. 4 vols. Paris: Cerf.

PLATO: Burnet, J. 1900–1907. *Platonis opera*. 5 vols. Oxford: Oxford University Press.

PORPHYRY: Edwards, M., trans. 2000. *Neoplatonic Saints. The Lives of Plotinus and Proclus by their Students*. Liverpool: Liverpool University Press (English translation of *Life of Plotinus* from 1–53).

PROCLUS: Dodds, E. R. 1933, 1963. *Proclus: The Elements of Theology*. Oxford: Clarendon Press.

(b) Gnostic

All references to the NAG HAMMADI texts (NHC) are to Robinson, J. M. 2000. *The Coptic Gnostic Library*. 5 vols. Brill: Leiden.

ALLOGENES: Funk, W.-P. et al. 2004. *L'Allogène (NH XI, 3)*. Québec: Les presses de l'Université Laval; Leuven: Peeters.

BRUCE CODEX: Schmidt, C. and V. MacDermot. 1978. *The Books of Jeu and the Untitled Text in the Bruce Codex*. Brill: Leiden.

ZOSTRIANUS: Barry, C. et al. 2000. *Zostrien (NH VIII, 1)*. Québec: Les presses de l'Université Laval; Leuven: Peeters.

II. Editions and Translations of the *Enneads*

Armstrong, A. H. 1966–1982. *Plotinus*. Greek Text with English Translation and Introductions. Cambridge, MA: Harvard University Press.

Bouillet, M.-N. 1857–1861. *Les Ennéades de Plotin*. French Translation with Introduction and Notes. 3 vols. Paris: Librairie de La Hachette. Vol. 1 (1857) contains extensive notes (491–544) on II.9 that are still valuable.

Bréhier, E. 1924–1938. *Plotin Ennéades*. Greek Text and French Translation with Introduction and Notes. 7 vols. Paris: Les Belles Lettres.

Brisson, L. and, J.-F. Pradeau. 2002–2010. *Plotin. Traités* French Translation and Commentary. 8 vols. Paris: Flammarion. Vol. 5 (2006) contains treatises 30–37, with a translation and commentary on II.9 by R. Dufour.

Harder, R., R. Beutler, and W. Theiler. 1956–1971. *Plotin*. Greek Text with German Translation and Commentary. 12 vols. Hamburg: Felix Meiner Verlag.

Henry, P. and H.-R. Schwyzer (HS1). 1951–1973. *Plotini Opera* I–III (editio maior). Bruxelles Edition Universelle.

Henry, P. and H.-R. Schwyzer (HS_2). 1964–1982. *Plotini Opera* I–III (editio minor, with revised text). Oxford: Clarendon Press.

Igal, J. 1982–1998. *Enéades*. 3 vols. (v. 1.I–II; v. 2.III–IV; v.3.V–VI). Madrid: Editorial Gredos. Vol. 1 (1982) contains a translation with notes of II.9.

MacKenna, S. 1962. *Plotinus. The Enneads*. English Translation revised by B. S. Page. London: Faber and Faber.

III. Studies on *Ennead* II.9 and Related Works

Abramowski, L. 1983. "Nag Hammadi 8,1 'Zostrianos,' das Anonymum Brucianum, Plotin *Enn.* 2,9 (33)." In *Platonismus und Christentum: Festschrift für Heinrich Dörrie* [Jahrbuch für Antike und Christentum, 10], edited by H.-D. Blume and F. Mann. Muenster: Aschendorff, 1–10.

Alt, K. 1990. *Philosophie gegen Gnosis: Plotin Polemik in seiner Schrift II, 9* [Abhandlungen der Akademie der Wissenschaften in Mainz, 8]. Stuttgart: Steiner.

Armstrong, A. H. 1973. "Man in the cosmos. A study of some differences between pagan Neoplatonism and Christianity." In *Romanitas et Christianitas*, edited by W. de Boer, P. G. van der Nat *et al.* Amsterdam: North Holland Publishing Co., 5–14.

Brisson, L. 2013. "Plotinus and the magical rites practiced by the Gnostics." In *Gnosticism, Platonism and the Late Ancient World. Essays in Honour of John D. Turner*, edited by K. Corrigan and T. Rasimus. Leiden: Brill, 443–458.

Bury, R. G. 1945. "Two notes on Plotinus." In *The Classical Review* 59.2: 53.

Cilento, V. 1971. *Paideia antignostica: Ricostruzione d'un unico scritto da Enneadi III 8, V 8, V 5, II, 9.* Firenze: F. Le Monnier.

Cornea, A. 2013. "Plotinus, Epicurus, and the Gnostics: On Plotinian classification of philosophies." In *Gnosticism, Platonism and the Late Ancient World. Essays in Honour of John D. Turner*, edited by K. Corrigan and T. Rasimus. Leiden: Brill, 465–484.

Dillon, J. 2009. "St John in Amelius' Seminar." In *Late Antique Epistemology. Other Ways to Truth*, edited by P. Vassilopoulou and S. R. L. Clark. Basingstoke: Palgrave MacMillan, 30–43.

Dodds, E. R. 1922. “Plotiniana.” In *Classical Quarterly* 16: 93–97.

Edwards, M. J. 1989. “*Aidôs* in Plotinus *Enneads* II, 9, 10.” In *Classical Quarterly* 39.1: 228–232.

Elsas, C. 1975. *Neuplatonische und gnostische Weltablehnung in der Schule Plotins* [Religionsgeschichtliche Versuche und Vorarbeiten, 34]. Berlin: de Gruyter.

Ferroni, L. 2013a. “Trois passages problématiques liés à la gnose chez Plotin: 33 (II 9) 13, 25–33; 33 (II 9) 9, 80; 30 (III 8) 9, 29–32.” In *Mnemosyne* 64: 399–410.

———. 2013b. “Where did Matter appear from? A Syntactic Problem in a Plotinian anti-Gnostic Treatise.” In *Gnosticism, Platonism and the Late Ancient World. Essays in Honour of John D. Turner*, edited by K. Corrigan and T. Rasimus. Leiden: Brill, 459–463.

Fleet, B. 2012. *Plotinus Ennead IV.8: On the Descent of the Soul into Bodies*. Las Vegas: Parmenides Publishing.

García Bazán, F. 1974. “Gnóstica: El Capítulo XVI de *La Vida de Plotino* de Porfirio.” In *Salesianum* 36: 463–78.

———. 1977. “Sobre la noción de *epinoiai* en *Enneada* II, 9 (33), 2, 1.” In *Cuadernos de Filosofía* 17: 83–94.

Gerson, L. 2013. *Plotinus Ennead V.5: That the Intelligibles are not External to the Intellect, and on the Good*. Las Vegas: Parmenides Publishing.

Gertz, S. R. P. 2016. "The Decline of Sophia and a Misleading Gloss in Plotinus *Enn*. II.9 [33].10.25." In *Classical Quarterly* 66.1: 413–417.

Hadot, P. 1999. "Plotin et les Gnostiques." *Plotin, Porphyre: Études néoplatoniciennes*. Paris: Les Belles Lettres, 211–223.

Igal, J. 1977. "Observaciones a las Enéadas I–II de Plotino: Texto y Fuentes." In *Helmantica* 28: 241–252.

———. 1981. "The Gnostics and 'The Ancient Philosophy' in Plotinus." In *Neoplatonism and Early Christian Thought: Essays in Honour of A. H. Armstrong*, edited by H. J. Blumenthal and R. A. Markus. London: Variorum, 138–149.

Irwin, T. H. 2010. "The Sense and Reference of *Kalon* in Aristotle." In *Classical Philology* 105.4: 381–396.

Jonas, H. 2001. *The Gnostic Religion*. Boston: Beacon Press.

Kalligas, P. 2000. "Plotinus Against the Gnostics." In *Hermathena* 169: 115–128.

———. 2014. *The* Enneads *of Plotinus: A Commentary, Volume 1*, translated by E. K. Fowden and N. Pilavachi. Princeton: Princeton University Press.

King, K. L. 2005. *What is Gnosticism?* Cambridge, MA: Harvard University Press.

Kobusch, Th. 2007. "Die Epinoia—Das menschliche Bewusstsein in der antiken Philosophie." In *Gregory of Nyssa Contra Eunomium II: An English version with supporting studies* [Proceedings of the 10th International Colloquium on Gregory of Nyssa (Olomouc, September 15–18, 2004)], edited by L. Karfíková, S. Douglas and J. Zachhuber. Leiden: Brill, 3–20.

Meyer, M. W. and R. Smith. 1999. *Ancient Christian Magic: Coptic Texts of Ritual Power.* Princeton: Princeton University Press.

Narbonne, J.-M. 2011. *Plotinus in Dialogue with the Gnostics* [Studies in Platonism, Neoplatonism, and the Platonic Tradition vol. 11]. Leiden: Brill.

———. 2013. "The Neopythagorean backdrop to the fall (σφάλμα/νεῦσις) of the soul in Gnosticism and its echo in the Plotinian treatises 33 and 34." In *Gnosticism, Platonism and the Late Ancient World. Essays in Honour of John D. Turner,* edited by K. Corrigan and T. Rasimus. Leiden: Brill, 411–425.

O'Brien, D. 1990. "The Origin of Matter and the Origin of Evil in Plotinus' Criticism of the Gnostics." In *Herméneutique et ontologie: mélanges en hommage à Pierre Aubenque,* edited by R. Brague and J.-F.

Courtine. Paris: Presses universitaires de France, 181–202.

———. 1993. *Théodicée plotinienne, théodicée gnostique.* Leiden: Brill.

O'Meara, D. J. 1980. "Gnosticism and the Making of the World in Plotinus." In *The Rediscovery of Gnosticism, Proceedings of the International Conference on Gnosticism at Yale, New Haven, Connecticut, March 28–31, 1978,* vol. 1 [Studies in the History of Religions, 41], edited by B. Layton. Leiden: Brill, 364–378.

Orbe, A. 1954. "Variaciones gnósticas sobre las Alas del Alma." In *Gregorianum* 35: 18–55.

———. 1976. *Cristologia Gnostica. Introducción a la soteriologia de los siglos II y III.* Vol. II. Madrid: EDICA, S. A.

Pasquier, A. 2006. "La réflexion démiurgique ou la 'terre étrangère' chez les gnostiques (Ennéade II.9.10–12)." In *Coptica, Gnostica, Manichaica: Mélanges offerts à Wolf-Peter Funk,* edited by L. Painchaud and P.-H. Poirier. Leuven: Peeters, 647–661.

Pépin, J. 1992. "Theories of Procession in Plotinus and the Gnostics." In *Neoplatonism and Gnosticism* [Studies in Neoplatonism: Ancient and Modern, 6], edited by R. T. Wallis and J. Bregman. Albany: State University of New York Press, 297–335.

Poirier, P.-H. 2012. "À propos de la νεῦσις dans les textes de Nag Hammadi." In *Laval théologique et philosophique* 68.3: 619–26.

Puech, H.-C. 1960. "Plotin et les Gnostiques." In *Les sources de Plotin* [Entretiens sur l'Antiquité classique, 5]. Vandoeuvres–Genève: Fondation Hardt, 161–190.

Roloff, D. 1970. *Die Großschrift: III,8; V,8; V,5; II,9* [Untersuchungen zur antiken Literatur und Geschichte 8]. Berlin: De Gruyter.

Rudolph, K. 1983. *Gnosis. The Nature and History of Gnosticism.* Edinburgh: T&T Clark.

Schmidt, C. 1900. *Plotins Stellung zum Gnosticismus und kirchlichen Christentum* [Texte und Untersuchungen zur Geschichte der altchristlichen Literatur, N. F., V, 4]. Leipzig: H.C. Hinrichs.

Spanu, N. 2012. *Plotinus, Ennead II 9 [33] "Against the Gnostics": A Commentary.* Leuven: Peeters.

———. 2013. "The Magic of Plotinus' Gnostic Disciples in the Context of Plotinus' School of Philosophy." *In Journal for Late Antique Religion and Culture* 7: 1–14.

———. 2014. "The Concepts of 'Power' and 'Mass' in Plotinus' Metaphysics." In *Journal for Late Antique Religion and Culture* 8: 14–25.

Stead, G. C. 1980. "In search of Valentinus." In *The Rediscovery of Gnosticism. Volume 1: The school of Valentinus*, edited by B. Layton. Leiden: Brill, 75–102.

Tardieu, M. 1992. "Les Gnostiques dans la *Vie de Plotin*." In *Porphyre: la Vie de Plotin*, vol. 2 [Histoire des doctrines de l'Antiquité classique, 16], edited by L. Brisson, J.-L. Cherlonneix, M.-O. Goulet-Cazé, R. Goulet, M. D. Grmek, J.-M. Flamand, S. Matton, J. Pépin, H. D. Saffrey, A.-P. Segonds, M. Tardieu, and P. Thillet. Paris: Vrin, 546–563.

———. 2013. "Écho et les antitypes." In *Gnosticism, Platonism and the Late Ancient World. Essays in Honour of John D. Turner*, edited by K. Corrigan and T. Rasimus. Leiden: Brill, 427–441.

Turner, J. D. 2000. "The Setting of the Platonizing Sethian Treatises in Middle Platonism." In *Gnosticism and Later Platonism: Themes, Figures, Texts* [Society of Biblical Literature Symposium Series, 12], edited by J. Turner and R. Majercik. Atlanta: Society of Biblical Literature, 179–224.

———. 2001. *Sethian Gnosticism and the Platonic Tradition* [Bibliotèque copte de Nag Hammadi, Section "Études" 6]. Québec: Les presses de l'Université Laval; Leuven: Peeters.

Vollenweider, S. 2009. "Der Logos als Brücke vom Evangelium zur Philosophie. Der Johannesprolog in der Relektüre des Neuplatonikers Amelios." In *Studien zu Matthäus und Johannes. Festschrift für Jean Zumstein zu seinem 65. Geburtstag / Études sur Matthieu et Jean. Mélanges offerts à Jean Zumstein pour son 65e anniversaire,* edited by A. Dettwiler, A and U. Poplutz. Zürich: Theologischer Verlag Zürich, 377–397.

Williams, M. A. 1996. *Rethinking "Gnosticism." An Argument for Dismantling a Dubious Category.* Princeton: Princeton University Press.

Wolters, A. M. 1981. "Notes on the Structure of *Enneads* II, 9." In *Life is Religion. Essays in Honor of H. Evan Runner,* edited by H. V. Goot. St. Catherine's, Ontario: Paideia, 83–96.

IV. General Publications

Alt, K. 1993. *Weltflucht und Weltbejahung. Zur Frage des Leib-Seele Dualismus bei Plutarch, Numenius, Plotin.* Stuttgart: Franz Steiner Verlag.

Armstrong, A. H. 1966–1982. *The Architecture of the Intelligible Universe in the Philosophy of Plotinus.* Cambridge: Cambridge University Press.

Armstrong, A. H., ed. 1967. *The Cambridge History of Later Greek and Early Medieval Philosophy.* Cambridge: Cambridge University Press.

Arnou, R. 1968. *Le Désir de Dieu dans la philosophie de Plotin.* 2nd ed. Rome: Presses de l'Université Grégorienne.

Dillon, J. 1977/1996. *The Middle Platonists: A Study of Platonism, 80 B.C.–A.D. 220,* London: Duckworth, 1977, 1996[2].

Dodds, Eric R. 1965. *Pagan and Christian in an Age of Anxiety: Some Aspects of Religious Experience from Marcus Aurelius to Constantine.* Cambridge: Cambridge University Press.

Emilsson, E. K. 1988. *Plotinus on Sense-Perception.* Cambridge: Cambridge University Press.

———. 2007. *Plotinus on Intellect.* Oxford: The Clarendon Press.

Gatti, M. L. 1996. *Plotino e la metafisica della contemplazione.* Milan: Vita e Pensiero.

Gerson, L. P. 1994. *Plotinus.* London/New York: Routledge.

———, ed. 1996. *The Cambridge Companion to Plotinus.* Cambridge: Cambridge University Press.

———, ed. 2010. *The Cambridge History of Philosophy in Late Antiquity.* 2 vols. Cambridge: Cambridge University Press.

Gottschalk, H. B. 1980. *Heraclides of Pontus.* Oxford: Oxford University Press.

Guthrie, W. K. C. 1967–1978. *A History of Greek Philosophy.* 5 vols. Cambridge: Cambridge University Press.

Hadot, Pierre. 1993. *Plotinus on the Simplicity of Vision.* Translated by M. Chase. Chicago: Chicago University Press.

Inge, W. R. 1948. *The Philosophy of Plotinus.* 3rd ed. London: Longmans, Green.

Les Sources de Plotin. 1960. Entretiens Fondation Hardt V. Vandoeuvres-Genève.

Lloyd, Anthony C. 1990. *The Anatomy of Neoplatonism.* Oxford: Clarendon Press.

Meijer, P. A. 1992. *Plotinus on the Good or the One (Enneads VI, 9): An Analytical Commentary.* Amsterdam: J. C. Gieben.

O'Daly, G. 1973. *Plotinus' Philosophy of the Self.* Shannon: Irish University Press.

O'Meara, Dominic J. 1993. *Plotinus: an Introduction to the Enneads.* Oxford: Oxford University Press.

Pépin, J. 1958. *Mythe et allégorie: les origins grecques et les contestations judéo-chrétiennes.* Paris: Aubier.

Remes, Pauliina. 2007. *Plotinus on Self: The Philosophy of the 'We.'* Cambridge: Cambridge University Press.

Remes, Pauliina. 2008. *Neoplatonism.* Berkeley: University of California Press.

Rist, John M. 1967. *Plotinus: The Road to Reality.* Cambridge: Cambridge University Press.

Schniewind, Alexandrine. 2003. *L'Éthique du Sage chez Plotin.* Paris: J. Vrin.

Smith, A. 1974. *Porphyry's Place in the Neoplatonic Tradition: A Study in Post-Plotinian Neoplatonism.* The Hague: Nijhoff.

———. 1981. "Potentiality and the Problem of Plurality in the Intelligible." In *Neoplatonism and Early Christian Thought,* edited by H. J. Blumenthal and R. A. Markus. London: Variorum, 99–107.

————. 2004. *Philosophy in Late Antiquity.* London: Routledge.

Theiler, W. 1960. "Plotin zwischen Platon und Stoa." In *Les Sources de Plotin.* Entretiens Fondation Hardt V, Vandoeuvres-Genève: Fondation Hardt, 63–103.

Wallis, R. T. 1995. *Neoplatonism.* 2nd ed. London: Duckworth.

West, M. L. 1966. *Hesiod* Theogony, *Edited with Prolegomena and Commentary.* Oxford: Clarendon Press.

Index of Ancient Authors

Index of Names and Subjects

• ALSO AVAILABLE FROM PARMENIDES PUBLISHING •

PRE-SOCRATICS

By Being, It Is: *The Thesis of Parmenides* by Néstor-Luis Cordero

The Fragments of *Parmenides*: *A Critical Text with Introduction and Translation, the Ancient Testimonia and a Commentary by A. H. Coxon. Revised and Expanded Edition edited with new Translations by Richard McKirahan and a new Preface* by Malcolm Schofield

The Legacy of Parmenides: *Eleatic Monism and Later Presocratic Thought* by Patricia Curd

Parmenides and the History of Dialectic: *Three Essays* by Scott Austin

Parmenides, Venerable and Awesome: *Proceedings of the International Symposium* edited by Néstor-Luis Cordero

Presocratics and Plato: *A Festschrift in Honor of Charles Kahn* edited by Richard Patterson, Vassilis Karasmanis, and Arnold Hermann

The Route of Parmenides: *Revised and Expanded Edition, With a New Introduction, Three Supplemental Essays, and an Essay* by Gregory Vlastos by Alexander P. D. Mourelatos

To Think Like God: *Pythagoras and Parmenides. The Origins of Philosophy. Scholarly and fully annotated edition* by Arnold Hermann

The Illustrated To Think Like God: P*ythagoras and Parmenides. The Origins of Philosophy* by Arnold Hermann (with over 200 full color illustrations)

PLATO

A Stranger's Knowledge: *Statesmanship, Philosophy, and Law in Plato's Statesman* by Xavier Márquez

God and Forms in Plato by Richard D. Mohr

Image and Paradigm in Plato's Sophist by David Ambuel

Imperial Plato: Albinus, Maximus, Apuleius by Ryan Fowler

Interpreting Plato's Dialogues by J. Angelo Corlett

One Book, the Whole Universe: *Plato's Timaeus Today* edited by Richard D. Mohr and Barbara M. Sattler

Platonic Patterns: *A Collection of Studies* by Holger Thesleff

Plato's Late Ontology: *A Riddle Resolved* by Kenneth M. Sayre

Plato's Parmenides: *Text, Translation & Introductory Essay* by Arnold Hermann. Translation in collaboration with Sylvana Chrysakopoulou with a Foreword by Douglas Hedley

Plato's Universe by Gregory Vlastos

The Philosopher in Plato's Statesman by Mitchell Miller

ARISTOTLE

Aristotle's Empiricism: Experience and Mechanics in the Fourth Century B.C. by Jean De Groot

One and Many in Aristotle's Metaphysics—*Volume I: Books Alpha-Delta* by Edward C. Halper

One and Many in Aristotle's Metaphysics—*Volume 2: The Central Books* by Edward C. Halper

Reading Aristotle: Physics VII.3 "What is Alteration?" *Proceedings of the International ESAP-HYELE Conference* edited by Stefano Maso, Carlo Natali, and Gerhard Seel

HELLENISTIC PHILOSOPHY

A Life Worthy of the Gods: *The Materialist Psychology of Epicurus* by David Konstan

THE *ENNEADS* OF PLOTINUS

Translations with Introductions & Philosophical Commentaries
Series edited by John M. Dillon and Andrew Smith

Ennead* I.6: *On Beauty by Andrew Smith

Ennead* II.5: *On What Is Potentially and What Actually by Cinzia Arruzza

Ennead* IV.3–IV.4.29: *Problems concerning the Soul by John M. Dillon and H. J. Blumenthal

Ennead* IV.4.30–45 & IV.5: *Problems concerning the Soul by Gary M. Gurtler

Ennead IV.7: *On the Immortality of the Soul* by Barrie Fleet

Ennead* IV.8: *On the Descent of the Soul into Bodies by Barrie Fleet

Ennead* V.1: *On the Three Primary Levels of Reality by Eric D. Perl

Ennead* V.5: *That the Intelligibles are not External to the Intellect, and on the Good by Lloyd P. Gerson

Ennead* VI.4 & VI.5: *On the Presence of Being, One and the Same, Everywhere as a Whole by Eyjólfur Emilsson and Steven Strange

ETHICS

Sentience and Sensibility: *A Conversation about Moral Philosophy* by Matthew R. Silliman

PHILOSOPHICAL FICTION

Pythagorean Crimes by Tefcros Michaelides

The Aristotle Quest: A Dana McCarter Trilogy. Book 1: Black Market Truth by Sharon M. Kaye

AUDIOBOOKS

The Iliad (unabridged) by Stanley Lombardo

The Odyssey (unabridged) by Stanley Lombardo

The Essential Homer by Stanley Lombardo

The Essential Iliad by Stanley Lombardo

FORTHCOMING

Ennead* I.1: *What Is the Living Being, and What Is Man? by Gerard O'Daly

Ennead* I.2: *On Virtues by Suzanne Stern-Gillet

Ennead* I.3: *On Dialectic by Pauliina Remes

Ennead* I.4: *On Well-Being by Kieran McGroarty

Ennead* I.5: *On Whether Well Being Increases With Time by Danielle A, Layne

Ennead* I.8: *On the Nature and Source of Evil by Anne Sheppard

Ennead* II.4: *On Matter by Anthony A. Long

Ennead* II.9: *Against the Gnostics by Sebastian Ramon Philipp Gertz

Ennead* III.4: *On Our Allotted Guardian Spirit by Wiebke-Marie Stock

Ennead* III.5: *On Love by Sara Magrin

Ennead* III.7: *On Eternity and Time by László Bene

Ennead* III.8: *On Nature and Contemplation by George Karamanolis

Ennead* V.3: *On the Knowing Hypostases by Marie-Élise Zovko

Ennead* V.8: *On Intelligible Beauty by Andrew Smith

Ennead* V.9: *On Intellect, Ideas, and Being by Matthias Vorwerk

Ennead* VI.1-2: *On the Genera of Being (I+II) by Damien Caluori & Regina Füchslin

Ennead* VI.3: *On the Genera of Being (III) by Riccardo Chiaradonna

Ennead* VI.7: *The Forms and the Good by Nicholas Banner

Ennead* VI.8: *On Free Will and the Will of the One by Kevin Corrigan and John D. Turner

Ennead* VI.9: *On the Good or the One by Stephen R. L. Clark